The Bonds of Womanhood

The Bonds of Womanhood

"Woman's Sphere" in New England, 1780–1835

Nancy F. Cott

New Haven and London   Yale University Press

Designed by John O. C. McCrillis and set in Baskerville type. Printed in the
United States of America by The Alpine Press, South Braintree, Mass.

Published in Great Britain, Europe, Africa, and Asia (except Japan) by Yale
University Press, Ltd., London. Distributed in Australia and New Zealand
by Book & Film Services, Artarmon, N.S.W., Australia; and in Japan by
Harper & Row, Publishers, Tokyo Office.

Library of Congress Cataloging in Publication Data

Cott, Nancy F
    The bonds of womanhood.

    Bibliography: p.
    Includes index.
    1. Women–New England–Social conditions. 2. Women–New England–
History. I. Title.
HQ1418.C67   301.41'2'09   76-49728
ISBN: 0-300-02023-6 cloth
       0-300-02289-1 paper

To my parents
Estelle Hollander Falik
and
Max E. Falik

CONTENTS

ACKNOWLEDGMENTS

The curators, archivists, and librarians in the libraries listed on the following page, and Faith L. Pepe of Westminster, Vermont, kindly assisted me in my search for source materials. I am also obliged to those libraries for permission to quote from documents in their collections.

I remain indebted to John P. Demos for his suggestions and encouragement while I was writing my Ph.D. dissertation, which was the first version of this book. To the mentors and friends who generously commented on that earlier work and helped me to improve this one—especially Sacvan Bercovitch, Laurie Crumpacker, Ellen DuBois, David H. Fischer, Tamara K. Hareven, Aileen S. Kraditor, Mary Beth Norton, Kathryn Kish Sklar, Judith Smith, Alan Trachtenberg, and Lise Vogel—and to Lynn Walterick of Yale University Press, who leavened the process of book production with both faith and work, I hope to express here some fraction of my sincere thanks; and to Lee Cott, a longer-standing appreciation, for improving the environment in more ways than one.

LIST OF ABBREVIATIONS

Locations of manuscripts cited:

AAS   American Antiquarian Society, Worcester, Massachusetts

BPL   Boston Public Library Rare Book Room, Boston, Massachusetts

CHS   Connecticut Historical Society, Hartford, Connecticut

CL   Congregational Library, Boston, Massachusetts

CSL   Connecticut State Library, Hartford, Connecticut

EI   James Duncan Phillips Library, Essex Institute, Salem, Massachusetts

HCL   Houghton Library, Harvard University, Cambridge, Massachusetts

HD   Historic Deerfield Library, Deerfield, Massachusetts

MHS   Massachusetts Historical Society, Boston, Massachusetts

MeHS   Maine Historical Society, Portland, Maine

NEHGS   New England Historic Genealogical Society, Boston, Massachusetts

NHHS   New Hampshire Historical Society, Concord, New Hampshire

SL   Arthur and Elizabeth Schlesinger Library on the History of Women in America, Radcliffe College, Cambridge, Massachusetts

SML   Sterling Memorial Library, Yale University, New Haven, Connecticut

VHS   Vermont Historical Society, Montpelier, Vermont

WHS   Worcester Historical Society, Worcester, Massa-
           chusetts

Journals cited:

AHR   *American Historical Review*
AQ   *American Quarterly*
FS   *Feminist Studies*
JAH   *Journal of American History*
JIH   *Journal of Interdisciplinary History*
JSH   *Journal of Social History*
MVHR   *Mississippi Valley Historical Review*
NEHGR   *New England Historic Genealogical Register*
WMQ   *William and Mary Quarterly*

INTRODUCTION

"Thine in the bonds of womanhood" Sarah M. Grimké signed the letters to Mary Parker which she published in Boston in 1838 as *Letters on the Equality of the Sexes and the Condition of Women*. Grimké had left behind the South Carolina plantation of her birth and become one of the first women to speak publicly against slavery. "Bonds" symbolized chattel slavery to her. She must have composed her phrase with care, endowing it intentionally with the double meaning that womanhood bound women together even as it bound them down.

It is a central purpose of mine to explain why an American feminist of the 1830s would have seen womanhood in that dual aspect. When I began, I had a slightly different intent. I wanted to know how a certain congeries of social attitudes that has been called the "cult of true womanhood" and the "cult of domesticity," and first became conspicuous in the early nineteenth century, related to women's actual circumstances, experiences, and consciousness.[1] Within this "cult" (it might almost be called a social

1. William R. Taylor, I believe, was the first among recent scholars to use the term "domesticity" in this sense, in an unpublished paper prepared for the Symposium on the Role of Education in Nineteenth-Century America, at Chatham, Mass., 1964, "Domesticity in England and America, 1770-1840." I thank Prof. Taylor for lending the paper to me in 1973. Barbara Welter named the "cult of true womanhood" in an article of that title, in *AQ* 18 (1966): 151-74. Aileen S. Kraditor introduced the phrase "cult of domesticity" in her introduction to *Up from the Pedestal: Selected Writings in the History of American Feminism* (Chicago: Quadrangle Books, 1968).

1

ethic), mother, father, and children grouped together in the private household ruled the transmission of culture, the maintenance of social stability, and the pursuit of happiness; the family's influence reached outward, underlying success or failure in church and state, and inward, creating individual character. Not the understanding of families as cells making up the body of society but the emphasis placed on and agencies attributed to the family unit were new, and the importance given to women's roles as wives, mothers, and mistresses of households was unprecedented. The ministers, educators, and pious and educated women in the northern United States whose published writings principally documented this ethic made women's presence the essence of successful homes and families. Conversely, the "cult" both observed and prescribed specific behavior for women in the enactment of domestic life. I began (as had others before me) by investigating the literature in the antebellum United States that so strikingly glorified the home and women's roles in it. But that method would not suffice, since I was interested in women's lives, not just what was written about them. Besides, I inclined to concur with G.R. Taylor that such popularized didactic writings "by and large . . . do not bring about changes, though they may hasten and clarify a change which is already in progress. They are only bought because they express something which people, however obscurely, feel."[2] The literature becomes popular, in other words, because it does not have to persuade—it does not innovate—it addresses readers who are ready for it.

It made sense, then, to look at the years before 1830, to find out what had happened that might clarify the reception of or the need for a "cult" of domesticity. I turned to women's personal documents (such as diaries and letters) in preference to published, prescriptive works, in order to

2. Gordon Rattray Taylor, *The Angel-Makers: A Study in the Psychological Origins of Historical Change* (London: Heinemann, 1958), p. 109.

broaden my inquiry into the relation between change in the material circumstances of women's lives and their outlook on their place as women. Recent historical research which has discovered shifts in family and sexual patterns in the late eighteenth century encouraged me to begin in that period. For the case of the United States—and notably New England—David Hackett Fischer's new work confirms what recent students of historical modernization have been discerning: that the period between 1780 and 1830 was a time of wide- and deep-ranging transformation, including the beginning of rapid intensive economic growth, especially in foreign commerce, agricultural productivity, and the fiscal and banking system; the start of sustained urbanization; demographic transition toward modern fertility patterns; marked change toward social stratification by wealth and growing inequality in the distribution of wealth; rapid pragmatic adaptation in the law; shifts from unitary to pluralistic networks in personal association; unprecedented expansion in primary education; democratization in the political process; invention of a new language of political and social thought; and—not least—with respect to family life, the appearance of "domesticity."[3]

3. David Hackett Fischer, "America: A Social History, Vol. I, The Main Lines of the Subject 1650-1975,", unpublished MS draft, 1974, esp. chap. 4, pp. 42-43, chap. 12, pp. 20-22. Some recent writings useful for their treatment of historical modernization and personal relations are Richard D. Brown, "Modernization and the Modern Personality in Early America, 1600-1865: A Sketch of a Synthesis," *JIH* 2 (1972):201-28, and *Modernization: The Transformation of American Life* (New York: Hill and Wang, 1976); Herman R. Lantz, et al., "Pre-Industrial Patterns in the Colonial Family in America: A Content Analysis of Colonial Magazines," *Amer. Sociological Review* 33 (1968):413-26; Edward N. Shorter, *The Making of the Modern Family* (New York: Basic Books, 1975); Daniel S. Smith, "Parental Power and Marriage Patterns—An Analysis of Historical Trends in Hingham, Massachusetts," *Journal of Marriage and the Family* 35 (1973):419-28; Daniel S. Smith and Michael Hindus, "Premarital Pregnancy in America, 1640-1966: An Overview and Interpretation," *JIH* 6 (1975):537-71; Robert V. Wells, "Family History and Demographic Transition," *JSH* 9 (1975):1-21, and "Quaker Marriage Patterns

Such considerations made it all the more important to begin my investigation of women's particular needs and demands, the requirements of them and ideology regarding them, with the late eighteenth century. Historians often compare "colonial women" with "nineteenth-century women" in order to clarify dimensions and directions of change in women's lives in the United States, in work opportunities, family patterns, social status, and ideology. Obviously, this scheme slights the diversity encompassed between 1607 and 1775, and between 1800 and 1900; but if it works at all it must point out that in pace and intensity the change in women's experience (as in other areas), between approximately 1780 and 1830, outran that for considerably more than a century preceding and half a century following. I have seized on the "Revolutionary" in-between period for just such a reason. It also seems to epitomize the prevailing direction of social development. The beginning and end of the period can serve as reference points, clarifying the extent of continuity as well as change. In referring to the early years (the 1780s) I mean also to look back to, and sum up to some extent, what came before; and in referring to later circumstances (the 1830s) I mean to look ahead, to suggest future patterns. My sources begin in the late colonial period but I am aiming at the first recognizably "Victorian" decade. This is an essay in nineteenth-century more than in eighteenth-century history, if such a distinction need be made: my purpose is more to comprehend the shape women's experience was taking than to illuminate what it had been. I have assumed all along that women were neither victims of social change—passive receivers of changing definitions of themselves—nor totally mistresses of their destinies. Women's roles did not develop

in a Colonial Perspective," *WMQ,* 3d ser., 29 (1972):415-42; E. A. Wrigley, "The Process of Modernization and the Industrial Revolution in England," *JIH* 3 (1972):225-60.

in a unilinear pattern. Social and economic change included alteration of family structure, functions, and values, which affected women's roles in manifold ways. These alterations could be turned to constrain women's autonomy and effect conservative intents, or women could grasp them as cause and opportunity for further change, even for assertion of new social power.

It is fitting to begin with the decade of the 1830s in view although it is the end point of this study, for it presents a paradox in the "progress" of women's history in the United States. There surfaced publicly then an argument between two seemingly contradictory visions of women's relation to society: the ideology of domesticity, which gave women a limited and sex-specific role to play, primarily in the home; and feminism, which attempted to remove sex-specific limits on women's opportunities and capacities. Why that coincidence? Objectively, New England women in 1835 endured subordination to men in marriage and society, profound disadvantage in education and in the economy, denial of access to official power in the churches that they populated, and virtual impotence in politics. A married woman had no legal existence apart from her husband's: she could not sue, contract, or even execute a will on her own; her person, estate, and wages became her husband's when she took his name. Divorce was possible—and, in the New England states, available to wives on the same terms as husbands—but rare. Women's public life generally was so minimal that if one addressed a mixed audience she was greeted with shock and hostility. No women voted, although all were subject to the laws. Those (unmarried or widowed) who held property had to submit to taxation without representation.

This was no harsher subordination than women knew in 1770, but by 1835 it had other grievous aspects. When white manhood suffrage, stripped of property qualifications, became the rule, women's political incapacity appeared more conspicuous than it had in the colonial period. As occupations in trade, crafts, and services diversified the agricultural base of New England's economy, and wage earning encroached on family farm production, women's second-class position in the economy was thrown into relief. There was only a limited number of paid occupations generally open to women, in housework, handicrafts and industry, and school-teaching. Their wages were one-fourth to one-half what men earned in comparable work. The legal handicaps imposed by the marriage contract prevented wives from engaging in business ventures on their own, and the professionalization of law and medicine by means of educational requirements, licensing, and professional societies severely excluded women from those avenues of distinction and earning power. Because colleges did not admit women, they could not enter any of the learned professions. For them, the Jacksonian rhetoric of opportunity had scant meaning.[4]

The 1830s nonetheless became a turning point in women's economic participation, public activities, and social visibility. New textile factories recruited a primarily female labor force, and substantial numbers of young women left home to live and work with peers. In the mid-1830s oc-

4. For a general review of women's status, including their legal status, see Eleanor Flexner, *Century of Struggle* (New York: Atheneum, 1970). It is useful to look at mid-nineteenth-century feminists' appraisals of the condition of women; see the Declaration of Sentiments (1848) from the Seneca Falls Convention, and Lucy Stone's marriage protest, both reprinted in Kraditor, *Up from the Pedestal,* pp. 184-86, 148-50. On changes in women's opportunities and constraints from the late eighteenth to the early nineteenth century, see Gerda Lerner, "The Lady and the Mill-Girl: Changes in the Status of Women in the Age of Jackson," *Mid-Continent American Studies Journal,* 10 (1969): 5-15 and Elisabeth Anthony Dexter, *Career Women of America* (Francestown, N.H.: Marshall Jones, 1950). On divorce, see George E. Howard, *A History of Matrimonial Institutions* (New York: Humanities Press, 1964; orig. 1904), 3: 11-17; on women's wages, Edith Abbott, *Women in Industry* (New York: D. Appleton, 1918), pp. 76n, 157, 192, 249, 262-316.

curred the first industrial strikes in the United States led and peopled by women. "One of the leaders mounted a pump," the Boston *Evening Transcript* reported during the first "turn-out" in Lowell, Massachusetts, to protest wage reductions, "and made a flaming Mary Woolstonecraft [*sic*] speech on the rights of women."[5] Middle-class women took up their one political tool, the petition, to demand legislation enabling wives to retain rights to their property and earnings. So many women pursued the one profession open to them, primary-school teaching, that their entry began to look like a takeover, although (or, to be accurate, because) they consistently commanded much lower salaries than men. Secondary schools and academies which could prepare young women to teach multiplied. Women's growing literacy, owed in part to the employment of some as teachers of girls, swelled the audience for female journalists and fiction writers. While it had been unprecedented for Hannah Adams to support herself by her writing in the first decade of the nineteenth century, that possibility came within more women's reach. Several ladies' magazines began publication during the decade, thereby increasing the editorial and publication possibilities for women authors and causing a female audience to coalesce.

Women also entered a variety of reform movements, to pursue objects in their own self-interest as well as to improve their society. Health reformers spotlighted women's physical condition. "Moral reformers" attacked the double standard of sexual morality and the victimization of prostitutes. Mothers formed societies to consult together on the rearing of children. Even larger numbers of women joined Christian benevolent associations, to reform the world by the propagation of the faith. An insistent minority of wo-

5. Quoted in Thomas L. Dublin, "Women at Work: The Transformation of Work and Community in Lowell, Massachusetts, 1826–1860" (Ph.D. diss., Columbia University, 1975), p. 111.

men became active in the antislavery movement, where they practiced tactics of recruitment, organization, fund raising, propagandizing, and petitioning—and initiated the women's rights movement in the United States, when some of them took to heart the principles of freedom and human rights. Although the Seneca Falls Convention of 1848 usually marks the beginning of organized feminism in this country, there were clearly feminist voices in the antislavery movement by the late 1830s.

At the same time, an emphatic sentence of domesticity was pronounced for women. Both male and female authors (the former mostly ministers) created a new popular literature, consisting of advice books, sermons, novels, essays, stories, and poems, advocating and reiterating women's certain, limited role. That was to be wives and mothers, to nurture and maintain their families, to provide religious example and inspiration, and to affect the world around by exercising private moral influence. The literature of domesticity promulgated a Janus-faced conception of women's roles: it looked back, explicitly conservative in its attachment to a traditional understanding of woman's place; while it proposed transforming, even millennial results. One might assume that this pervasive formulation was simply a reaction to—a conservative defense against—expansion of women's nondomestic pursuits. But women's educational, reform, labor force, and political activities were just beginning to enlarge in the 1830s when the concept of domesticity crystallized. Several decades' shift in the allotment of powers and functions inside and outside the household had created the constellation of ideas regarding women's roles that we call domesticity. It was hardly a *deus ex machina*. The particularization and professionalization taking place in the occupational structure between 1780 and 1835 affected women's domestic occupation as

well as any other; and concomitant subtle changes in women's view of their domestic role established a substructure
for their nondomestic pursuits and self-assertion. The ideology of domesticity may seem to be contradicted func-
tionally and abstractly by feminism, but historically—as
they emerged in the United States—the latter depended on
the former.

In order to pursue questions about women's experience,
consciousness, and outlook in the decades leading to the
1830s, I have relied on their own private writings, and have
also drawn on words spoken to and published about women by ministers, educators, and other authors. These
sources themselves indicate that the study will not investi-
gate the condition of the whole female sex but will be
limited to the literate (and, perhaps, writing-prone) portion
of it, particularly those whose lives conformed to the ruling norms of American life. The women to whom I will
refer throughout this work when I speak of "women" were,
with few exceptions, white, middle-class or wealthier
(though not the very elite), of English Protestant heritage,
American-born, resident on farms, in rural towns, and
cities. These were the women who supplied scholars for
female academies and members for evangelical churches,
religious voluntary associations, reform movements, and
eventually feminist meetings; the kind who read ladies'
magazines, who became schoolteachers, who spent their
adult lives as mothers of families. "Middle-class" women
was not a synonym for "leisured" women in this period,
however (if ever it is, in fact). These women worked. While
unmarried, they engaged in schoolteaching, domestic work,
handicraft and industrial labor. When married they kept
house, reared children, manufactured household goods,
supplied boarders. Individual women's economic burdens
varied, depending on their families' wealth, the location of

their homes, and the decades in which they lived. Some of them had to support themselves entirely, but most made their economic contribution within a family circle.

While this study must exclude the poor and illiterate, it covers a broad middle-to-upper range of the population. The cultural hegemony of that class from which prevalent conceptions of women's roles were derived, and promulgated, suggests also that these conceptions created constraints or opportunities for all women. Because literacy and methods of communication were improving rapidly in early nineteenth-century New England it is all the more likely that dynamic ideas about women, formulations of their roles, and even their ways of thinking about their status would resound beyond the specific points of their class and geographical origin.[6]

I have focused on New England because it seemed the most effective, limited testing ground: its culture generated in profusion the kind of documents—private writings, organizational records, prescriptive literature—that promised to contain answers to my inquiry. Most of the literature constituting the "cult of domesticity" in the United States originated in the New England states, although there is reason to consider it a national phenomenon. New England had the most influential regional culture in the country's early history. In the period under consideration here New Englanders proselytized so vigorously on behalf of their religious and secular values, through the dissemination of printed literature, and migrants, that they consciously contributed to the making of a nation (the Northern part of it, at least) in their image. Until tested further my conclusions must be confined to the New England case, although they

6. Jacob Abbott, in *New England and her Institutions by One of her Sons* (Boston, 1835), p. 25, claimed that even in outlying or newly settled areas there was hardly a log or frame dwelling "in which some periodical print is not taken. The newspapers of the day are scattered far beyond the route of the mails, and the region of passable roads."

apply implicitly to the rest of the North as it recapitulated the conditions obtaining in New England, and contrast implicitly to the slaveholding South.[7]

The New England diaries, memoirs, and letters preserved to the present day do not, of course, compose a scientific random sample of the category "middle-class women." They compose *a* sample. In order to describe what kind of sample that is, with what biases, I have tried to classify my sources—a tentative endeavor at best, because collateral information about the diarist or correspondent so often is lacking. Reviewing the 100 women whose documents provided my chief (though not entire) source material, and weighing such rough indices as occupation of husband, amount of leisure and education, types of work, expenditures, and family name, I judged half (51) of them "middle-class." Some of this group were struggling to maintain respectability. The other half (49) I considered "upper-middle-class"; some of these were quite well-to-do, and a

7. To put it schematically, the Northern "cult of true womanhood" and the Southern image of the lady may be seen in at least three relations. They could neither be indigenous but both be "the nineteenth century's" conception of the female role, as William R. Taylor has asserted in *Cavalier and Yankee: The Old South and American National Character* (Garden City, N.Y.: Anchor Books, 1963), p. 143. They could be separate traditions depending on the same or similar patterns of causation, with perhaps different timing. Or they could be separate, indigenous traditions with different origins. I tend to support the last view. As I will propose, the New England concept initially was bourgeois, and prescribed a role of utility, not leisure, decoration, or helplessness for women. The Southern image, as I understand it, belonged more directly to the historical tradition immortalizing the aristocratic lady. Its origins and appearance rested on the purposive establishment of a slaveholding "cavalier" society—and specifically on the presence of black women slaves plus, in some places, a disproportionate ratio of men to women among whites—rather than to an ongoing social transformation. It seems to me highly possible that the Southern tradition influenced Northern conceptions of women's roles more than vice versa; that would explain why by mid-century Northern rhetoric on woman's role sounded increasingly like Southern. As Taylor himself has deftly shown, the "cavalier" affected the Yankee's conception of the good life in other significant respects.

few were among the elite. The 100 women were unevenly distributed through New England, more than half (53) living in Massachusetts, more than another quarter (26) in Connecticut, and the remainder divided among Rhode Island, Vermont, New Hampshire, and Maine. The New England population at large was also concentrated in Massachusetts and Connecticut, but less so: the proportion in Massachusetts barely exceeded one-third, and that in Connecticut never exceeded one-fifth of the total New England population at any time between 1800 and 1830.[8]

The sources were also considerably more urban than the general population. I am certain that 17 lived on farms, although more *probably* did. By comparison, in 1820 over 80 percent of the whole labor force in Maine, New Hampshire, and Vermont, over 70 percent in Connecticut, and over 55 percent in Rhode Island and Massachusetts pursued agricultural occupations.[9] Of those women whose town residence is clear, 40 lived in towns of less than 2500 persons, 23 in towns of between 2500 and 6000, and 26 in the larger cities of Boston (11), Salem (6), and Lowell (3), Massachusetts; Hartford, Connecticut (3); and Newport, Rhode Island (3).[10] Thus, by the census definition, 55 per-

8. I was able to determine state of residence for 97 of the 100. Population figures for the New England states appear in J. Potter, "Growth of Population in the United States, 1700–1860," in David V. Glass and D. Eversley, eds., *Population in History* (London: Arnold, 1965), p. 664. I have noted residence, wherever possible, in the List of Women's Documents Consulted (see pp. 207–13).

9. Yasukichi Yasuba, *Birth Rates of the White Population in the United States, 1800–1860* (Baltimore: Johns Hopkins University Press, 1962), p. 154.

10. These are population *estimates* for the towns of women's residence. In the case of women whose documents pertained mainly to the years before 1812, I used the *Second Census, 1800: Return of the Whole Number of Persons* (Washington, D.C., 1801) to figure the size of the towns in which they lived. In the case of women whose documents pertained mainly to the period between 1812 and 1840, I used the *Fifth Census; or Enumeration of the Inhabitants of the U.S. as Corrected at the Department of State, 1830* (Washington, D.C. 1832).

cent of the sources resided in "urban" places—of 2500 persons or more. It is important to recognize that about half of the "urban" sources lived in towns such as Beverly, Massachusetts, or Glastonbury, Connecticut, or Concord, New Hampshire, not in the cities of Boston or Newport. Nevertheless, in 1830 even in Rhode Island, the most "urban" state, only 31 percent of the population lived in towns of 2500; in Massachusetts, the proportion was 21 percent, and in the other New England states, less than 10 percent. The more-than-usually urban and nonfarm character of the sample is an added reason to see in this study the shape of things to come after 1830. By 1850 over 55 percent of the Massachusetts population and over 50 percent of the Rhode Island population were "urban," and in Connecticut and New Hampshire the proportion had risen above 15 percent; more than half of the labor force in New England—over two-thirds in Connecticut and over three-quarters in Massachusetts and Rhode Island—engaged in nonagricultural occupations.[11]

The time spanned by individual women's documents varies, from a few months to a half-century. Twenty-two of their lives and accounts pertain to years between 1750 and 1795; 27, to years between 1795 and 1810; 45, to years between 1810 and 1825; and 32, to years between 1825 and 1840.[12] In 15 cases one can view a woman's passage from youth through marriage and, in 5 of these, through motherhood. Slightly more than half of the women—53—were single. For the most part these were young women in their late teens and early twenties who had not yet married, rather than confirmed middle-aged spinsters. (New England women married at an average age of 22 or

---

11. Yasuba, *Birth Rates*, pp. 143, 154.

12. The total adds up to more than 100 because many individuals' documents cross the boundaries of these chronological divisions.

23 during this period.[13]) The rest (47) were married—I include here the 15 who moved from girlhood to marriage—and 34 of them were mothers; 5 became widows.

The frequency of single women might suggest that the sample fails to represent women's typical experience (since more than 90 percent of American women married), until one takes into account the age structure of the population. Between 1800 and 1840 more than two-thirds of the white American population was under the age of 24. The proportion between the ages of 14 and 24, which would include most single women, was rising from slightly under one-fifth of the total population, in 1800, to approximately one-quarter, in 1840. The proportion between 24 and 44, which would include most married women and mothers, was one-fifth in 1800, and fell slowly during the next few decades.[14] Since there was approximately the same number of women between 14 and 24 as between 24 and 44—and the former outnumbered the latter as the decades passed—the slight majority of unmarried women among the sources accurately renders the age structure of the population at one point in time.

Ideal sources, however, would trace almost all women from girlhood through marriage and motherhood in order to recapitulate the typical life cycle. Why do more private writings from women's youth than from their maturity survive? The simplest answer is that they had more time when unmarried, or thought they had more time, to ponder and record their thoughts. Sarah Ripley Stearns, who kept a diary more or less faithfully from the age of fourteen, wrote when she was thirty, married for three years, and a mother, "I do not find so much time to write in my jour-

13. This is an estimate. Research on average marriage age has generally been confined to the period before 1800. See Wells, "Quaker Marriage Patterns in a Colonial Perspective," esp. pp. 428-31, and Bernard Farber, *Guardians of Virtue: Salem Families in 1800* (New York: Basic Books, 1972), pp. 41-43.
14. Potter, "Growth of Population," p. 271.

nal as formerly when I lived in my father's house—the cares of a rising family & a feeble state of health, take up much time & day after day, month after month passes away & I see but little that I have done."[15] A simple and direct correlation between private writing and leisure does not exhaust the question, however: individual inclination is involved. Unmarried women were "unsettled," in the language of the day, and had stronger motives for self-scrutiny—for the examination of their prospects—than did married women who already had made their most significant life-choice. Further to undermine the simple correlation of leisure with diary-keeping, some of the busiest possible women kept diaries: Sarah Snell Bryant, for example, who was household manager of a western Massachusetts farm, mother of half a dozen children, and yet never missed a daily entry in her diary between 1795 and 1847.[16]

The major source of energy for diary writing in this period, I think, was one somewhat abstracted from circumstances of leisure or marital or wealth status: religion. The Calvinist tradition encouraged self-examination and exposure of one's self to God. An individual's written record of her life aided her in monitoring her progress toward salvation. This was a long-standing tradition, but one that prevailing illiteracy had prevented most women from practicing during the colonial period. By 1840, however, almost all women in New England could read and write, women's literacy having approximately doubled since 1780.[17] Growing numbers of women could take this path of reli-

15. Diary of Sarah Ripley Stearns, Jan. 1, 1815, Stearns Collection, SL. It is likely that she meant pregnancy by her reference to a "feeble state of health," for she bore three children between 1813 and 1816.

16. Diary of Sarah Snell Bryant, Cummington, Mass., 1795–1847, HCL.

17. See Kenneth A. Lockridge, *Literacy in Colonial New England* (New York: Norton, 1974), pp. 38–42, 57–58, on women's literacy in 1780; and Maris Vinovskis and Richard M. Bernard, "Women in Education in Ante-Bellum America," unpubl. Working Paper 73–7, Center for Demography and Ecology, University of Wisconsin, Madison, June 1973, on the later period.

gious or self-expression, and might appreciate it as did Sophronia Grout, who wrote in 1823, "A retired chamber is one of the choicest blessings I enjoy. . . . Here, may I review my feelings, mourn over my numerous imperfections. . . . Veiled from the world I vent my feelings on paper for I do find relief in recording the exercises of my mind."[18] The Protestant tradition produced two main sorts of diaries. One was the laconic account of tasks performed (such as Sarah Snell Bryant's), in which the motive to disclose one's progress to one's self and God was tacit, even buried. The other was the explicit record of self-examination and often self-castigation, which could also have a secular aspect. Each of these has its virtues and defects from the historian's point of view: the former is likely to be more informative about the person's work than her thoughts, the latter vice versa.

I have introduced these considerations here to suggest that the causes that allowed or encouraged women to leave personal records do not lend themselves to efficient weighting and ordering. One might want to say that women who left diaries were more self-conscious than those who were their peers in other respects and did not do so, but even that element is imponderable because other variables, such as a family tradition of diary-keeping, or particular religious scruples, might have exerted equal influence. Busyness, level of uncertainty, desire for expression, religious conscience, sense of tradition, self-consciousness might each and all have pertained, in addition to literacy. I thought that I would be most likely to comprehend the experience of this class of women as a whole by examining the private records of a large and varied number of them, with all their idiosyncrasies, including the impoverished evangelist's wife, the industrious rural household manager, the once-

18. Diary of Sophronia Grout, Hawley, Mass., Feb. 9, 1823, Pocumtuck Valley Memorial Association Library Collection, HD.

genteel seamstress, the carefree daughter of a wealthy lawyer, as well as the contentedly domestic mother of three.
The drawbacks and virtues of these sources are identical:
they give account not of mass behavior nor generalized
norms but of a small number (relative to the whole population) of discrete, individual psyches. Such documents
have a unique combination of assets, because they were
unintended for strangers' eyes, yet attempted to communicate something of the authors' selves. No other historical
source is more likely to disclose women's consciousness.
On the other hand, they lack completeness, and thus are
not strictly comparable one with the other. One diarist
may record every day, another every week, another more
sporadically through the years. One may record every task
accomplished, while another may do more but disdain to
write about it. Without some corollary information a pres-
ent-day reader cannot tell what was left out of a diary,
letter, or memoir, and whether items were left out because
they were unimportant or the very most important to the
writer. (In an ironic sense, the writers thus protect their
"unknownness" from historians' prying.)

Personal documents of middle-class women are not sufficient, although they are essential, to reconstruct the social
history of New England women between 1780 and 1835.
Contemporary published views about and advice to women, on which I have also relied, help to establish the cultural milieu in which women found themselves but leave
their actual behavior to inference. My intent, guided by
the limits and assets of my sources, is to provide an inter-
pretative framework for a thorough social history which
has yet to be written. My theme concerns the social deriva-
tion of a concept of "womanhood" rooted in the experience of Yankee middle-class mothers but applied to the
female sex as a whole. I hope to show the emergence of
this formulation and to analyze and explain its coherence,

plausibility, and usefulness. These purposes demand doubling back and forth between evidence and interpretation, between circumstance and ideology, between experience and consciousness, and repeatedly reviewing the same chronology with reference to different topics in order to establish overlapping patterns which should reinforce and help to explain one another. This is an essay in the true sense—an attempt at understanding and interpretation—an effort to make sense of women's lives in an era of social transformation in which we can recognize the outlines of our own time.

1

WORK

"A woman's work is never done," Martha Moore Ballard wrote in her journal one November midnight in 1795, having been busy preparing wool for spinning until that time, "and happy she whos[e] strength holds out to the end of the [sun's] rays." Ballard was sixty years old that year—a grandmother several times over—though she still had at home her youngest child of sixteen. Housekeeper and domestic manufacturer for a working farm where she baked and brewed, pickled and preserved, spun and sewed, made soap and dipped candles, she also was a trusted healer and midwife for the pioneer community of Augusta, Maine. During a quarter-century of practice continuing past her seventieth year, she delivered more than a thousand babies. The very processes of her work engaged her in community social life. In her medical work she became acquainted with her neighbors as she provided services for them, and domestic crafts, such as quilting and spinning, also involved her in both cooperative and remunerative social relationships.[1] The pattern of her life was not atypical for the matron of a farm household, particularly in a frontier community, in the late eighteenth century.

My investigation of women's roles and consciousness

1. Diary of Martha Moore Ballard, 1785-1812, in Charles Elventon Nash, d., *The History of Augusta [Maine]* (Augusta: Charles Nash and Sons, 1904), pp. 229-464; quotation, Nov. 26, 1795, p. 348.

begins with their work, on account of several interrelated assumptions. A person's work, or productive occupation, not only earns a living and fills time but also contributes to self-definition and shapes social identity. A characteristic occupation enforces habits that tend to dominate a person's whole approach to life. The more complex and specialized a society becomes, the more numerous and diverse kinds of work are required, and the more discrete the relation between work and social identity. If an individual's work changes, or the work typically associated with a social group does, wider-ranging change in the person's or group's role in society can be expected.

If there was intensive social change between 1780 and 1835, that at once makes shifts in women's patterns of work likely; but before investigating change it is valuable to recognize continuity. Certain influential but taken-for-granted conditions continuously affected women's work. The most pervasive was that women were considered adjunct and secondary to men in economic life. From the earliest years of New England, women's labor was crucial to prosperous settlement and "industry" was praised in either sex. But long-standing tradition gave men the importance and the burden of "providing." As early as 1692 Cotton Mather described women's economic activity in Boston as being only "to Spend (or . . . Save) what others *Get*." Divorce records of the eighteenth century clearly differentiated the two spouses' economic roles: the husband's, to supply or provide; the wife's, to use goods frugally and to obey.[2] If both sexes were expected to make themselves useful, nevertheless the man had the initiating and central economic role.

2. Cotton Mather, *Ornaments for the Daughters of Zion* (Cambridge, 1692), p. 45. On marital norms revealed in divorce records, see Nancy F. Cott, "Divorce and the Changing Status of Women in Eighteenth-Century Massachusetts," *WMQ* 3rd ser., 33 (1976); esp. 611-14, and "Eighteenth-Century Family and Social Life," *JSH* 10 (1976), esp. 30-31.

The legal conditions of marriage embodied women's economic status. A wife's property and earnings belonged to her husband. Only when single and over eighteen, or widowed, did a woman own her own labor power and property. Women thus found little incentive for economic ambition, since on the whole they planned and wished to marry. Nor did women have much opportunity for economic achievement. Wage rates reflected the expectation that they would rely on men as providers. Marriage placed legal obstacles in the way of women's entrepreneurship. Higher education for scholarly professions was unavailable to them.[3]

The norm for an adult woman remained household occupation, which implied dependence on a man's initiating economic activity. Because of its relation to men's provider role in marriage, women's productive work retained a secondary character even when carried outside the home and performed for wages. Thus a historian writing about the cotton-mill system of the early nineteenth century and its female operatives can assert, "it was not their turnover rate but the girls' status as secondary earners that gave the system its distinctive character."[4] During the years when

3. Richard B. Morris, "Women's Rights in Early American Law," in his *Studies in the History of American Law* (New York: Columbia University Press, 1930), pp. 126–200, has become the standard essay on colonial women under the common law. Mary Beard, *Woman as Force in History* (New York: Collier Books, 1962), chap. 6, also makes some provocative comments. See Alexander Keyssar, "Widowhood in Eighteenth-Century Massachusetts," *Perspectives in American History* 8 (1974), for an illuminating analysis which refines some of Morris's claims. On women's wage rates compared to men's through the early nineteenth century, see Edith Abbott, *Women in Industry*, (New York and London: D. Appleton, 1918), pp. 76n., 157, 192, 249, 262–316. For example, at the Merrimack mills in Lowell, Massachusetts, in 1824, women's wages ranged from $2.25 to $4.00 weekly; men's ranged from $4.50 to $12.00 weekly (p. 272).

4. Howard Gitelman, "The Waltham System and the Coming of the Irish," *Labor History* 8 (1967):235.

farm households which were self-contained productive units prevailed, the economic and productive interdependence of all members of a family diluted the meaning of women's economic status. Women depended on men to buy and work land and produce grain, but men had no bread without women baking it. Women's economic dependency was one strand in a web of interdependence of men's and women's typical work. It was when commercial farm production augmented subsistence, master craftsmen became bosses of journeymen and replaced custom work with work for the market, and wage earning or profit taking became characteristic ways of "providing" that women's economic role appeared singular, their dependency prominent.

Another allied but more impalpable element of continuity in women's work (as in their lives) was its constant orientation toward the needs of others, especially men. Ministers and other moralists always described women's duties in interpersonal terms. "Piety to God— reverence to parents—love and obedience to their husbands—tenderness and watchfulness over their children— justice and humanity to their dependents—" made up a New Hampshire pastor's definition of woman's role, in his *Female Guide* of 1793.[5] Woman's role in marriage —to serve her husband—again partially explains this characteristic of women's work. In its strictly economic aspect the traditional marriage contract resembled an indenture between master and servant. Both parties had rights and obligations. The wife (much like the servant) deserved provision and owed service and obedience.[6] Of course, in the larger sense, men also served their wives, by providing

5. John Cosens Ogden, *The Female Guide, or Thoughts on the Education of that Sex Accomodated [sic] to the State of Society, Manners, and Government in the United States* (Concord, N.H.: George Hough, 1793), p. 22.

6. See Cott, "Divorce and the Changing Status of Women," pp. 611-14.

for them; but their service was the price of an independent, superordinate role rather than the obligation of a dependent and subordinate one. This economic skeleton of marriage supported a broader cultural body of meaning. Denied the incentive and opportunity for economic (and, generally, public) ambition, women had instead the incentive and opportunity to serve others directly, within family relationships for the most part.

Catherine Sedgwick inadvertently highlighted this contrast when, in her youth (before her career as a novelist), she measured her own prospects against the accomplishments of her father Theodore Sedgwick, the Federalist statesman. "A life dignified by usefulness, of which it has been the object and the delight to do good, and the happiness to do it in an extended sphere, does," she reflected, "furnish some points of imitation for the most limited routine of domestic life. Wisdom and virtue are never at a loss for occasions and times for their exercise, the same light that lightens the world is applied to individual use & gratification. You may benefit a Nation, my dear Papa, I may improve the condition of a fellow-being."[7] A man served in "an extended sphere," in "the world," to benefit "a Nation"; a woman, in the "limited routine of domestic life," for "individual use and gratification," to benefit "a fellow-being," in Sedgwick's not uncommon view. The persistence of the household occupation of adult women reaffirmed their adjunct and service relationship to men in economic activity, even when new economic factors and opportunities intervened.

The basic developments hastening economic productivity and rationalizing economic organization in New England

7. Catherine Maria Sedgwick, New York, to Theodore Sedgwick, Stockbridge, Massachusetts, March 1, 1812; Sedgwick Collection, MHS.

between 1780 and 1835 were extension of the size of the market, increases in agricultural efficiency, reduction in transportation costs, and consequent specialization of economic function, division of labor, and concentration of industry. In late eighteenth-century towns, subsistence farming and household production for family use prevailed, supplemented by individual craftsmen (cobblers, coopers, blacksmiths, tailors, weavers, etc.) who were established or itinerant depending on density of population in their locale, and by small industrial establishments such as sawmills, gristmills, fulling mills, ironworks, and brickyards. The Revolutionary war stimulated some forms of household production (such as "homespun"), and so did the disruption of the international market during the Napoleonic wars, but more continuous lines of change moved the New England economy from its agricultural and household-production base and gave it a commercial and then industrial emphasis by 1835.

Merchant capitalism was a primary force in this transformation. Merchant capitalists took risks, supplied capital, searched out markets, and attempted to maximize profits by producing standardized goods at the least cost, thus organizing production on a larger scale than had previously been typical. Their actions commanded a shift away from home production for family use, and from local craftsmen's production of custom or "bespoke" work for known individuals, toward more standardized production for a wider market. Mercantile capitalism flourished during the enormous expansion of New England's carrying trade and re-export business that occurred from 1793 to 1807 because of the confusion of European shipping during the Napoleonic wars. This burst of shipping energy also caused subsidiary economic activities, such as shipbuilding, and complementary businesses, such as brokerage, marine insurance, warehousing, and banking, to grow. Under the brunt of the national embargo in 1807 and the subsequent war with England this blooming of the American carrying and re-export trade faded, but since much of the capital involved was transferred to manufacturing activity overall economic productivity did not diminish greatly.

The shift to market-oriented production under merchant capitalists prepared the way for the development of manufacturing and the factory system. Under the demand of the merchant capitalist for widely distributable goods, the craftsman's shop became a larger and more specialized unit, for production only rather than (as formerly) for production and retail sale. The master craftsman became the "boss" of a larger number of journeymen and apprentices. In New England another production system, limited mainly to shoes and textiles, also preceded and overlapped with industrial manufacture. This was the "putting-out" or "given-out" system, in which a merchant or master craftsman distributed materials to individuals to work on in their homes at piece-work rates, and collected and sold the finished goods. As the given-out system developed, the individuals (often women) it employed at home performed more and more specialized and fragmentary handicrafts. Indeed, the hallmarks of economic development in this period were functional specialization and division of labor. Where there had been "jacks-of-all-trades" there came specialized laborers; where there had been eclectic merchants there came importers and exporters, wholesalers and jobbers and retailers. Farmers who had produced only for subsistence trained their eyes on, and diverted some of their energies to, the market for commercial produce. New specialists appeared in fields from insurance to banking to transportation, as incorporations of businesses multiplied and turnpikes and bridges replaced wooded paths.[8] In order to understand shifts in women's work during these years, rapid changes of this type must be kept in mind. Whether a woman lived toward the beginning or toward the end of this half-century may have informed the character of her work as much as, or more than, her geographical location, wealth, or marital status, which were other significant factors. Comparison of the kinds of work recorded in women's diaries in the earlier and later years makes that clear.

During the late eighteenth century both unmarried and married women did their primary work in households, in families. Unmarried daughters might be called upon to help their fathers in a store or shop connected to the house: Sally Ripley, a tradesman's daughter in Greenfield, Massachusetts, more than once recorded in her diary, "This morning my Father departed for Boston, & I am again entrusted with the charge of the Store." But daughters' assistance in the housewife's realm of food preparation and preservation, dairying, gardening, cleaning, laundering, soap making, candle making, knitting, and textile and clothing manufacture was the more usual case. Mothers and daughters shared these labors. The continual and time-consuming work of spinning was the most readily delegated to the younger generation, it seems. Hannah Hickok Smith of Glastonbury, Connecticut, managed to avoid spinning, because she had five daughters at home. "The girls . . . have been very busy

8. For a fuller explanation of economic change during these years see George Rogers Taylor, *The Transportation Revolution*, vol. 4 of the *Economic History of the U.S.* (New York: Rinehart, 1951), pp. 10–14, 208–40, 250–52, 266–69; Stuart Bruchey, *The Roots of American Economic Growth, 1607–1861* (New York: Harper Torchbooks, 1968), esp. pp. 200–01; Douglass C. North, *The Economic Growth of the United States, 1790–1860* (New York: Norton, 1966), esp. pp. 9–11, 36–58, 156–59; Abbott, *Women in Industry*, pp. 66–71; Percy Wells Bidwell, "The Agricultural Revolution in New England," *AHR* 26 (1921):683–702.

spinning this spring," she reported to their grandmother in 1800, "and have spun enough for about seventy yards besides almost enough for another carpet." Spinning must have taken precedence in the daughters' work, for when they had "no spinning to do of any consequence" then Mrs. Smith admitted that she "lived very easy, as the girls have done every thing."[9]

Other unmarried daughters in the post-Revolutionary years, such as Abigail and Elizabeth Foote of Colchester, Connecticut, and Elizabeth Fuller of Princeton, Massachusetts, spent days and months engaged in cloth manufacture—carding, combing, and spinning the fiber, weaving, bleaching or dyeing the fabric—in addition to regular cutting, sewing, and quilting of articles for use.[10] Characteristically women's work, textile manufacture was especially characteristic for unmarried women. It was no accident that they came to be called spinsters. Women who remained unmarried into old age continued to be useful in the households of their kin because of the assistance they offered in textile manufacture.[11]

By selling the services or products of their spinning, weaving, or needlework, women could turn their usual domestic occupations into paid work. Elizabeth Foote "fix'd two Gown for Welch's Girls which came to 1'6″'" in 1775. Zeloda Barrett of New Hartford, Connecticut, knit mittens and stockings for sale; the daughter of the

9. Diary of Sarah Ripley (Stearns), May 21, 1809 (see also Oct. 17, 1808), Stearns Collection, SL; Hannah Hickok Smith, Glastonbury, to Abigail Mitchell, Southbury, June 5, [1800], and May 1810, CSL.

10. See diaries of Elizabeth and Abigail Foote, 1775-76, CHS; and diary of Elizabeth Fuller, 1790-92, in Francis E. Blake, *History of the Town of Princeton [, Mass.]* (Princeton, 1915), 1:302-23.

11. The *Oxford English Dictionary* points out that the word *spinster* shifted during the seventeenth century from its original meaning, female spinner, to become the legal term for an unmarried woman. The four-volume diary of Rebeccah Noyes, CHS, covering the years from 1801 to 1829, illuminates the experience of a "spinster" (in both senses) past middle age.

Reverend Mills, who lived near Hadlyme, Connecticut, knit gloves and stockings. Eliza Perkins Wildes, a married woman of Arundel, Maine, wove cloaks for sale. Sales of homespun yarn and home-woven cloth provided women with a major source of income through the eighteenth and very early nineteenth century. Theodora Orcutt's account with a local provisioner of Whately, Massachusetts, showed her sales of at least seven different weights of yarn in 1781. This common practice of exchanging homemade yarn or cloth for credit with neighborhood tradesmen gave over in the early nineteenth century to the pattern of domestic weaving of factory-made yarn put out by merchant capitalists. Zeloda's sister Samantha Barrett, a skilled weaver about thirty years old, added to the income of their farm household by weaving homespun for individuals and, after 1815, by making up cloth for "the Factory."[12]

Unmarried women also earned wages by performing their usual domestic tasks in households other than their own. At times Elizabeth Foote noted that "mr Wells owed me 2s 6p for my work being 1s per day" and that others "owed me 3 weeks and 2 days work." Zeloda Barrett worked sporadically in other households, at the rate of 5 shillings per week. In the well-to-do Porter household of Hadley, Massachusetts, young women periodically appeared to spin and "taylor." This kind of domestic service was a function of age as much as economic need; it formed part of a young woman's "apprenticeship" to womanly duties. Hiring was often casual. Elizabeth Wildes recorded on November 14, 1791, "I went to Mr. Mach-

12. Elizabeth Foote diary, March 7, 1775; diary of Zeloda Barrett, Dec. 7, 1820, CHS; diary of the daughter of the Rev. Mills, 1809, VHS; diary of Elizabeth Perkins Wildes, 1789-93 (see list of items sold, in center of volume) MeHS; Orcutt's account, reprinted in Abbott, *Women in Industry*, pp. 25-26; weaving account book of Samantha Barrett for 1812-16, CHS.

Collohs after a girl," and on the following day, "Molly Watson came here to stay." In and out of the farm household of Sarah Snell Bryant of western Massachusetts went a series of young women, "coming here to live" and then going off "bag and bagage [*sic*]."[13]

The mistress of a farm family usually considered domestic "helps" essential. When her five daughters were young, Hannah Hickok Smith commented anxiously on the presence or absence of a "hired girl" in her family in every letter she wrote to her mother. Long-term indentures avoided transiency in domestic workers, but might compound other problems if the mistress found her relationship with her "help" less than harmonious. Anna Bryant Smith of Portland, Maine, could hardly wait until Betsy Delano reached the end of her indenture at age twenty-one, because she felt the girl was "under no regulations" and "had no system in [her]." Mrs. Smith wearily complained from time to time that she had "set up till 11 o'clock waiting for Betsy Delano to come home but had to go to bed & leave her out to my Grief and mortification," and prayed that "we never have another night walker." The wife of the most eminent citizen of Sharon, Connecticut, had continual trouble with hired hands on their farm while her husband was absent, and lamented that "Silve," who helped her in the house, was "as bad as she can be." Martha Moore Ballard also expressed dissatisfaction with the standards of the younger generation. "I paid Elizabeth Taylor for what work she has done for me and dismist her," she recorded in December 1795. "I

13. Elizabeth Foote diary, April 13, April 9, 1775; Zeloda Barrett diary, June 29, July 27, Aug. 20, Dec. 11, 1804, March 9, July 10, 1820; Elizabeth Porter Phelps, "Diary, 1763-1805," ed. Thomas Eliot Andrews, *NEHGR* 18 (1964); Elizabeth Perkins Wildes diary, Nov. 14 and 15, 1791; diary of Sarah Snell Bryant, July 17, 1806, HCL—see also March 6 and 17, June 2, 1804, Feb. 8, March 29, Sept. 24, 1806, April 15, 1816.

am determined not to pay girls any more for ill manners."[14] The self-assertion of these "helps" hardly suggests
an obeisant temperament among young women who
earned their keep.

For rates of pay comparable to those in domestic work,
young women also taught summer sessions of primary
school. As early as the 1760s school districts began the
practice of hiring women rather than men as teachers for
summer sessions, which were primarily for very young
children and older girls, who were excluded from regular
winter terms. The move in a sense institutionalized the
private "dame" school, but put in the teacher's place
young and unmarried women rather than older matrons
or widows. The duration of the summer term varied from
two months to as much as six months (April to October)
by the end of the century. Several kinds of data suggest
that the summer scholars learned reading but not writing.
Hannah Adams remembered that in Medfield, Massachusetts, in the 1760s, "in the summer, the children were
instructed by females in reading, sewing, and other kinds
of work. The books chiefly made use of were the Bible,
and Psalter." In another New England woman's recollection, "in summer, it was simply reading and spelling, sewing and knitting. In summer they always employed female
teachers." More than half of New England women in the
eighteenth century could not sign their names, according
to the best recent estimate; yet perhaps not all of these
were "illiterate," if they learned to read without learning
to write, in summer sessions. Some summer sessions went
further. In 1760 three of the four precincts of Dedham,
Massachusetts, hired female teachers to offer reading, writ-

14. Letters from Hannah Hickok Smith to Abigail Mitchell, 1796–1800,
CSL; diary of Anna Bryant Smith, April 4, 1807, July 24, Dec. 31, 1806,
March 3, 1807, MeHS; diary of Margaret Everston Smith, Jan. 9, 11, 16, 1808,
CHS; Martha Moore Ballard diary, Dec. 19, 1795, in Nash, *History of Augusta*,
p. 349.

ing, and ciphering during the summer. (In the winter, schoolmasters equipped to teach Latin were employed.) The town of Manchester, Massachusetts, in 1763 authorized half of the school allotment—a serious investment, certainly—"to support four school Dames to keep a free schoole."[15]

The teachers of summer sessions were, by and large, unmarried daughters of farm families, between the ages of seventeen and thirty. Elizabeth Foote left her household work in Colchester and "set out for Gilead to keep school" in April 1776. Ruth Henshaw, who occupied her winter days on the family farm in Leicester, Massachusetts, with carding, spinning, sewing, and quilting—and also enjoyed herself entertaining and visiting—taught school in nearby Spencer or Brookfield every summer between 1791 and 1801, when she was in her twenties. She boarded with a family for the duration of the term from June to September, and sometimes for a term from April to June as well. Elizabeth Bancroft of Pepperell, Massachusetts, a contemporary of similarly well-established family, also boarded out and taught school in the mid-1790s. It was a "tiresome" task to her, and she rejoiced at the term's end, "I once more enjoy the sweets of liberty." Yet to the modern eye, these schools seem irregular, loosely organized, and subject to the teacher's whim. Both Ruth Henshaw and Elizabeth Bancroft taught from twenty to forty-five "scholars," and the number varied from day to day. The latter did not scruple against ending the school

15. *A Memoir of Miss Hannah Adams, written by Herself, with additional notices, by a friend* (Boston, 1832), p. 3; *Bessie; or, Reminiscences of a Daughter of a New England Clergyman of the Eighteenth Century*, by a Grandmother (New Haven: J. H. Benham, 1861), p. 66; Kenneth A. Lockridge, *Literacy in Colonial New England*, (New York: Norton, 1974), esp. pp. 38–42, 57–58; on Dedham, Lawrence Cremin, *American Education: The Colonial Experience* (New York: Harper Torchbooks, 1970), p. 525; on Manchester (and another example, Warwick, Massachusetts), Abbott, *Women in Industry*, p. 267n. I am indebted to Kathryn Kish Sklar for the reference to *Bessie*.

day early when she wanted to see visitors or prepare a dress to be made. In 1793, because her schoolhouse was closed for a while in the summer for repairs, she taught until mid-October, and in 1794 she created a fortnight's break at midsession. Schoolteaching in this period appeared less a means of essential support for unmarried women than a mode in which daughters of established families enacted their duty to the community.[16]

As family-centered production gave ground to market-oriented production and individual wage earning, school-teaching became a more important financial resource for young women. Both common schools and private seminaries and academies multiplied during the early national period, creating more frequent opportunities for employment.[17] During the early decades of the nineteenth century young women found teaching jobs of at least three kinds. First was traditional summer-school teaching, which was becoming more regularized as school boards pursued professionalism, licensing, and economy, but still retained elements of flexibility and casualness. On April 7, 1817, Amanda Elliott, thirty years old and the youngest of eleven siblings of a Guilford, Connecticut, family, noted "some talk that I should take a school." Twelve days later she recorded, "I determined on taking a school for a quarter," and on May 4, with some irony, "this day opened my school and should be glad were it the day that clos'd it; excellent feeling for the beginning of a three month job." She took schools at the same season in 1819 and 1820, nonetheless. Eighteen-year-old Eunice Wait left her "common labours & domestic avocations" at home in Hallowell, Maine, to teach school for the summer in Gerry,

16. Abigail Foote diary, April 1776; diary of Ruth Henshaw, 1791–1801, esp. June 18, 1792, April 18, 1796, July 8, 1800, AAS; diary of Elizabeth Bancroft, June 18 and 19, July 8, Aug. 20, Oct. 12, 1793, July 1 and 21, Sept. 6, 8, and 11, Nov. 1, 1794, March 18, May 6, Sept. 24, 1795, AAS.

17. See chapter 3, "Education."

fifteen miles away, in 1821. Pamela Brown of Plymouth Notch, Vermont, accepted when, in May 1836, "Mr. Green came and engaged me to teach school in his district for three months. I am to have a dollar a week and to begin next week." Her school went on until the end of August.[18]

Because of the repeated religious revivals of these decades and ministers' accompanying emphasis on the formative years of youth, some pious young women took schoolteaching responsibilities with new, religious seriousness. A minister's daughter began her third season of teaching in May 1821 by noting "when I look around on 30 children whose minds are susceptible of any impressions, either good or bad, I almost shrink at the task which devolves on me." A few days later she recorded, "Have felt very anxious for my little flock this day—How great are the duties incumbent upon an instructor of youth—Impressions made on young and tender minds often remain indelible." Her anxieties did not subside until the end of June.[19]

Another kind of teaching opportunity existed in the growing numbers of academies for girls. Some academies offered "accomplishments" such as fancy needlework, foreign languages, music, and painting, while others attempted a literary education. Lucinda Read followed a common course when she left her family's farm in Greenfield, Vermont, at eighteen, went to Canton, Connecticut, to attend an academy, and shortly afterward (1816) secured a job teaching in its lower school. She subsequently

18. Diary of Amanda Elliott, CSL; diary of Eunice Hale Wait Cobb, July 9, 1821, BPL; diary of Pamela Brown, May 23, 1836, in *The Diaries of Sally and Pamela Brown, 1832-1838; Hyde Leslie, 1887, Plymouth Notch, Vermont,* ed. Blanche Brown Bryant and Gertrude Elaine Baker (Springfield, Vt.: William L. Bryant Foundation, 1970), p. 41.

19. Diary of Sophronia Grout, May 15 and 19, June 13, 28, and 29, 1821, Pocumtuck Valley Memorial Library Collections, HD. Cf. the diary of Lavinia Bailey Kelly (Cilly), vol. 2, Oct. 13, 1834, NHHS.

taught in Plainfield, New Hampshire, and Montpelier, Vermont. Attending an academy was generally the appropriate preparation for teaching in one. Eliza Perkins, who had been to school in Hartford, Connecticut, left to teach at the Greenfield Female Academy in 1819. She complained that she could "barely get a support" there, however, and considered going South to become a private tutor in a family.[20]

Although women were not well paid for teaching they continued to seek it as respectable and intellectual work. Since women commanded a much lower salary than men, school districts under pressure of population and common-school expansion began to turn to them for regular winter-term instruction. This third kind of teaching job became available to women in the 1830s, setting them before classes of girls *and* boys in their teens. Pamela Brown not only taught in the summer of 1836; between January and March she taught in another school district at the higher rate of $1.50 per week. Her older sister Sally had taught in that district during December and January 1834–35. Mary Hall of Concord, New Hampshire, taught a district school for a brief winter session in 1829–30 after she had attended nearby Brackett Academy for four quarters. Rachel Stearns, in her mid-twenties, moved from Greenfield to Leominster, Massachusetts, to teach a district school for the winter term in 1834–35. She relied on her Methodist beliefs to give her the courage to speak at the head of a class that included "three great boys." Between 1825 and 1860, according to a recent inquiry, a quarter

20. Diary of Lucinda Read, vol. 1, Aug. 5, 1815, Jan. 19, Feb. 21, April 15, 1816, vol. 2 for later years, MHS; Eliza Perkins to Weltha Brown, May 19, 1819, July 18, 1819, and undated, Weltha Brown Correspondence in Hooker Collection, SL. The location of Greenfield Academy is unclear. See also Lydia Huntley, ed., *The Writings of Nancy Maria Hyde of Norwich, Connecticut, Connected with a Sketch of her Life* (Norwich: Russell Hubbard, 1816), on preparation for academy teaching; and chapter 3.

of all native-born New England women were schoolteachers for some years of their lives.[21]

The growth of schoolteaching provided one instance of the expansion of nondomestic occupations for women. In the late eighteenth century, young women found their chief social usefulness and most remunerative work in households—their own or other families'. But as population expansion, improvements in transportation, and the spur of merchant capitalism allowed market-oriented production to flourish, the importance of young women's traditional work in household manufacture diminished. Specialized production for commercial exchange was the rising norm. Industrialization, a giant step in this process, occurred first in textile manufacture, which was originally women's—and especially unmarried women's— household work.[22]

21. Pamela Brown diary, Jan. 17 and 18, 1836, Sally Brown diary, April 29, 1834, in *The Diaries of Sally and Pamela Brown*, pp. 31–33, 27; diary of Mary Hall, Dec. 21, 1829, Feb. 6, 1830, NHHS; diary of Rachel Willard Stearns, vol. 4, Nov. 17, 1834, Stearns Collection, SL—she also said, regarding the prayer she made to open the school day, "It is well I am a Methodist, otherwise I should think it wrong for a woman to pray before a man"; Maris Vinovskis and Richard M. Bernard, "Women in Education in Ante-Bellum America," unpublished Working Paper 73-7, June 1973, Center for Demography and Ecology, University of Wisconsin, Madison, pp. 13–14 and graph 6. On wages of schoolteachers, see Elisabeth A. Dexter, *Career Women of America* (Francestown, N.H.: Marshal Jones, 1950), pp. 6–8.

22. In his 1791 Report on Manufactures, Alexander Hamilton noted a "vast scene of household manufacturing" in the U.S., particularly of cotton, flax, and wool materials; travelers to the U.S. and legislative reports before 1810 remarked on the wearing of homespun fabrics in New England. Political and economic circumstances between 1790 and 1810 worked to stimulate household manufacture of textiles. During the Revolution, importation of British cloth was cut off. When, at the close of the war, foreign goods began to flood U.S. markets, legislatures of several New England states made special efforts to sustain the level of household manufacture. Patriotic motives, an unfavorable balance of trade, and uncertain trade relations with England and France during the 1790s encouraged this. Jefferson's Embargo and the wave of westward migration after 1800 also stimulated household textile manufacture, the former by cutting off imported goods and money income from England and

The first "manufactories" in the United States were places of business established in major cities in the 1760s to collect yarn spun and cloth woven by women in their homes by traditional hand methods. Some merchants soon put spinning wheels and looms on the premises of their manufactories, and hired women and children to work them there; but in general they employed a much larger proportion of women working in their own homes than on the manufactory premises. After Samuel Slater introduced industrial spinning machinery to New England in 1789, and other entrepreneurs established spinning mills, employing women to work the machinery, the proportions working at home and on the premises were reversed. The early mills (between 1790 and 1815) produced only yarn, which was distributed to domestic weavers like Samantha Barrett to be made into cloth. The power loom did not appear in New England until 1814. That year the Boston Manufacturing Company introduced it at Waltham, Massachusetts, uniting under one factory roof all the operations necessary to turn raw fiber into finished cloth. Factories mass-producing cotton cloth multiplied during the 1820s.[23]

By 1830, industrial manufacture had largely superseded home spinning and weaving in New England by producing cloth more cheaply. This changed women's work more than any other single factor, and likely had more emphatic impact on unmarried women than on mothers of families. Industrialization of textiles disrupted daughters' predictable role in the household first. Mothers' lives continued

France, the latter by providing a market for surplus household production in New England. But many of the factors which fostered home manufacture, in place of importation, also fostered industrial development. See Rolla M. Tryon, *Household Manufactures in the United States, 1640–1860* (New York: Augustus M. Kelley, 1966; orig. 1917), pp. 124–33, 142–47, 162, 245–52, 274–77.

23. Ibid., pp. 274–77; Taylor, *Transportation Revolution,* pp. 229–34; Abbott, *Women in Industry,* pp. 36–39, 41–47.

to be defined by household management and child rearing. Daughters, however, often had to earn wages to replace their contribution to family sustenance. Textile mill operatives, who were almost all between the ages of fifteen and thirty, were young women who followed their traditional occupation to a new location, the factory. New England textile factories from the start employed a vastly greater proportion of women than men.[24]

The economic and social change of the period injected uncertainty, variety, and mobility into young women's lives—into none more dramatically than the early mill operatives'. Mary Hall began industrial employment after her academy schooling and experience in schoolteaching. In November 1830 she started folding books at a shop in Exeter, New Hampshire, not happy to be removed from her family. "Yes, I shall probably be obliged to call this, to me a land of strangers, home for the present," she wrote in her diary. "But home sweet home can never be transfer'd in the affections of Me. . . . How often this day amidst its cares and business have I been in imagination under the paternal roof seeing, hearing and conversing with its lov'd inhabitants." She was twenty-four years old. After seven months she returned home, because several family members were ill. In September 1831, she went to Lowell, Massachusetts, for employment as a cotton-mill operative. She worked in Lowell for the next five years, except for returns home to Concord for more than a year between 1832 and 1833, for the summer in 1834, for weeks in

24. Abbott, *Women in Industry*, p. 121, on the age of operatives; pp. 89–92, on the proportion of women. Her summary of statistics on eight New England cotton mills between 1818 and 1833 shows that women constituted 87 percent of the operatives, on the average. The proportion of women workers in New England mills at this time was far greater than that in British mills, in part because British mills more frequently used mule-spinning machinery, which was difficult for women wearing long skirts to operate, while early American mills used frame-spinning machinery, which did not involve that difficulty.

November and December 1834 (because of deaths in her family), and in November 1835 and June 1836. During her years in Lowell she worked for at least three different corporations.[25]

Emily Chubbuck, whose family was probably poorer than Mary Hall's, had a more disjointed employment history. The fifth child in a New Hampshire family transplanted to upstate New York, she went to work in 1828, at the age of eleven, splicing rolls in a woolen factory. Her parents allowed her to keep her weekly wage of $1.25. When the factory closed in January 1829 she began attending a district school, to supplement the education she had received from an older sister. Two months later the factory reopened and she resumed work there. During the next three years, as her family moved several times in attempts to make a living, she intermittently worked for a Scottish weaver twisting thread, attended an academy, washed and ironed for her family's boarders, sewed for a mantua-maker, and attended a district school. At fourteen, despite her mother's advice to apprentice herself to a milliner, she lied about her age to obtain a schoolteaching job. Her wages were only 75 cents a week plus board. She knew that she "could earn as much with the milliner, and far more at twisting thread," but she hoped for a future in literary pursuits rather than manual employment.[26]

There was a large class of young women who would have spun at home in early decades but whose families'

25. Mary Hall diary, Nov. 11, 1830 (quotation) and passim. Her sister Judith joined her in work at Lowell (after brief industrial employment elsewhere) and died there, in Mary's arms. Mary also noted the arrival and departure of other young women from Concord.

26. A. C. Kendrick, ed., *The Life and Letters of Mrs. Emily C. Judson* (New York and Boston, 1861), pp. 15–29 (quotation, 28–29). Emily Chubbuck achieved a literary career, as "Fanny Forester," and later became the third wife of Adoniram Judson, the famous missionary to Burma.

incomes or priorities made factory work unlikely for them. Their work too became variable and sporadic, shifting among the options of schoolteaching, needle-work, domestic work, and given-out industry. None of these was really a full-time, year-round occupation. Women tended to combine them. Rachel Stearns, under pressure of necessity, became willing to intersperse sewing in another household with her schoolteaching, although earlier she had "thought it quite too degrading to go to Uncle F's and sew." Nancy Flynt, a single woman of Connecticut, wrote to her married sister around 1810, "[I am] a tugging and a toiling day and night to get a maintenance, denying myself the pleasure of calling on my nearest neighbors. . . . I would tell you how much work I have dispatched since I saw you, I have a great deal of sewing on hand now." The twenty-five-year-old daughter of the minister in Hawley, Massachusetts, decided she should learn to support herself "by the needle" and therefore began to learn the milliner's trade, but her health failed, preventing her from continuing. "Perhaps [I] flattered myself too much with the idea of being able to bear my own expenses," she reflected somewhat bitterly.[27]

Given-out industry, which constituted a significant stage in the industrial development of New England, enabled women to earn money while staying at home. Two kinds of production organized this way drew heavily on women's labor: the stitching and binding of boots and shoes (con-centrated in eastern Massachusetts) and the braiding, or plaiting, of straw bonnets. The latter was a handicraft designed before 1800 by New England women who used native rye straw for the material. By 1830 thousands car-ried it on in the employ of entrepreneurs who imported

27. Rachel Willard Stearns diary, vol. 5, Oct. 19, 1835; Nancy Flynt to Mercy Flynt Morris, undated (1810s), CHS; diary of Esther W.T. Grout, Feb. 13, 1831, Pocumtuck Valley Memorial Library Collection, HD.

palm leaves from Cuba and distributed them to farm-
houses to be made up into hats.[28] Eliza Chaplin and her
sister Caroline of Salem, Massachusetts, made and sold
bonnets during the 1820s, the same years that they taught
school. Julia Pierce taught school in the summer and had
"plenty of work" to do in the winter, she said: "I have
braided more than 100 hats and the other girls as many
more." The working life of Amanda Elliott of Guilford,
Connecticut, exemplifies the variety of this transitional
period. Within six months in 1816–17 she devoted considerable time to splitting straw and braiding hats; noted
five new boarders; taught school; and mentioned binding
shoes, in addition to usual domestic needlework, knitting,
washing, and ironing. For some fortunate young women,
of course, the diminution of household manufacture for
the family meant greater leisure and opportunity for education. Hannah Hickok Smith's letters after 1800 revealed
that spinning gradually dwindled in importance in her
daughters' occupations. "As we have had much leisure
time this winter," she wrote in 1816, "the girls have employed themselves chiefly in reading writing and studying
French Latin and Greek."[29]

While economic modernization changed young unmarried women's work more conspicuously than their mothers'
at first, the disruption of the integral relation between the
household and the business of society was bound to re-
define matrons' occupations too. Wife-and-motherhood in
a rural household of the eighteenth century implied re-

28. Abbott, *Women in Industry*, pp. 66–73; Taylor, *Transportation Revolution*, pp. 218-19.

29. Eliza Chaplin to Laura Lovell, June 24, 1821, and April 9, 1824, Chaplin-Lovell Correspondence, EI; Julia Pierce to Sally Smith, March 24, 1842,
Hooker Collection, SL; Amanda Elliott diary, Nov. 1816 to May 1817; Hannah Hickok Smith to Abigail Mitchell, March 16, 1816. As adults, Hannah
Smith's daughters—the "Smith sisters" of Glastonbury—became well-known
for their erudition and self-assertive spirit.

sponsibility for the well-being of all the family. Upon marriage a woman took on "the Cares of the world," Elizabeth Bowen admitted as she recounted her past life, at midcentury. Fond as Esther Edwards Burr was of improving her mind, she declined an opportunity to take French lessons in the 1750s with the forceful comment, "The married woman has something else to care about besides lerning [sic] French!" Sarah Snell Bryant's daily diary reported in straightforward fashion her matronly duties in an educated, respectable, but impecunious farm family in western Massachusetts. During the 1790s and early 1800s she bore and nursed six children (usually returning to household cares within a few days after childbirth), and taught them all to read the Bible before sending them to school. Generally she occupied every day in making cloth and clothing—from the "hatcheling" of flax and "breaking" of wool to the sewing of shirts, gowns, and coats—knitting gloves and stockings, baking, brewing, preserving food, churning butter, gardening, nursing the sick, making candles or soap, washing, ironing, scouring, quilting with neighbors, and even entertaining visitors. During a summer when her husband was traveling, she also taught school.[30] Contemporaries of Sarah Snell Bryant who lived in more densely populated and commercial locations might have less labor to perform, especially if their husbands' wealth allowed their families to purchase goods and services. Martha Church Challoner, who lived in Newport, a lively Rhode Island port, in the 1760s, was able to buy various fabrics, shoes, and some basic foods. She had two black women in her house as servants (or slaves, possibly), and hired others to do washing, mending, spinning, carding,

30. Diary of Elizabeth Bowen, undated (c. 1750s), EI; diary of Esther Edwards Burr, June 17, 1755, Beinecke Rare Book Library, Yale University; Sarah Snell Bryant diary, 1795-1810 (for her schoolteaching see June 26 and 27, July 3, 18, and 20, Aug. 23, Sept. 13, 1797).

sewing, and nursing. Still, she herself made candles, knit stockings, sold butter and eggs, and sewed household linens, while supervising the household.

The diminished need for domestic manufacture in a commercial town enabled some wives to engage in business, usually alongside their husbands. Lydia Hill Almy of Rhode Island wished to "do something towards earning [her] living" while her husband was on a whaling voyage in 1797-99, and so she assisted at a tanyard, and also let rooms in her house.[31] The latter was always appropriate as a means for married women to earn income becuase it did not take them away from home. Wives of tradesmen might be found carrying out retail sales or wholesale purchases. Abigail Brackett Lyman reported to her mother back in Northampton how busy she and her husband, a merchant-shopkeeper, were on their trip to Boston, she "in chusing [sic] articles in the shoping [sic] way" to stock their store. Anna Bryant Smith of Portland, Maine, went "behind the Counter" in her husband's store when necessary. When she "called to the store, [and] found customers who wanted waiting on," she worked there "till [her] head went round like a top." Not infrequently she doubled as "Maid about house, & Cleark [sic] in the store." The business needed her presence most when Mr. Smith was absent, but occasionally they worked together. In May 1806 the couple went to Boston, and Anna Smith spent her time "selecting goods" for stock; six months later she made the purchasing trip alone, sending the goods back to her husband in Portland. When she stayed at home her routine was monotonous, which pleased her. Her typical daily round sounded remarkably like a modern housewife's: "Am finely this Morn, Washed my breakfast

31. Diary of Martha Church Challoner, 1765-70, CHS; diary of Lydia Hill Almy, Dec. 21, 1797, Feb. 28, Jan. 24. March 7, 1798, EI.

dishes, cleaned the Parlour, Made beds, Cook'd dinner, &c
&c." Her domestic activities, however, also included weaving carpets, sewing linens, baking bread, preserving fruit
in jams and jellies, brewing beer, curing bacon, making
candles, and knitting. She favored these over the store.
"A Storm is most welcome," she noted in January 1807,
"for then I stay at *home* which has more charms for me
than any other place."[32]
Well into the middle decades of the nineteenth century
married women's work remained centered on household
management and family care, although the growing ramifications of the market economy diminished the importance of household manufacture and enlarged families'
reliance on money to purchase basic commodities. Greater
population density, commercial expansion, technological
advances in transportation and communication, specialization in agriculture, and involvement of rural residents in
given-out industry all contributed to the demise of the self-
contained household economy. "There is no way of living
in this town without cash," Abigail Lyman reported from
Boston in 1797, and smaller towns rapidly manifested
the same commercial spirit and need. Hannah Hickok
Smith's account book for the years 1821-24 points out
the extent to which a prosperous farm matron in an
"urban"-sized commercial town—Glastonbury, Connecticut—was involved in commercial transaction. She recorded
the purchase of edibles and baking supplies (spices, plums,

32. Abigail Brackett Lyman to Mrs. Brackett, Oct. 11, 1797, in Helen
Roelker Kessler, "The Worlds of Abigail Brackett Lyman," (M.A. thesis, Tufts
University, 1976), appendix B; Anna Bryant Smith diary, Jan. 1, 1806, Jan.
23, 1807 (quotations), Aug. 26, 1806, May 1806 and Oct. 1806 (on work
with her husband, and trips to Boston), Jan. 27, 1806, Jan. 28, 1807 (quotations), April 8 and 9, Aug. 19, 1806, Jan. 21, 1807 (for examples of household activities). I am indebted to Douglas L. Jones of Tufts University for
loaning me a copy of Ms. Kessler's thesis.

currants, raisins, sugar, molasses, salt, wine, coffee, tea);
of household items (teacups, platters, chest, jug, box,
coffeepot, tinware, pins) and construction materials (pine
boards, nails, steel); of writing accoutrements (paper, pen-
knife, spelling book), nursing supplies (camphor, plaister)
and soap, and some luxuries (snuff, tobacco, shell combs,
parasol). Furthermore, she purchased at least eleven different kinds of fabric (such as dimity, brown holland,
"factory cloth"), four kinds of yarn and thread, leather,
and buttons; bought silk shawls, bonnets, dresses, stockings, and kid gloves, and also paid for people's services
in making clothing. The farm produced the marketable
commodities of grain (oats, rye, corn) and timber, animals (calves, turkeys, fowl) and animal products (eggs,
hens' feathers, quills, wool, pork), and other farm produce which required more human labor, such as butter,
cider, lard, and tallow.[33]

If married women's occupations no longer predictably
consisted of domestic productive activities such as spinning, soap making, or brewing, nevertheless they were
identified with *being at home,* an essential responsibility
because of household upkeep and child care. "I have been
so entirely engrossed today by domestic avocations, that
I have hardly had time for reflection," noted the young
wife of a lawyer in Haverhill, Massachusetts, in 1802, yet
without specifying her activities: "domestic duties, though
the discharge of them affords great pleasure, . . . [are] not
of that kind which would 'figure in narration.'" Susan
Huntington, the wife of a Boston minister, laid out her
opinion of a wife's duties in 1815: "a woman's *first* active duties belong to her own family . . . [in] the ordering
of domestic affairs, the regulation of servants, the care &
culture of children, the perusal of necessary works to assist

33. Abigail Brackett Lyman to Mrs. Brackett, Oct. 11, 1797; account book
of Hannah Hickock Smith, 1821-24, CSL.

in the all important concern of education, & of other
necessary books, including the Scriptures."[34]

The growing availability of goods and services for purchase might spare a married woman from considerable
drudgery, if her husband's income sufficed for a com-
fortable living. It also heightened her role in "shoping,"
as Abigail Brackett Lyman spelled it (her consumer role),
although that was subject to her husband's authority over
financial resources. In colonial America husbands, as
"providers," typically were responsible for purchasing
goods—including household goods, furniture, and food
staples, if they were to be bought—but in commercial
towns of the late eighteenth and early nineteenth century
wives more frequently became shoppers, especially for
articles of dress and food. The increasing importance of
monetary exchange bore hard on those who needed to replace their former economic contribution of household
manufacture with income-producing employment, while
meeting their domestic obligations. Taking in boarders
was one alternative. Betsey Graves Johnson did that while
she brought up the five children born to her between 1819
and 1830. Otherwise, married women had the same options for wage earning as single women who wished to stay
at home: to take in sewing, or work in given-out industry.
Schoolteaching, a slight possibility for wives, was a likelier
one for widows whose children had reached school age.
One widow's "cares," as described by her sister in 1841,
were "enough to occupy all her time and thoughts almost.
. . . [She] is teaching from 16 to 20 sholars [sic] boarding
a young lady, and doing the housework, taking care of her
children, &c."[35]

34. Diary of Mary Orne Tucker, April 14, 1802, EI; diary of Susan Mansfield Huntington, Jan. 5, 1815, SML.

35. The dating and scale of the shift from husband to wife as purchaser of
domestic necessaries is largely unexplored. Cf. Mary P. Ryan's comments on
women's growing consumer role, 1750–1820, in *Womanhood in America:*

These constants—"doing the housework, taking care of her children"—persisted in married women's lives. Child care required their presence at home. This responsibility revealed itself as the heart of women's domestic duties when household production declined. After four years of marriage Sarah Ripley Stearns regretfully attributed her neglect of church attendance and devotional reading not to household duties but to "the Care of my Babes, which takes up so large a portion of my time of my time [*sic*] & attention." More than ever before in New England history, the care of children appeared to be mothers' sole work and the work of mothers alone. The expansion of nonagricultural occupations drew men and grown children away from the household, abbreviating their presence in the family and their roles in child rearing. Mothers and young children were left in the household together just when educational and religious dicta both newly emphasized the malleability of young minds. Enlightenment psychology drew tighter the connection between early influence on the child, and his or her eventual character, just as mothers' influence on young children appeared more salient.[36]

From *Colonial Times to the Present* (New York: Franklin Watts, 1975), pp. 96–97. There are extensive examples, in the well-known lives of such men as Benjamin Franklin, of eighteenth-century men's concern and responsibility for household purchases. The early nineteenth-century genre paintings displayed in *The Painter's America: Rural and Urban Life, 1810–1910*, ed. Patricia Hills (New York: Praeger and the Whitney Museum of Art, 1974), give interesting visual evidence of women's role as consumers.

Diary of Betsy Graves Johnson, 1812-30, MHS; Mary Irwin, Felicity, Ohio, to Eliza W. Pitkin, Mt. Vernon, Ohio, Jan. 2, 1841, Hooker Collection, SL. Cf. Lucy Larcom's mother, who, when widowed, moved from Beverly to Lowell, Massachusetts, to keep a boardinghouse while raising her children. Lucy Larcom, *A New England Girlhood* (New York: Corinth Books, 1961; orig. 1887), pp. 145–46.

36. Sarah Ripley Stearns diary, Oct. 13, 1816, SL. On developments in the mother's role, see chapter 2, "Domesticity"; Nancy Osterud, "The New England Family, 1790-1840," unpublished paper OSV 590.1, Museum Education

Mothers, especially religious ones, felt their responsibilities keenly. "There is no subject concerning which I feel more anxiety than the proper education of my children," Susan Huntington recorded in 1813. "Governors & kings have only to enact laws & compel men to observe them—mothers have to implant ideas and cultivate dispositions which can alone make good citizens or subjects—. . . the mothers task is to mould the infants character into whatever shape she pleases." Abigail Bradley Hyde, the wife of a struggling minister in Bolton, Connecticut, and mother of five youngsters, confessed to her parents her sense of inadequacy: "I am so far from discharging the duties of my station or from meeting the high responsibilities which devolve on me as a mother, that the conviction of my deficiencies which sometimes forces itself on me is sometimes overwhelming." "O how solemn, how great the responsibilities of a Mother," wrote Mary Hurlbut, an evangelically-minded mother of four in New London who viewed her tasks with more confidence, "—how great, how arduous & yet delightful work to teach and train these dear Children aright—I desire to feel it in all its length and breadth—& feel *I* am in a great measure responsible for their future conduct & destiny."[37]

Dept., Old Sturbridge Village, April 1972; Ryan, *Womanhood in America*, pp. 124–26; and Anne L. Kuhn, *The Mother's Role in Childhood Education: New England Concepts 1830–1860* (New Haven: Yale University Press, 1947). The proportion of persons employed in nonagricultural pursuits among all employed persons (white and black, male and female) rose between 1820 and 1840 from 17.9 percent to 26.9 percent in Maine, from 17.3 percent to 21.6 percent in New Hampshire, from 15.4 percent to 18.2 percent in Vermont, from 42.4 percent to 58.7 percent in Massachusetts, from 36.6 percent to 60.1 percent in Rhode Island, and from 29.5 percent to 38.5 percent in Connecticut. Yasukichi Yasuba, *Birth Rates of the White Population in the U.S. 1800–1860* (Baltimore: Johns Hopkins University Press, 1962), p. 154.

37. Susan Mansfield Huntington diary, Feb. 7, Oct. 25, 1813; Abigail Bradley Hyde to Mr. and Mrs. Bradley, April 5, 1829, Bradley-Hyde Collection, SL; diary of Mary Hurlbut, April 23, Nov. 11, 1831, CHS.

Child care and housekeeping, including sewing, remained demanding enough to consume most of married women's time and energy. Women's domestic occupations have been confused with leisure because of the contrast they offered to men's occupations outside the home, and because of the conflation of the two contrasts, work/leisure, work/home. But only the small elite who could employ numerous servants had leisure to speak of. Mary Jackson Lee, of Boston's mercantile aristocracy, felt "removed from care & responsibility" while her husband was absent on business in the early years of their marriage, since servants kept her house and cared for her only child. "Return to me," she entreated her husband in a letter, "and give me the delightful occupation of attending to you, and feeling my presence *at home* of some importance." Most middle-class women were much busier, even when their children were few. Eliza Perkins Gunnell apologized to a former school friend for her sporadic correspondence with the explanation, "when you are a wife, and mother of a crying babe, and feel it necessary to curtail your expenses as it respects help, your own feelings will supply a sufficient excuse."[38]

Fragmentary evidence suggests that domestic help was difficult to obtain by the third decade of the nineteenth century, even in cities where needy female immigrants had little choice but to take employment in housework. Abigail Alcott wrote to her sister-in-law from Boston in June 1830, "respecting a girl or woman—Can find no such body to be had for love or money." In country towns the situation was apparently even more difficult. When newly-

38. Mary Jackson Lee to Henry Lee, in journal format, Sept. 1, 1813, Aug. 12, 1814, in Frances Rollins Morse, ed., *Henry and Mary Lee: Letters and Journals* (Boston, 1926), pp. 202, 214; Eliza Perkins Gunnell to Weltha Brown, Dec. 10, 1821, Hooker Collection, SL.

married Eliza Chaplin Nelson moved from the commercial seaport of Salem, Massachusetts, to tiny Canaan, New Hampshire, she was chagrined at her failure to find a woman who would "take the place of a servant."[39] The rise of industrial employment thwarted the casual hire of young women for domestic service so typical of the eighteenth century. Sarah Parrott, twenty-three-year-old daughter in an influential Portsmouth, New Hampshire, family, wrote to her brother in 1823 of how busy she had been, "particularly in respect to the girls we have had with us & those who have left us entirely alone at various times. New Hampshire has become a manufacturing State, & the demand for girls has been such that almost every family has been in want of domestics it is really a severe affliction." A book on *New England and Her Institutions* written by "one of her sons" in 1835 claimed that country girls rarely went "out to service," because they preferred factory work or given-out industry. "Perhaps the difficulties of modern housekeepers did begin with the opening of the Lowell factories," Lucy Larcom, who had been an operative in the 1830s, later proposed. "Country girls were naturally independent, and the feeling that at this new work the few hours they had of every-day leisure were entirely their own was a satisfaction to them. They preferred it to going out as 'hired help.' It was like a young man's pleasure in entering upon business for himself." The relative lack of domestic help may thus have magnified mar-

39. Abigail Alcott to Lucretia May, June 15, 1830, Alcott Family Papers, 1, folder 25, HCL; Eliza Chaplin Nelson, Canaan, N.H., to Laura Lovell, Fall River, Mass., Sept. 24, 1832, EI. Among the voluntary associations begun by women in this period (see chapters 4 and 5) were societies for encouraging "faithful domestics"; see, e.g., the "Constitution of the society for the mutual benefit of female domestics and their employers instituted in Boston, April 11, 1827," MHS.

ried women's domestic obligations at the same time that
the commercial economy was reducing their scope.[40]

Differences observable in women's work earlier and later
in these years are more or less recapitulated if one com-
pares a rural, commercially undeveloped area with a con-
temporaneous urban, commercial location. The more
densely populated and commercially advanced an area, the
greater was families' reliance on purchasing power and
money income, and the less the need for wives' household
manufacture; the greater the ramifications of business outside the household and the less within it. Martha Church
Challoner's production and consumption patterns contrasted with Sarah Snell Bryant's in the latter part of the
eighteenth century. The work Margaret Everston Smith of
Sharon, Connecticut, did in her husband's absence in 1807-
08 provides a similarly telling comparison with the leisure
of Bostonian Mary Jackson Lee in 1813-14. Margaret's
husband John Cotton Smith was a wealthy lawyer and
political officeholder—in fact the most notable man in
town—but he was also a farmer. While he was absent she
supervised the operation of the farm and handled pay-
ments, credits, and debts. She had no children to tend,
since her son was off with his father, but she had to
direct three male "hands" and two female "helps" to
make sure that the wheat was threshed, washed, and

40. Sarah Parrott, Portsmouth, to Cadet Robert P. Parrott, West Point, Nov.
27, 1823, Parrott Family Collection, NHHS; [Jacob Abbott], *New England
and her Institutions by One of her Sons* (Boston, 1835), pp. 28-29; Larcom,
New England Girlhood, p. 199. In her widely read *Treatise on Domestic Economy* (1842), Catharine Beecher observed that "the number of those, who are
compelled to go to service, is constantly diminishing. Our manufactories, also,
are making increased demands for female labor, and offering larger compensation." American women suffered "endless" "anxieties, vexations, perplexities,
and even hard labor . . . from this state of domestic service," in Beecher's view.
Beecher, *Treatise on Domestic Economy* (rev. ed., New York, 1847) reprinted
in Nancy F. Cott, ed., *Root of Bitterness: Documents of the Social History of
American Women* (New York: Dutton, 1972), p. 176.

milled, that animals were slaughtered, and meat preserved, that ice was stored, the house cleaned, clothing made. Mary Lee, in contrast, ruefully acknowledged, "I so much desire to feel as if I was of consequence to someone that if the child has the finger-ache, or nurse looks pale, I immediately think I cannot possibly leave them and thus gain my point."[41]

It was wealth, of course, that gave Mary Lee her leisure, as it was wealth that allowed Margaret Smith to direct rather than perform the work of the farm. Wealth determined the character of an individual woman's work as strongly as her geographical location. In unmarried women's lives it made especially conspicuous differences. In the 1790s Elizabeth Fuller, daughter of a minister in straitened circumstances, had to be busy with spinning, weaving, and cleaning house. At the same time Betsey Cranch, daughter of a successful lawyer, occupied herself in receiving and making visits, reading novels, painting, and playing the piano (although she also accomplished some needlework, ironing, and cooking). "All the habits of debilitating softness" characterized Hannah Adams's youth, during the pre-Revolutionary prosperity of her father's store in Medfield; but when his wealth collapsed during the war she taught school and wove bobbin lace.[42]

In the early nineteenth century, young women such as Eliza and Caroline Chaplin and Eliza Perkins took in handiwork and taught school to support themselves. Others, with more urgent need, went into factory work. Unmarried daughters of wealthy urban families, meanwhile, spent their time in social life. Eunice Callender, who

41. Margaret Everston Smith diary, 1807–08; on John Cotton Smith, see Charles Sedgwick, *General History of the Town of Sharon* (Amenia, N.Y., 1898), p. 152; Mary Lee to Henry Lee, Sept. 1, 1813.

42. Elizabeth Fuller diary, 1790–92, in Blake, *History of the Town of Princeton*, 1:302–23; diary of Elizabeth Cranch (Norton), 1781–89, MHS; *Memoir of Hannah Adams*, p. 2.

lived with her parents in Boston and never married, occupied herself wholly with social visits, attendance at church and lectures, shopping, walks, and charity organization meetings. Sarah Connell, in Newburyport, alternated schooling at several different academies with minimal domestic duties, frequent social visiting, jaunts, dances, French lessons, shopping, and reading (chiefly Gothic fiction).[43]

The characteristic "work" of unmarried women of the elite largely consisted in maintaining social contacts. Diaries such as those of Margaret Searle of Newburyport, Mary Tappan Pickman of Salem, or Lucilla Parker of Boston indicate that the unmarried daughters of mercantile wealth were the most leisured and the most involved in "society" of all New England women. Whether they enjoyed their role is a separate question. At eighteen Mary Pickman discounted a sermon that admonished youth to repudiate the sin of frivolity. "Frivolity to be sure ought not to be the occupation of a moral and immortal being," she said, "but it is not sin and is I think in youth particularly excusable." Amelia Lee Jackson—of the Boston "clan" of Lowells, Lees, Cabots, Jacksons, and Tracys—displayed much more ambivalence, confiding to a cousin, "I think a girl's life at my age [21] isn't the most pleasant by any means; she is in the most unsettled state: a young man can occupy himself with his business, and look forward to his life and prospects, but all we have to do is to pass our time agreeably to ourselves. . . . I think everyone likes to feel the *necessity* of doing something, and I confess that I have sometimes wished

43. Diary of Eunice Callender, 1808-18, and letters of Eunice Callender to Sarah Ripley Stearns, Stearns Collection, SL; *Diary of Sarah Connell Ayer, 1805-1835* (Portland, Me., 1910), before 1810.

I could be poor to have the pleasure of exerting my self."[44]

Married women of any rank or location were likely to have less leisure than their unmarried peers. Marital status as well as date, place, and wealth affected the nature of a woman's work, partially because of actual demands and partially because of societal expectations. "Betsy's season for gaiety is passing away, she is in the road to matrimony, and will not find so much leisure to frolic," Mary Orne Tucker commented on a friend's impending marriage. For herself, at twenty-six, she could not "approve the same conduct in a wife, which is allowable in a gay girl." "To restrain my own mirth," she admitted, "I have had to teach my heart many lessons." Between the frivolity allowed to girls and the devotion to home duties expected of married women there was a serious disjunction. Years before she became Mrs. Stearns, Sarah Ripley tried to convince herself that it was an advantage to spend less

44. Diary of Margaret Searle (Curson), Jan.–Nov. 1809, Jan. 1812–July 1813, Curson Family Papers, HCL; diary of Mary Tappan Pickman, 1831–34, Nov. 2, 1834 (quotation), EI; diary of Lucilla Parker (Quincy), 1832–33, HCL; Amelia Lee Jackson to Henry Lee, Jr., Sept. 21, 1838, in Morse, *Henry and Mary Lee*, pp. 269–70. Judged by the comments of Amelia Jackson and her aunt, Mary Jackson Lee, the women of the Jackson family seem to have believed wholeheartedly in the "Protestant ethic" of the sacred duty of work, for women as well as men. During Henry Lee's business travels in 1812–13 (which were made because of his financial losses in 1811), his wife Mary wrote to him, "I think I should be better satisfied [in your absence] if I were obliged daily to make some efforts, either to gain or to avoid spending money—but my friends all think that I am spending as little as I can, and I suppose the pride of some of them would be sadly wounded if I were to do anything to gain—this is a pride I cannot conceive of. I know not why the wife should not work *a little* as well as the husband *labour so hard,* and did I feel a certainty that you would agree with me upon the subject, I should most certainly act upon the principle." Mary Lee to Henry Lee, Feb. 28, 1813, in Morse, ed., *Henry and Mary Lee,* p. 178. Her words are also arresting because they reveal the assumption—how well entrenched?—among the mercantile aristocracy that women "do not work," at least not for gain.

time "in Company" than her girlfriends did, for "those who spend a great proportion of time in paying & receiving visits of ceremony lose their relish for domestic enjoyments, while those who are more at home grow more and more attach'd to their situation."[45]

Unquestionably, women associated marriage with demanding duties. Although Nancy Flynt had to toil to support herself as a single woman, she commented acidly to her married sister on "the many hours of confinement and other necessary duties that deprive the married woman of a thousand innocent girlish enjoyments." Since her sister had married, Flynt objected, her letters were "short and unfrequent [sic]" and their "most important subjects" related to "domestic affairs." Sarah Connell Ayer, newly married, admitted to a friend, "I look forward to *housekeeping* with much anxiety. My daily prayers are that I may be enabled to discharge the many and important duties of a wife so as to gain the approbation of my husband, my conscience, and above all of my God." Another new bride, urging a friend to visit, warned her, "if you are thinking of entering the matrimonial state, you had better come while you can, as there is no certainty attending that but confinement." Betsey Cranch's life drew the contrast between daughter and wife vividly. Disheartened with her monotonous leisure in her father's house, in the privacy of her diary she complained, "how small, few and uninteresting, are the events & occurrences which my secluded life affords—I sometimes wonder if my faculties & affections will not rust & grow useless for want of something to exert them upon." But in

45. Mary Orne Tucker diary, May 13, 1802; diary of Sarah Ripley, June 10, 1800, AAS. (The diaries of Sarah [called Sally] Ripley, later Mrs. Stearns, are divided between AAS, which has the volumes for 1799-1801 and 1805-08, and SL, which has the volumes for 1801-04, 1808-12, and 1813-18.)

the sixth year of her marriage she was so busy caring for three sons, making clothing, doing laundry, cooking, baking, cleaning, making household articles, spinning, and overseeing hired spinsters, that she occasionally protested at being mistress and servant in one.[46]

Ideally, a woman's life followed a continuum from childhood upbringing in a family, through adolescent "apprenticeship" in nurturing and household duties, to wife-and-motherhood. But social and economic change resulted in sharper distinctions between the roles (particularly the work roles) of young, unmarried women and those of matrons. As unmarried women sought to replicate their household usefulness in factory, shop, or school, they experienced greater variety, mobility, independence, and more insecurity as well.[47] Those who earned income outside the household setting might defy the rules of women's economic dependence and absorption in family service. In fact, however, they usually engaged in wage earning in order to help sustain their families: to support younger siblings, pay off the farm's mortgage, or provide for their brothers' educations. Mary Hall's periodic returns from Lowell to her family in Concord, New Hampshire, symbolized the continuing interdependence between the employed daughter and the parents and siblings at home. Mill operatives' stories in the famous Lowell magazines

46. Nancy Flynt to Mercy Flynt Morris, undated (1810s), CHS; Sarah Connell Ayer to Maria Kittredge, April 25, 1811, in *Diary of Sarah Connell Ayer*, p. 375; Rebeccah Root Buell to Weltha Brown, June 24, 1822, Hooker Collection, SL; Elizabeth Cranch Norton diary, March 4, 1787 (quotation) and 1794–95.

47. I have drawn connections between the disruption of young women's traditional work-roles in this period and their adherence to religion in "Young Women in the Second Great Awakening in New England," *FS* 3 (1975):15–29.

often portrayed heroines who took up factory employment
for the benefit of their kin at home.[48]

Still, the significance for unmarried women of new wage-
earning employment outside the household should not be
minimized. It meant disposable income, it usually meant
distance from home, it meant association with one's peers
in age.[49] It could mean the start of unforeseen careers in
literature, education, or religion. Salome Lincoln of Rayn-
ham, Massachusetts, the daughter of pious Baptists, went
to a common school and then began work, at age fourteen,
in a factory village called Hopewell. As a weaver (the best-
paid of textile-factory occupations) she supported herself
for ten years. Apparently a commanding figure, she led a
"turn-out" (strike) in 1829; about the same time she
experienced a divine "call," and began to preach among
the factory workers. By 1831 contributions supported the
Freewill Baptist "female preacher" Salome Lincoln, and
she gave up factory work. Lucy Larcom, who began mill
work at age eleven to help support her widowed mother
and family, later claimed that it had been a "great advantage" for factory operatives to be "brought together, away
from their own homes," and to learn "to go out of themselves, and enter into the lives of others." During her own
years as an operative she was glad to return to the factory
after spending a period of months assisting a married

48. E.g., see "Susan Miller," by F.G.A., a Lowell operative, reprinted in
Cott, *Root of Bitterness,* pp. 130–40, and other stories collected in *Mind
among the Spindles: a Miscellany wholly composed by the factory girls, selected from The Lowell Offering* (Boston, 1845). Those operatives who were
minors—such as Lucy Larcom, when she first came to Lowell—of course owed
their wages to their parents.

49. Abbott, *Women in Industry,* p. 113, reports that of 6320 women residing
in Lowell, Massachusetts, in 1840, only one-eighth were from the state, and
the great majority had come from Maine, New Hampshire, and Vermont. See
also, especially with regard to the peer community created at work, Thomas L.
Dublin, "Women at Work: The Transformation of Work and Community in
Lowell, Massachusetts, 1826-1860" (Ph.D. diss., Columbia University, 1975).

sister with housework and child care. "I found that I enjoyed even the familiar unremitting clatter of the mill," she later wrote, "because it indicated that something was going on. I liked to feel the people around me, even those whom I did not know. . . . I felt that I belonged to the world, that there was something for me to do in it, though I had not yet found out what. Something to do: it might be very little but still it would be my own work."[50]

While changes in economy and society made young women's work more social, more various and mobile, the same developments reduced the social engagement, variety, and mobility in the work of wives and mothers. House-keeping and child care continued to require married women's presence at home, while the household diminished in population, kinds of business, and range of contacts. In an intriguing development in language usage in the early nineteenth century, "home" became synonymous with "retirement" or "retreat" from the world at large. Mary Tucker quoted approvingly in 1802 an author's assertion that "a woman's noblest station is retreat." On a cousin's approaching marriage she remarked, "Sally has passed her days in the shade of *retirement* but even there many virtues and graces have ripened to perfection, she has every quality necessary for a *good wife*." Salome Lincoln's marriage to a fellow preacher in 1835 virtually ended her extradomestic pursuits; she subsequently used her preaching talents only on occasional travels with her husband. The shifting emphasis among married women's occupations emerges clearly in the comparison of Lydia Hill Almy's occupations in 1797–99 with Mary Hurlbut's in the 1830s. The former not only kept house but let rooms, col-

50. Almond H. Davis, *The Female Preacher, or Memoir of Salome Lincoln* (Providence, R.I., 1843); Larcom, *New England Girlhood,* pp. 178–79, 193. The Freewill Baptists, unlike traditional denominations, allowed women to preach. See Dexter, *Career Women of America,* pp. 59–60.

lected firewood, attended to livestock, and arranged to sell tanned skins; she considered her two children "grown out of the way" and "very little troble [*sic*]" when the younger was not yet weaned. Mary Hurlbut, in contrast, appeared solely concerned with her children's lives and prospects.[51]

Married women's work at home distinguished itself most visibly from men's work, especially as the latter began to depart from the household/farm/craftshop to separate shops, offices, and factories. The rhythms of adult men's and women's work diverged even as did their places of work. During the eighteenth century, in agricultural towns, men and women had largely shared similar work patterns; their work, tied to the land, was seasonal and discontinuous. It was conditioned by tradition, family position, and legal obligation as well as by economic incentive.[52] E.P. Thompson has called the dominant characteristic of work in such an agricultural/artisanal economy its "task-orientation," in contrast to the "time-discipline" required under industrial capitalism. Task-orientation implies that the worker's own sense of customary need and order dictates the performance of work. Intensification or delay occurs as a response to perceived necessity: in farming, for instance, the former occurs in harvest time, or the latter during stormy weather. Irregular work patterns typically result. "Social intercourse and labour are intermingled," Thompson also has pointed out, "the working-day lengthens or contracts according to the task—and there is no great sense of conflict between labour and 'passing the time of day.'" Persons accustomed to

51. Mary Orne Tucker diary, May 14, April 13, 1802; Davis, *Memoir of Salome Lincoln;* Lydia Hill Almy diary, Jan. 28, 1798 (quotation)—she weaned her daughter late, however, when the child was about two years old—see July 16, 1798; Mary Hurlbut diary, 1830-36.

52. See Keith Thomas, "Work and Leisure in Pre-Industrial Society," *Past and Present* 29 (1964):50-66.

time-discipline, however, may consider task-oriented work patterns "wasteful and lacking in urgency." Thompson's analysis derived from his study of eighteenth-century English farmers, artisans, and laborers but can be applied to their contemporaries in New England. Even eighteenth-century colonial merchants, who, as risk-taking capitalists, might be expected to initiate disciplined work habits, structured their work lives in what Thompson would denote "preindustrial" ways, intermingling their work with recreation and with the conduct of their households. "The Founding Fathers, after all, lived in a preindustrial, not simply an 'agrarian' society," as Herbert Gutman has remarked, "and the prevalence of premodern work habits among their contemporaries was natural."[53]

The social transformation from 1780 to 1835 signalled a transition from preindustrial to modern industrial work patterns.[54] The replacement of family production for direct use with wage earning, the institution of time-discipline and machine regularity in place of natural rhythms, the separation of workplaces from the home, and the division of "work" from "life" were overlapping layers of the same phenomenon. Richard D. Brown, who has described a "modernization" of personal outlook taking place among white Americans in the post-Revolutionary generation, uses evidence that individuals then adopted occupational ambition, planned ahead systematically, took risks for economic ends, and attuned themselves to time-

53. E.P. Thompson, "Time, Work-Discipline, and Industrial Capitalism," *Past and Present* 38 (1967):56-59, 60 (quotation), 70-79; Arthur Cole, "The Tempo of Mercantile Life in Colonial America," *Business History Review,* 33 (1959):277-99; Herbert G. Gutman, "Work, Culture and Society in Industrializing America, 1815-1919," *AHR* 78 (1973):532.

54. In "Time, Work-Discipline and Industrial Capitalism," pp. 80-90, Thompson cites division and supervision of laborers, punitive use of bells, clocks, and fines, money incentives, preaching and schooling, and suppression of irregularities such as holidays or sports as the immediate means used to impose time-discipline and form new labor habits in industry.

discipline. "Americans organized their use of time on an unprecedented scale," he points out:

> Almanacs, which plotted the weather in relation to the calendar, had first been published in the mid-1700's but now they were printed by the thousands, becoming every farmer's companion. One English traveler observed that whever he had been, "... in every cabin where there was not a chair to sit on, there was sure to be a Connecticut clock." The same man also remarked that the phrase "I calculate" had become the American synonym for "I believe" or "I think."[55]

Were Americans—or primarily *male* Americans—moving toward calculated, time-disciplined work habits? Household work, still the chief work of adult women, retained the irregularity, the responsiveness to immediate and natural demands, and the intermixture with social occasion common to preindustrial occupations. Even when domestic employments diminished in scope they were task-oriented. Not the clock, but human need, regulated preparation of meals, sewing of garments, and tending of children. Care of children is "the most task-oriented of all," as E. P. Thompson has acknowledged.[56] Habits such as the alternation between intense work and leisure, and the use of social occasions for work or work for social occasions (as in quilting bees), persisted in women's lives. Even their work for pay, when it was performed intermittently and in the household, conformed to the traditional rhythms,

---

55. Richard D. Brown, "Modernization and the Modern Personality in Early America, 1600–1865: A Sketch of a Synthesis," *JIH* 2 (1972):219–20. See also his *Modernization: The Transformation of American Life, 1600–1865* (New York: Hill and Wang, 1976), esp. pp. 95, 134–35. The English traveler made his remarks in 1844.

56. "Time, Work-Discipline and Industrial Capitalism," p. 79.

although given-out industry imposed on them the demands of entrepreneurs and distant marketplaces rather than familiar needs. Female mill operatives and other industrial workers outside the household, on the contrary, were subject to time-discipline. The repeated difficulties New England mill owners had in making operatives conform to clock-time and machine regularity testified to the rootedness among them of a different, longer-standing approach to work.[57] Because young women's employment outside the household was sporadic, it did not easily or quickly convert them to time-discipline. The turnover rate among mill operatives was notably high.[58] Most women who were employed away from home periodically returned to family and to household work. The vast majority eventually married. Recurrent opportunities or requirements to help in family-related tasks—such as Lucy Larcom's stint with her married sister—reaffirmed accustomed domestic patterns of work for them.

Despite the changes in its social context adult women's work, for the most part, kept the traditional mode and location which both sexes had earlier shared. Men who had to accept time-discipline and specialized occupations may have begun to observe differences between their own work and that of their wives. Perhaps they focused on the remaining "premodern" aspects of women's household work: it was reassuringly comprehensible, because it responded to immediate needs; it represented not strictly "work" but "life," a way of being; and it also looked unsystematized, inefficient, nonurgent. Increasingly men did distinguish women's work from their own, in the early nineteenth century, by calling it women's "sphere," a "separate" sphere.

57. See Gutman, "Work, Culture, and Society," pp. 544–45.
58. See Gitelman, "The Waltham System," and Dublin, "Women at Work," p. 68.

Women's sphere was "separate" not only because it was at home but also because it seemed to elude rationalization and the cash nexus, and to integrate labor with life. The home and occupations in it represented an alternative to the emerging pace and division of labor. Symbol and remnant of preindustrial work, perhaps the home commanded men's deepest loyalties, but these were loyalties that conflicted with "modern" forms of employment. To be idealized, yet rejected by men—the object of yearning, and yet of scorn—was the fate of the home-as-workplace. Women's work (indeed women's very character, viewed as essentially conditioned by the home) shared in that simultaneous glorification and devaluation.

2

DOMESTICITY

In 1833, when Esther Grout returned to Hawley, Massachusetts, from her travels in search of employment, and wrote in her diary "Home is sweet"—"there is no place like home"—those phrases were freshly minted clichés.[1] A host of New Englanders were using the printed word to confirm and advance her sentiments. Essays, sermons, novels, poems and manuals offering advice and philosophy on family life, child rearing and women's role began to flood the literary market in the 1820s and 1830s, with a tide that has not yet ceased. These early works fall into five categories. There were those primarily on the mother's (less frequently, the father's) responsibilities, such as the Reverend John S.C. Abbott's *The Mother at Home,* Lydia Maria Child's *The Mother's Book,* William Alcott's *The Young Mother,* and Theodore Dwight's *The Father's Book.* A closely related group, including Heman Humphrey's *Domestic Education,* Louisa Hoare's *Hints for the Improvement of Early Education,* and—a fictional version—Catherine Sedgwick's *Home,* offered principles for child rearing. Others such as Sally Kirby Fales's *Familiar Letters on Subjects Interesting to the Minds and Hearts of Females* and Lydia H. Sigourney's *Letters to Young Ladies* assessed women's social role in a general way. A fourth sort more specifically considered the appropriate education for women: Abigail Mott's *Observations on the Importance of Female Education* and Almira

1. Diary of Esther Grout, Aug. 4, 1833, Pocumtuck Valley Memorial Association Library Collections, HD.

Phelps's *The Female Student,* for instance, did so. A slightly different number, with titles such as *The Young Lady's
Home* or *The Young Lady's Friend,* followed the etiquette
tradition, prescribing manners for women and men.[2] At
the same time, magazines addressing an audience of "ladies" multiplied rapidly, carrying essays, stories, and advice
of a similar domestic slant. Despite some minor differences
and contradictions among the views expressed in this rash
of words, altogether they revealed a single canon—of domesticity.

The central convention of domesticity was the contrast
between the home and the world. Home was an "oasis in
the desert," a "sanctuary" where "sympathy, honor, virtue are assembled," where "disinterested love is ready to
sacrifice everything at the altar of affection." In his 1827
address on female education a New Hampshire pastor proclaimed that "It is at home, where man . . . seeks a refuge
from the vexations and embarrassments of business, an
enchanting repose from exertion, a relaxation from care by
the interchange of affection: where some of his finest
sympathies, tastes, and moral and religious feelings are
formed and nourished;—where is the treasury of pure disinterested love, such as is seldom found in the busy walks of
a selfish and calculating world." The ways of the world, in
contrast, subjected the individual to "a desolation of feeling," in the words of the *Ladies' Magazine;* there "we behold every principle of justice and honor, and even the dictates of common honesty disregarded, and the delicacy of

2. All of the titles mentioned were published in New England (primarily Boston) between 1830 and 1840, except Hoare's, published in London in 1819,
republished in New York, 1820, and then in Salem in 1829; Mott's, published
in New York in 1825; and Sedgwick's 1835 novel—though a New Englander
she published with Harper & Bros. in New York.

our moral sense is wounded; we see the general good, sacrificed to the advancement of personal interest, and we turn
from such scenes, with a painful sensation. . . ."[3]

The contradistinction of home to world had roots in religious motives and rhetoric. Christians for centuries had de-
preciated "the world" of earthly delights and material pos-
sessions in comparison to Heaven, the eternal blessings of
true faith. In the 1780s and 1790s British Evangelicals
doubled the pejorative connotation of "the world," by
preferring bourgeois respectability above the "gay world"
of aristocratic fashion. Living in an era of eroding public
orthodoxy, they considered family transmission of piety
more essential than ever to the maintenance of religion;
consequently they conflated the contrasts of Heaven versus
"the world" and bourgeois virtue versus the "gay world"
with the contrast between the domestic fireside and the
world outside.[4] In that tradition, when Esther Grout
wrote in her diary, "oh how sweet is retirement. The pleas-
antest & I think some of the most profitable moments of
my life have been spent in retirement," she was referring
to her withdrawal from the world in solitary religious
devotion and *also* to her repose *at home.*[5]

The rhetorical origins of the contrast between home and

3. "Home," by L.E., *Ladies' Magazine* 3 (May 1830):217-18; Charles Burroughs, *An Address on Female Education, Delivered in Portsmouth, N.H.,
Oct. 26, 1827* (Portsmouth, 1827), pp. 18-19.

4. For examples of Evangelical writings see Thomas Gisborne, *An Enquiry
into the Duties of the Female Sex* (London, reprinted Philadelphia, 1798), and
Hannah More, *Strictures on the Modern System of Female Education,* vol. 1,
9th ed. (London, 1801); see also M.G. Jones, *Hannah More* (Cambridge,
1952); Gordon Rattray Taylor, *The Angel-Makers: A Study in the Psychological Origins of Historical Change 1750-1850* (London: Heinemann, 1958) esp.
pp. 12-36; Christopher Hill, "Clarissa Harlowe and her Times," *Essays in
Criticism* 5 (1955):320, Keith Thomas, "The Double Standard," *Journal of
the History of Ideas* 20 (1959): 204-205; and Ian Watt, "The New Woman,
Samuel Richardson's Pamela," R.L. Coser, ed., *The Family: Its Structure and
Functions* (New York: St. Martin's, 1964), pp. 286-88.

5. Esther Grout diary, Sept. 13, 1830.

world demand less interpretation than the canon of domesticity built upon it. That contrast infused the new literature
because, in simplest terms, it seemed to explain and justify
material change in individual's lives. Between the Revolution and the 1830s New England's population became
more dense and more mobile, its political system more
representative and demanding of citizens, its social structure
more differentiated and its economic structure more complex than in earlier years when the business of "the world"
had mostly taken place in households. Economic growth
and rationalization and the entry of the market mechanism
into virtually all relations of production fostered specialized and standardized work and a commercial ethic. Because of regional division of production and marketing,
agricultural production itself became more specialized and
more speculative. The farmer's success was not in his own
hands when he produced for distant markets. In handicrafts
the functional differentiation of wholesale merchant, retail
merchant, contractor or "boss," and pieceworker replaced
the unified eighteenth-century pattern in which an artisan
made and sold his wares from his residence. Masters (now
employers) and their journeymen or apprentices no longer
assumed a patriarchal relationship; wages and prices defined their relationship to one another and to the merchants above them. Trends such as the decline of traditional
determinants of deference, the assertion of an individualist
ethos, increasing extremes of wealth and poverty, and replacement of unitary association networks by pluralistic
ones, indicated deep change in social relations.[6] Differentiation and specialization characterized this transformation

6. See works cited in chapter 1, note 8, and David Montgomery, "The Working Classes of the Pre-Industrial American City," *Labor History* 9 (1968):3–22;
John R. Commons, "American Shoemakers, 1648–1895," *Quarterly Journal
of Economics* 24 (1909):39–84; and David Hackett Fischer, "America: A
Social History, Vol. 1, The Main Lines of the Subject 1650–1975," unpublished MS draft, 1974, esp. chap. 4, pp. 42–43, chap. 12, pp. 20–22.

of society. These were portrayed and symbolized most powerfully in the separation of production and exchange from the domestic arena—the division between "world" and "home."

The canon of domesticity encouraged people to assimilate such change by linking it to a specific set of sex-roles. In the canon of domesticity, the home contrasted to the restless and competitive world because its "presiding spirit" was woman, who was "removed from the arena of pecuniary excitement and ambitious competition." Woman inhabited the "shady green lanes of domestic life," where she found "pure enjoyment and hallowed sympathies" in her "peaceful offices." If man was the "fiercest warrior, or the most unrelenting votary of stern ambition," "toil-worn" by "troubled scenes of life," woman would "scatter roses among the thorns of his appointed track." In the "chaste, disinterested circle of the fireside" only—that is, in the hearts and minds of sisters, wives, and mothers—could men find "reciprocated humanity . . . unmixed with hate or the cunning of deceit."[7] The spirit of business and public life thus appeared to diverge from that of the home chiefly because the two spheres were the separate domains of the two sexes.

In accentuating the split between "work" and "home" and proposing the latter as a place of salvation, the canon of domesticity tacitly acknowledged the capacity of modern work to desecrate the human spirit. Authors of domestic literature, especially the female authors, denigrated business and politics as arenas of selfishness, exertion, embarrassment, and degradation of soul. These rhetoricians suggested what Marx's analysis of alienated labor in the

7. Quotations from "Woman," probably by S.J. Hale, *Ladies' Magazine* 3 (Oct. 1830):441, 444; "Influence of Woman—Past and Present," *Ladies' Companion* 13 (Sept. 1840):245; Virginia Cary, *Letters on Female Character* (2d ed., Philadelphia, 1830), p. 47; *The Discussion: or the Character, Education, Prerogatives, and Moral Influence of Woman* (Boston, 1837), pp. 225-26.

1840s would assert, that "the worker . . . feels at ease only
outside work, and during work he is outside himself. He is
at home when he is not working and when he is working
he is not at home."[8] The canon of domesticity embodied a
protest against that advance of exploitation and pecuniary
values. Nancy Sproat, a pious wife and mother who published her own family lectures in 1819, warned that "the
air of the world is poisonous. You must carry an antidote
with you, or the infection will prove fatal." (A latter-day
Calvinist, she clearly gave "the world" dual meaning, opposing it to both "home" and "Heaven." Her antidote,
likewise, was a compound, of domestic affection and religious faith.) No writer more consistently emphasized the
anti-pecuniary bias of the domestic rhetoric than Sarah
Josepha Hale, influential editor of the Boston *Ladies' Magazine* from 1828 to 1836 and subsequently of *Godey's
Lady's Book* in Philadelphia. "Our men are sufficiently
money-making," Hale said. "Let us keep our women and
children from the contagion as long as possible. To do
good and to communicate, should be the motto of Christians and republicans." She wished "to remind the dwellers
in this 'bank-note world' that there are objects more elevated, more worthy of pursuit than wealth." "Time is
money" was a maxim she rejected, and she urged mothers
to teach their children the relative merits of money and of
good works.[9]

8. Karl Marx, "Alienated Labor" (1844), in *Writings of the Young Marx on
Philosophy and Society,* ed. and trans. Loyd D. Easton and Kurt H. Guddat
(Garden City, N.Y.: Anchor Books, 1967), pp. 292-93.

9. Mrs. N. Sproat, *Family Lectures* (Boston, 1819), p. 81; *Ladies' Magazine,* 3 (Jan. 1830):42-43; 3 (July 1830):325; 3 (Feb. 1830):49-55. Hale
maintained that women's empire in the home was "purer, more excellent and
spiritual than the worldly scope of regulating by laws the intercourse of business," *Ladies' Magazine* 5 (Feb. 1832):87. Cf. Catharine Beecher's declaration
in *Suggestions Respecting Improvements in Education* (Hartford, Conn.,
1829), p. 53: "The dominion of woman [in contrast to man's] may be based
on influence that the heart is proud to acknowledge."

Yet the canon of domesticity did not directly challenge
the modern organization of work and pursuit of wealth.
Rather, it accommodated and promised to temper them.
The values of domesticity undercut opposition to exploita-
tive pecuniary standards in the work world, by upholding a
"separate sphere" of comfort and compensation, instilling
a morality that would encourage self-control, and fostering
the idea that preservation of home and family sentiment
was an ultimate goal. Family affection, especially maternal
affection, was portrayed as the "spirit indefatigable, de-
lighting in its task," which could pervade and "regenerate"
society. Furthermore, women, through their reign in the
home, were to sustain the "essential elements of moral
government" to allow men to negotiate safely amid the
cunning, treachery, and competition of the marketplace.[10]
If a man had to enter the heartless and debasing world,
his wife at home supplied motive and reward for him, to
defuse his resentment:

> O! what a hallowed place home is when lit by the smile
> of such a being; and enviably happy the man who is
> the lord of such a paradise. . . . When he struggles on in
> the path of duty, the thought that it is for *her* in part
> he toils will sweeten his labors. . . . Should he meet
> dark clouds and storms abroad, yet sunshine and peace
> await him at home; and when his proud heart would

10. *Woman's Mission* (New York, 1840), pp. 20–21; *The Discussion*, p. 225.
Cf. Mary Ryan's conclusion, in "American Society and the Cult of Domesticity, 1830–1860" (Ph.D. diss., University of California, Santa Barbara,
1971), esp. pp. 70–71, 337, that the literature of domesticity of the 1840s included a complete theory of the psychologically specialized and socially
integrative functions of the family in industrial society. Ryan observes that
women in the home instilled in their husbands and children national values
and an ethic of social control; "by sustaining their husbands through the dis-
comforts of modern work situations, and gently restraining them from anti-
social behavior, American women facilitated the smooth operation of the
industrial system." The nineteenth-century definition of "social integration"
was "the moral power of woman" (pp. 70, 337).

resent the language of petty tyrants, "dressed in a little brief authority," from whom he receives the scanty remuneration for his daily labors, the thought that she perhaps may suffer thereby, will calm the tumult of his passions, and bid him struggle on, and find his reward in her sweet tones, and soothing kindness, and that the bliss of home is thereby made more apparent.[11]

The literature of domesticity thus enlisted women in their domestic roles to absorb, palliate, and even to redeem the strain of social and economic transformation. In the home, women symbolized and were expected to sustain traditional values and practices of work and family organization. The very shrillness of the *cri de coeur* against modern work relations, in the canon of domesticity, meant that women's role in the home would be inflexibly defined.

Recoiling from the spirit of self-interest and self-aggrandizement they saw in the marketplace, rhetoricians of domesticity looked to the home for a sanctuary of "disinterested" love; because women at home presumably escaped exposure to competitive economic practices, they became representatives of "disinterestedness." (In fact, women at home who engaged in "given-out" industry, as increasing numbers did, brought the economic world into the home.) More profoundly and authentically, married women represented "disinterestedness" because they were economically dependent. Because their property and earnings by law belonged to their husbands, married women could not operate as economic individuals.[12] Wives lacked the means and mo-

11. "Essay on Marriage," *Universalist and Ladies' Repository* 2 (April 19, 1834):371.

12. Nor did wives, on the whole, fail to understand their dependence. "First when I received the $5. bill I kissed it," a Cambridge woman wrote to her absent husband in thanks, "because it seemed to me a proof that my dear Husband did not lose me from his mind as soon as from his sight; then, I thought I would use it very prudently." Elizabeth Graeter, Cambridge, Mass., to Francis Graeter, Aug. 14, 1836, Hooker Collection, SL.

tive for self-seeking. The laws of marriage made the social model of striving for wealth irrelevant to them. Beyond equating wives' economic dependence with disinterestedness, the canon of domesticity went a further step and prescribed women's appropriate attitude to be selflessness. The conventional cliché "that women were to live for others" was substantially correct, wrote the author of *Woman's Mission,* for only by giving up all self-interest did women achieve the purity of motive that enabled them to establish moral reference points in the home.[13] Thus women's self-renunciation was called upon to remedy men's self-alienation.

Furthermore, the canon of domesticity required women to sustain the milieu of task-oriented work that had characterized earlier family organization. This requirement made service to others and the diffusion of happiness in the family women's tasks. Women's household service alone remained from the tradition of reciprocal service by family members. Since it highlighted that aspect of women's role, the canon of domesticity in its early formulation directed them not to idleness or superficial gentility but to a special sort of usefulness. Sarah Hale maintained, for instance, that women's principles of unselfishness and magnanimity should be manifest in their acts of service. A female author of *Letters on Female Character* similarly preferred to view woman as "a rational being, whose intelligent and active exertions are to afford a perennial source of comfort to mankind," rather than as a romantic goddess to be worshipped.[14]

Assuming that women would be happy insofar as they served others and made them happy, these writers reinforced women's orientation toward interpersonal goals in the emotional realm rather than self-reliant accomplish-

13. *Woman's Mission,* pp. 48–52.
14. *Ladies' Magazine* 3 (Oct. 1830):445; Cary, *Letters,* p. 174.

ment.[15] "In every thing I must consult the interest, the happiness and the welfare of *My Husband,*" Eunice Wait of Hallowell, Maine, wrote on the day she married a Universalist evangelist, ". . . may it be my constant study to make him contented and happy, and then will my own happiness be sure."[16] In a similar vein Mary Orne Tucker congratulated herself, after four years of marriage, on her husband's happiness at home: "His *happy home* I say, and I say it too with *pride,* and *pleasure;* it is no small compliment to my own abilities, to my own powers to please, my temper is somewhat wayward, but I hope it has not been discovered in scenes of domestic life, to shine as a good wife, is an object of my highest ambition, there are many humble duties to fulfill and to fulfill them with honor and chearfulness [*sic*] is a consideration which ought not to be beneath the notice of every reflecting woman."[17]

The amorphousness of such requirements as "to please" or "to serve" did not make women's role any less demanding. Ironically, the rhetoric that intended to distinguish "home" and "woman" from "the world" and "man" tended to make the two spheres analogous and comparable. It

15. In children's books in the 1840s, there is a discernible contrast between the achievement motivation encouraged in boys and the affiliation motivation encouraged in girls. J. S. C. Abbott's *The School Boy,* for instance, stressed that the boy must aim for correctness and truth, even at the expense of popularity. Girls' books by Lydia Maria Child and Lydia Sigourney also advocated purity and correct principle, but stressed that girls should attain these by loving others, treating them nicely, following the Golden Rule, etc. In his *Rollo* series, Jacob Abbott portrayed Rollo (nine years old) as an independent little man who followed the truth and wished to succeed, but made Rollo's sister Jane passive, cautious, nervous, and dependent on her brother. Bernard Wishy discusses these books in *The Child and the Republic* (Philadelphia, 1968), pp. 57-58.

16. Diary of Eunice Hale Wait Cobb, vol. 1, p. 29, Sept. 10, 1822, BPL.

17. She continued, "I am every day amply repaid for all my endeavors to please, every look from my master is a certificate of my success, and the plaudit of my own conscience affords sweet peace." Diary of Mary Orne Tucker, EI, May 1, 1802.

was the paradox of domesticity to make women's work-
roles imitate men's; despite the intent to stress how they
differed, domestic occupations began to mean for women
what worldly occupations meant for men. A businessman
in a *Godey's Lady's Book* story admonished his young
wife, who had repeatedly neglected to have his midday
meal ready on time:

> Your error lies in a false idea which you have enter-
> tained, that your happiness was to come somewhere
> from out[side] of your domestic duties, instead of in
> the performance of them—that they were not part of a
> wife's obligations, but something that she could put
> aside if she were able to hire enough servants. I cannot,
> thus, delegate my business duties to any one; without
> my governing mind and constant attention, every thing
> would soon be in disorder, and an utter failure, instead
> of prosperity, be the result of my efforts. By my care-
> fulness and constant devotion to my business, I am
> enabled to provide you with every comfort; surely,
> then, you should be willing also to give careful atten-
> tion to your department, that I may feel home to be a
> pleasant place.[18]

Business provided one analogy, politics another. "I think
it is my humble desire to be as a wise Legislator to my
little province," wrote Susan Huntington, a minister's wife
who knew the domestic canon by heart before publications
rehearsed it, "to enact as few statutes as possible, & those
easy and judicious—to see that all things are done at the
proper time, & in the proper way, so far as is practicable,
that our family may be a quiet, well organized, regular
family."[19]

18. T. S. Arthur, "Sweethearts and Wives," *Godey's Lady's Book* 23 (Dec.
1841), reprinted in Nancy F. Cott, ed., *Root of Bitterness: Documents of the
Social History of American Women* (New York: Dutton, 1972), p. 169.
19. Diary of Susan Manfield Huntington, June 14, 1819, SML.

Defining it as her province, the canon of domesticity
made woman's household occupation her vocation. The
very attempt to immobilize woman's role in the home
transformed her household duties into a discrete, specialized, and objective work-role. Domesticity as a vocation
meant, furthermore, that woman's work-role imitated
man's while lacking his means of escape. If man could
recover from his work "at home," woman's work was "at
home." She provided for his relief. Since her sex-role contained her work-role, for her there was no escape. "A law
of her being" appointed her vocation, according to the
canon. "To render *home* happy, is woman's peculiar
province; home is *her* world." She was "neither greater nor
less than man, but different, as her natural vocation is different, and . . . each is superior to each other in their
respective departments of thought and action." Even if
woman's vocation was "natural," however, it required
preparation and instruction. Not only the numerous books
of advice to the wife and mother but also new institutions
to educate girls for those roles, heralded the rationalization
of women's domestic occupations into a "profession."[20]

The canon of domesticity created great expectations in
and of women to excel in their vocation. When family life

20. Quotations from *Ladies' Magazine* 3 (May 1830):218; Caleb Cushing,
"The Social Condition of Woman," from the *North American Review,* April
1836, reprinted in Allen Thorndike Rice, ed., *Essays from the North American Review* (New York, 1879), p. 67. See chapter 3, below, on the movement
to educate girls for domestic responsibilities. Catharine Beecher popularized
the idea that wife-and-motherhood was woman's "profession" in the mid-
nineteenth century, but that usage began, I believe, with Hannah More's
Strictures on the Modern System of Female Education, originally published in
1799 and widely read by women in the United States for decades after. More
wrote, "The profession of ladies, to which the bent of their instruction should
be turned, is that of daughters, wives, mothers, and mistresses of families"
(vol. 1, 9th ed. [London, 1801], p. 112).

fulfilled these expectations the ideological gloss probably heightened its gratifications, as in Mary Orne Tucker's case. Eunice Wait Cobb, too, recorded in her diary, "Yes the happiness which we enjoy in our little family may well be termed *uninterrupted* happiness. All is *harmony, peace,* and *contentment,*" shortly after she bore her second son. A few months later she confirmed, "Indeed *our* family may *well* be called a little heaven below for health and plenty happiness & contentment are the constant inmates of our dwelling." The self-sacrifice inherent in the vocation, however, combined with unpredictable difficulties in household management and child rearing, made strenuous demands. At nineteen, Mehitable Dawes had read didactic literature on woman's role "to form . . . myself to confer happiness in domestic life." At thirty-five, after thirteen years of marriage, she confessed "often wish myself a smarter body, & able to be a first rate mother, wife, mistress, & every thing—sometimes am quite discouraged on this matter—the difficulty is I do not look above for support—am apt to depend on myself—oh that I could sincerely ask for aid—so many important duties press upon me I am almost bewildered." Even so supremely pious a woman as Susan Huntington found it impossible to maintain equanimity in the face of family illnesses and transient domestic help. "It really depresses my spirits so as to affect my appetite and strength," she confessed to her diary, "Oh that I *could* rise above these vexations & distresses & be happy in the recollection that God governs." How difficult it was to conform to the model of domesticity, especially because of the "many little vexing worrying circumstances," as Susan Huntington put it, "continually taking place in this world in conducting the management of a family."[21]

21. Eunice Hale Wait Cobb diary, Sept. 1825, Jan. 1826; diary of Mehitable May Dawes Goddard, Aug. 11, 1815, Jan. 1, 1831, May-Goddard Collection, SL; Susan Mansfield Huntington diary, Aug. 13, 1817, May 2, 1819.

Marriage initiated women's vocation. The romantic-love sentiments which had been conveyed in imaginative literature since the eighteenth century influenced women to hope for an ideal mate, although reality was always more contrary, as some acknowledged:

> While we may think "there is a *magic* in that little word *home*," there are many within my knowledge, are never so happy as when exiled from thence. . . . *Many,* I believe, submit to the chains of hymen, and verbally acknowledge them *silken,* but their conduct tells another tale. The society of *entire* strangers and those perhaps not possessing half the merit or attractions of their companions is constantly courted, while the presence of the husband, or wife, awakens no senssations of pleasure. Well, perhaps if it were *only* this. But feelings of disgust—nay—even of *contempt,* are sometimes visible in the countenances of the married pair, when subjected to an interview. Whose heart would not revolt at such a state?

This observation led the writer, Eliza Chaplin, not to abandon but to enlarge the ideal. She would never marry for "interest," she said—would never marry at all unless she could give her whole heart. For years she had imagined an ideal mate who was noble, ingenuous, the possessor of "every quality I could desire." She said she would "ever remain in 'single blessedness' and deem it felicity thus to live," rather than endure "the unhappiness that exists where minds are 'fettered to different moulds'—and rather than be subject to the 'eternal strife' which in such cases prevails."[22] Such protestations rested on women's aware-

22. Eliza Chaplin to Laura Lovell, July 27, 1820, Chaplin-Lovell Correspondence, EI. On romantic love ideals see Herman R. Lantz et al., "Pre-Industrial Patterns in the Colonial Family in America: A Content Analysis of American Magazines," *American Sociological Review* 33 (1968):413–26; Ian Watt, "The New Woman: Samuel Richardson's Pamela," pp. 268–73; Edward Shorter,

ness that marriages were often contracted for economic rather than romantic motives. *"Souls* must be *kindred* to make the bands silken," Mary Orne Tucker insisted; "all other I call unions of *hands,* not *hearts,*—I rejoice that the knot which binds me was not tied with any mercenary feelings, and that my *heart* is under the same *sweet* subjection as my *hand.*"[23]

The choice of a mate was fateful, women recognized, because marriage bound both man and woman and subjected her to him. In Mary Tucker's view, marriage could prove "a galling chain" for the unfortunate or heedless; those who married "from proper motives" would be "insensible of the bondage, but if beauty alone seduces, or gold allures, it will 'prove that plague of iron' which the poet sings." Lucy Beckley wrote verses to her "New-Married Sister" warning, "Now you have left your parents wing,/Nor longer ask their care./It is but seldom husbands bring/A lighter yoke to wear." Even the sentimental women novelists who glorified marriage also saw its other aspect. "There is no tyranny so perfect as that of a capricious and alienated husband," wrote Lydia Huntley Sigourney in a story titled "The Intemperate." Catherine Sedgwick pitied her married sister Frances, who had to accede to her husband's disastrous financial decisions: "[She] cannot consent to it but in *obedience* to his wish, which she thinks she has no right to withhold." "Poor Frances! My heart bleeds for her, when I think to what thraldom her noble spirit is subjected."[24]

As long as the wife's legal subordination persisted, in

The Making of the Modern Family, (New York: Basic Books, 1975), chaps. 2, 3, 4.

23. Mary Orne Tucker diary, April 17, 1802.

24. Ibid., April 28, 1802; journal-book of Lucy Beckley, 1819, CHS; Lydia H. Sigourney, "The Intemperate," *Universalist and Ladies' Repository* 2 (March 22, 1834):336; Catherine Maria Sedgwick to Robert Sedgwick, Oct. 8, 1817, Sedgwick Collection, MHS. A New York judge, who advocated wives'

combination with romantic love ideals that stressed personal attraction and emotional motivation for both part-
ners, women faced an overwhelming irony: they were to
choose their bondage. "In America the independence of
woman is irrecoverably lost in the bonds of marriage,"
noticed Alexis de Tocqueville, among other visitors to the
United States in the early nineteenth century, but she
"voluntarily and freely enters upon this engagement," in
full knowledge of her destiny. "She has learned by the use
of her independence to surrender it without a struggle and
without a murmur when the time comes for making the
sacrifice."[25] Not wholly accurate—he probably exaggerated
both the young unmarried woman's independence and the
wife's willingness to bend to subordination—but nevertheless perspicacious, Tocqueville seized on a central paradox
of domesticity, that women were expected to make a voluntary choice amounting to self-abnegation. That "sacrifice" was impossible for some. Eliza Perkins Cabot recalled
of her adolescence in the early nineteenth century, "My
mother thought any of her daughters were fools to marry

---

ownership of their own property, asserted in 1837 that the laws of marriage
gave the husband "so much, and such uncontrolled, indefinite, irresponsible
and arbitrary power over [the wife's] person, and subject[ed] her to such an
abject state of surveillance to the will, commands, caprices, ill humours,
angry passions, and mercenary, avaricious and selfish disposition, conduct and
views of her husband," that marriage for women approximated slavery for
blacks. Marriage legally subjected a woman "to privations of the like character,
and to a greater extent, than if she had committed a criminal and indictable
offense," i.e., by depriving her of her liberty and property. *Remarks Compris-
ing in Substance Judge Hertell's Argument in the House of Assembly of the
State of New York, in the Sessions of 1837, in support of the bill to restore to
married woman "The Right of Property"*. . . (New York, 1839), pp. 41-43.

25. Alexis de Tocqueville, *Democracy in America,* ed. Phillips Bradley, (New
York: Vintage Books, 1945), 2:212-13. Frank Furstenburg, "Industrialism
and the American Family: A Look Backward," *American Sociological Review*
31 (1966):330-32, notes that foreign visitors to America in the early nineteenth century often commented on the difference between a young woman's
freedom and a married woman's confinement.

anybody. They had all they wanted at home."[26] The great majority, of course, found it possible. But what tensions complicated that choice, which was also the most important one a woman would make? "The contract is so much more important in its consequences to females than to males," a young man in 1820, a law student, wrote, comparing the significance of marriage to the two sexes, "for besides leaving everything else to unite themselves to one man they subject themselves to his authority—they depend more upon their husband than he does upon the wife for society & for the happiness & enjoyment of their lives—he is their all—their only relative—their only hope—but as for him—business leads him out of doors, far from the company of his wife . . . & then it is upon his employment that he depends almost entirely for the happiness of his life."[27]

26. "Reminiscences of Eliza Perkins Cabot," typescript, Cabot Family Collection, folder 9, SL. Single women occasionally contrasted the married woman's role unfavorably with their own. At twenty-one, in 1796, Abigail May remarked on meeting an old acquaintance, "the lady was Mrs. Poor—Meriam Fullerton—that gay sprightly Meriam Fullerton that was—but oh! how alter'd— she looks dull, dejected, in short, like a *married woman. I'll say* with Solus— 'oh! I'll never be married' if such sower [sic] looks comes [sic] of matrimony." Journal from Portland, 1796, p. 19, MeHS. Cf. Catherine Sedgwick's comment, after surveying society at a New York dinner party in 1833, "a married woman past thirty in America is the same nonentity that a French girl of sixteen is—but the one is sustained by hope—she is looking into a world in which she is to be an actor—Our poor married lady has played out the play & what so dull as a theatre when the curtain has fallen!" Diary of Catherine Maria Sedgwick, April 19, 1833.

27. Journal of George Younglove Cutler, 1820, quoted in Emily Vanderpoel, ed., *Chronicles of a Pioneer School* (Cambridge, Mass.: University Press, 1903), p. 196. Certainly Hannah Emery of Exeter, New Hampshire, saw the fateful aspect of her decision to marry, in 1791. "The die is about to be cast which will probably determin [sic] the future happiness or misery of my life," she wrote to a friend. "Yesterday our names were published, and the week after next the connection will be formed which only Death can separate. I have always anticipated the event with a degree of solemnity almost equal to that which will terminate my present existence." Hannah T. Emery to Mary Carter, Oct. 17, 1791, Cutts Family Manuscripts, EI. She seems to have been eerily prescient, for she died in childbirth shortly after her marriage.

The canon of domesticity and its enveloping social circumstances freighted women's marriage choice with unprecedented meaning. Marrying meant beginning a vocation
imbued with significance for society, as well as fitting
one's neck to a "yoke" that could not be broken (in ac-
cord with conventional propriety); and the separation of
the home from "the world" isolated women in their roles
as wives and mothers. All this followed the "romantic"
acceptance of a husband. Young women's awareness of the
conflict between romantic and economic elements in the
marriage choice, and of the heavy social consequences of
marriage (probably compounded by the contrast between
single and married women's lives), seems to have resulted
in an emotional reaction or "marriage trauma" in the
minds of some by the 1820s and 1830s. Women who sincerely envisioned *beaux ideals* and neither found them in
reality nor would settle for less refused ever to marry.[28]
The "marriage trauma" may have also enhanced the sense
of fulfillment of those who found seemingly perfect part-
ners, whether consciously anticipated or not.[29] But the
most frequent manifestation of the "marriage trauma," I
suspect, was a withdrawal of emotional intensity from the
too-burdened marriage choice, and also from the marital

28. Mrs. A.J. Graves (pseud.), the author of *Girlhood and Womanhood; or
Sketches of my Schoolmates* (Boston, 1844), p. 210, admitted that her highly
romantic view of love had made it impossible for any man to meet her standards. Catherine Sedgwick, at forty-five, paused when she "heard or read a
remark that struck me—that romantic imaginative persons formed a *beau
ideal* to which nothing in life approximated near enough to satisfy them—,"
and thought that "This may account for my never responding to the sentiments of those who sought me." Catherine Maria Sedgwick diary, May 24,
1834. See also her account of a dream that seems to express her horror at the
possibility of marrying a less-than-perfect man, Oct. 12, 1836.

29. The courtship of reformers Angelina Grimké and Theodore Weld comes
to mind. See *The Letters of Theodore Dwight Weld, Angelina Grimké Weld,
and Sarah Grimké*, ed. Gilbert H. Barnes and Dwight L. Dumond (New York:
Appleton-Century-Crofts, 1934), vol. 2:532–678.

relationship.[30] Two examples from the 1830s suggest two possible patterns.

Rachel Stearns, Sarah Ripley Stearns's daughter, was descended from genteel Congregationalist families but had experienced impoverishment and isolation since her father's death when she was five. At age twenty-one, self-supporting (although still resident at home with her mother), she converted to Methodism. On a journey to a Methodist meeting slightly more than a year later, one of her "brethren" engaged her in conversation about his duty to marry and unexpectedly asked her to marry him. She was shocked—having viewed her role in the conversation "in the light of an aged maiden lady [at twenty-three!] giving advice to a young man"—and wrote in her diary her initial reaction: "I marry a mason!" (Later she crossed this out and replaced it with "I marry a journeyman mechanic.") She gave him her reasons against it: she loved him as a Christian, and hoped for no other connection; her mother was dependent on her; moreover she had never thought of marrying, and did not expect to be asked. "I told him I was destined to lead a single life, my mother had always told me no one would want me, and I had not qualified myself for that station." In her dreams that night she relived the situation. Shortly afterward, coincidentally, she lost her schoolteaching job, and for days an inner voice nagged her, "'Now you have left the school, you have nothing to do, go and marry that man, and let the trouble for schools be at rest.'" She worried whether God or the

30. Women's investment of emotion in their relationships with other women may have stood out all the more clearly—especially during adolescence and young womanhood—because of this "marriage trauma" effect. On women's relationships with one another see chapter 5, "Sisterhood," below, and also the richly rendered description in Carroll Smith-Rosenberg, "The Female World of Love and Ritual," *Signs: A Journal of Women in Culture and Society* 1(1975):1–29.

devil had sent such an urge. "I feel in a perfect maze," she wrote in her diary, "there is a bewildering feeling in my head which I cannot account for, I can do [no] more work in one day, than I formerly could in three. I don't know but I am actually insane, sometimes I think I am." While she was moving about in search of a school during the next month, she wrote nothing in her diary. Never again, when she resumed writing, did she mention the marriage offer.[31]

Lavinia B. Kelly of Northwood, New Hampshire, who lived comfortably at home with parents and three younger siblings, reacted differently to an unforeseen suitor. In 1837, when she was nineteen, she was "astonish[ed]" to receive a proposal of marriage in a letter from J.S. Cilly (her diary never reveals his first name). "I had been acquainted with Mr. Cilly for a long time but it had never occurred to me that he regarded me with any particular partiality and I was therefore wholly unprepared for such a declaration." In her reply, she said she was undecided but would consider his offer and continue to see him on the previous friend-of-family terms. The two saw each other seldom in the next weeks, but three months after the proposal they went on an outing to the beach and had a long talk. "Before I came home I had engaged myself to him," Lavinia's diary records. "It was a serious business but I had the approbation of my parents and I felt that I could love him as well as woman ought to love a husband." Ten weeks later they married. On her husband's first extended absence from home, on business, two months after the wedding, the bride reported, "*I miss him a little bit.*"[32]

Rachel Stearns in her almost neurotic bewilderment and

31. Diary of Rachel Willard Stearns, vol. 7, Nov. 22, 1836, Stearns Collection, SL. Cf. the only comment recorded by her mother, Sarah Ripley, regarding her own decision (at age twenty-seven) to marry Charles Stearns, whom she had known for five years: "Our constancy has been tried & our affection proved." Diary of Sarah Ripley Stearns, Nov. 10, 1812, Stearns Collection, SL.

32. Diary of Lavinia Bailey Kelly Cilly, vol. 2, June 12, Sept. 6, Nov. 22, 1837; Jan. 17, 1838; NHHS.

Lavinia Kelly in her seeming denial of the importance of
the event disclosed two responses to the pressure of the
marriage decision. For them and their contemporaries that
pressure was especially (perhaps uniquely) concentrated.
The marriage choice determined women's life experience
to a greater extent than it had earlier, when married women's household roles were less specialized, the conjugal relationship more dependent on wider kin connections,
and the ideologies of individualism and romantic love
less dominant. It was also more conclusive than in a later
period when the incidence of divorce increased.[33]

Both strong and weak, happy and unhappy marriages resulted, as one would expect. A woman might call her husband her "best and dearest friend," say that she missed
him with "longing desires" when he was absent, declare
that "every year I feel more endeared to him whom I love
better than myself," regret "having a whole day pass without seeing so good a friend," or, in the tradition of Calvinist self-criticism, berate herself for allowing her earthly
love to overshadow religion: "My heart is too much devoted to creature objects. I think I am not so eager after
the wishes & honours of the world as to please a beloved
creature object." Others might refer to their husbands not
at all, only as "Mr. A." (or whatever his initial), or even
with a touch of sarcasm as "my liege lord."[34]

33. The "marriage trauma" response applies to the early part of the nineteenth century. Toward the later part of the century, more women actually
declined to marry; its last decades witnessed the highest proportion of women
never-marrying in all of American history. Toward the turn of the twentieth
century, when the frequency of divorce rose, the proportion of women marrying returned to more typical levels. Daniel Scott Smith conveniently includes a
table of proportions of U.S. women ever-marrying in "Family Limitation,
Sexual Control, and Domestic Feminism," in Mary Hartman and Lois Banner,
eds., *Clio's Consciousness Raised* (New York: Harper Torchbooks, 1973),
p. 121.

34. Quotations are (in order) from diary of Ruth Henshaw (Miles), April 6,
1806, AAS—regarding her husband's death within their first year of marriage;
diary of Lydia Hill Almy, Nov. 1797, EI—after her husband had been gone for

As the start of woman's vocation, marriage held out promise as well as anxiety. Legally and economically the husband/father controlled the family, but rhetorically the vocation of domesticity gave women the domestic sphere for their own, to control and influence. Motherhood was proposed as the central lever with which women could budge the world and, in practice, it offered the best opportunity to women to heighten their domestic power. The authors of "domestic education" books assumed that children lived mostly in the presence of their mothers, not their fathers, even though final authority (legally and conventionally) was patriarchal. Fathers' interaction with young children tended to diminish when they engaged in commercial and industrial work more often away from the household.[35] As women and children were segregated at home, and women's domestic manufacture diminished, motherhood stood out as a discrete task. The increasingly generous appraisals of mothers' authority denoted the transformation of domesticity into a specialized vocation.

Declaring that parents—particularly mothers—could decide their children's fate, and warning that they could produce misery or joy for themselves through their own parental acts, the domestic educators of the 1820s and 1830s displayed their acceptance of the Lockean idea that early influences on a child directly and inevitably decided his or her later character. They also suggested that parents lacked (or shunned) contributions from relatives, neighbors,

the first seven weeks of an eighteen-month trip; diary of Mary Hurlbut, June 19, 1831, CHS—after seven years of marriage; diary of Anna Bryant Smith, March 11, 1807, MeHS—respecting her husband's absence at his store all day (they had been married more than twenty years); diary of Eliza Ann Hull Staples, July 3, 1828, CSL—after eight months of marriage. Luella Case, in her correspondence with Sarah Edgarton, Hooker Collection, SL, referred to her husband as her "liege lord."

35. See chapter 1, note 36.

servants, boarders, or masters of apprentices, and had become exclusively responsible themselves for the rearing of
their children. In *Fireside Education* Samuel Goodrich observed that parental education "adjust[ed] itself" to the
needs of society: "with the advance of refinement and
knowledge the family circle is drawn closer together, and
the solicitude of parents for their children and their influence over them are proportionally increased." He concluded, as did so many of his contemporaries, that parenthood
involved a "fearful charge." "Parents are to their children,
fortune, fate, and destiny."[36] Because of the mother's
primary role in the child's early years, most of the domestic educators reasoned further, "Mothers have as powerful
an influence over the welfare of future generations as all
other earthly causes combined."[37]

That emphasis did not originate in works of the 1830s.
From the turn of the century New England ministers had
pointed out the importance of the mother's role. Many
endorsed their colleague William Lyman's pronouncement
of 1802: "Mothers do, in a sense, hold the reins of government and sway the ensigns of national prosperity and
glory. Yea, they give direction to the moral sentiments of
our rising hopes and contribute to form their moral state.
To them therefore our eyes are turned in this demoralizing
age, and of them we ask, that they would appreciate their
real worth and dignity, and exert all their influence to
drive discord, infidelity and licentiousness from our
land."[38] The ministers' sense that religion was under attack urged them on, and they viewed their congregations,
in which women formed the strong majority, pragmatically.

36. Samuel Goodrich, *Fireside Education* (New York, 1838), p. 17.
37. J. S. C. Abbott, *The Mother at Home; or, the Principles of Maternal Duty
Familiarly Illustrated* (New York, 1833), p. 152.
38. William Lyman, *A Virtuous Woman the Bond of Domestic Union, and
the Source of Domestic Happiness* (New London, Conn., 1802), pp. 22-23.

Through mothers ministers could influence the next generation, an aim which took on crucial dimensions in an era of national expansion and individual mobility. Mothers moved around the country, and their teachings were presumably lifelong. Domestic education promised to affect individual character in its formative years and to implant lessons that geographical relocation would not destroy.

In the two decades after 1800 New England ministers fervently reiterated their consensus that mothers were more important than fathers in forming "the tastes, sentiments, and habits of children," and more effective in instructing them.[39] Their emphasis departed from (and undermined) the patriarchal family ideal in which the mother, while entrusted with the physical care of her children, left their religious, moral, and intellectual guidance to her husband. Without certain shifts in prevailing doctrine about salvation and in their views of childhood, ministers could not have thus turned their attention to mothers. During the "Great Awakening" of the early nineteenth century the orthodox view—that an individual's award of saving grace was purely God's work—relaxed, permitting new emphasis on the propriety and utility of human efforts to complement God's will. Though all was ultimately in God's hands, the Reverend Increase Graves of Bridport, Vermont, pointed out, humans were obliged "to do all they are able, just as much as if they could save themselves by their own works."[40] Just as individuals were obligated to help themselves through piety and re-

39. For amplification see Nancy F. Cott, "In the Bonds of Womanhood: Perspectives on Female Experience and Consciousness in New England, 1780–1830" (Ph.D. diss., Brandeis University, 1974), chap. 3, "Ministers' View of Women," esp. pp. 114-23. Quotation is from George Keely, *The Nature and Order of a Gospel Church . . . with an appendix containing an enquiry into the Standing of Females in a Christian Church . . .* (Haverhill, Mass., 1819), p. 6.

40. Quoted from the Rev. Increase Graves' description of a revival in Bridport, Vt., in 1813-14, in Bennet Tyler, *New England Revivals . . .* (Boston, 1846), pp. 366-67.

pentance, parents were obligated to aid in the salvation of their children. The implications about childhood in Lockean educational psychology also influenced the approach taken by the clergy, particularly Unitarians or Universalists, who rejected the idea of the depravity of the soul, and extreme Arminians. Even Congregationalists who considered themselves Calvinists, and evangelicals of several denominations who stressed natural depravity, assimilated some of the new emphasis on the formative importance of early childhood. In their search for ways to reinvigorate religion they called upon such ideas, concentrating new efforts on the "virtuous education" of children and proposing mothers as educators.[41]

Without denying paternal authority, the pastors' appeals acknowledged that child rearing had become a specialized domestic process carried on by mothers. "It seems as if all my occupation is gone," Mary Lee wrote sadly to her sister in 1811, when her first child died at the age of one.[42] Mehitable Dawes Goddard wrote with a plaintive tone to her mother-in-law, a few months after she bore her first child, that she had been doing no reading, writing, or sewing but only tending the infant. "I am very fidgetty I think —& make a world of fuss over the poor little thing—but as I've nothing else to occupy me, I ought not to be too devoted—You see tho' that she is uppermost in my mind or I should not have begun with talking of her."[43]

41. See Cott, "In the Bonds," pp. 116-20; cf. John Lathrop, "A Sermon Preached before the Members of the Boston Female Asylum, September 1815," BPL; and Thomas Barnard, *A Sermon Preached before the Salem Female Charitable Society . . . July 6, 1803* (Salem: William Carlton, 1803).

42. "I have still much to do for myself and others," she tried to convince herself, "and in employment will seek relief." Mary Lee to Hannah Lowell, May 25, 1811, in Frances Rollins Morse, ed., *Henry and Mary Lee: Letters and Journals* (Boston: T. Todd, 1926), p. 103.

43. Mehitable May Dawes Goddard to A. Goddard, February 16, 1820, May-Goddard Collection, Box 1, SL. Since Goddard and her husband were living in Manchester, England, when she wrote the letter, her routine may have been more heavily concentrated on child care than if she were living at home.

Motherhood evoked conscientious effort. "My time is abundantly occupied with my babies," wrote Abigail Alcott to her brother and sister-in-law, when her Anna was two and Louisa six months.

It seems to me at times as if the weight of responsibility connected with these little immortal beings would prove too much for me—Am I doing what is right? Am I doing enough? Am I not doing too much is my earnest enquiry. I am almost at times discouraged if I find the result prove unfavorable. . . . Mr. A aids me in general principles but no body can aid me in the detail—and it is a theme of constant thought—an object of mounting solicitude—If I neglect every thing else, I must be forgiven—I know you laugh at me and think me a slave to my children and think me foolishly *anxious*—I can bear it all, better than one reproach of conscience, or one thoughtless word or look given to my Anna's inquiry.[44]

Some mothers detailed in journals the daily progress of their infants (suggesting a new note of empiricism in child rearing) or repeatedly recorded pious hopes for them. Religious women accepted motherhood as a project in salvation. "I doubt not, if mothers would begin with their children when they are young, they might mould them

44. Abigail May Alcott to Lucretia and Samuel May, June 22, 1833, Alcott Family Papers, box 1, folder 25, HCL. At the time of Anna's birth she had written to the Mays (March 31, 1831): "that most interesting of all occupations is begun—the care of my child—and delightful it is—I would not delegate it to an angel—I am at times most impatient to dismiss my nurse that not even she should participate with me in this pleasure. . . . It is a happiness not to be communicated to every one—all could not understand the sacred, pure emotions which have filled and at times overwhelmed me." In this light, Charles Strickland's study of Bronson Alcott's child-rearing without reference to Abigail, in "A Transcendentalist Father: The Child-Rearing Practices of Bronson Alcott," *Perspectives in American History* 3 (1969):5–73, seems inherently faulty.

into any frame they chose," wrote Peggy Dow, wife of a Methodist evangelist, in 1813. In their diaries women transcribed extracts stressing the effects of pious education by mothers, "those angels of love and fidelity who first opened our senses to behold God in his works and word."[45]

Motherhood by this definition was no easy task. Mothers were to teach by both precept and example, Susan Huntington reminded herself, in line with the current wisdom. She summed up in her diary, "In short nothing but the most persevering industry in the acquisition of necessary knowledge—the most indefatigable application of that knowledge to particular cases—the most decisive adherence to a consequent course of piety—& above all the most unremitted supplications to Him who alone can enable us to resolve & act correctly—can qualify us to discharge properly those duties which devolve upon every Mother." Women's private writings attested to the heavy impression of maternal responsibilities on sensitive minds. "My Children how will they get along through this World of sin and vanity—" Mercy Flynt Morris worried. "I know not what they will be left to do—there are so many ways for there [sic] youthful minds to be led astray in all vices—It is my duty to warn them against those vices and try to instill into there [sic] minds the importance of seeking an interest in Christ—without which they will be miserable."[46]

Women found their joys as well as their burdens in motherhood, bound to it as they were. Elizabeth Graeter

45. Peggy Dow, "Vicissitudes, or the Journey of Life," in Lorenzo Dow, *History of Cosmopolite* (Cincinnati, 1859), p. 669; diary of Elizabeth Cleveland, undated (c. 1824), EI. In *The Mother at Home* (Boston, 1833), the Reverend J.S.C. Abbott recommended that mothers keep journals of their children's development. See Elizabeth Ellery Sedgwick's journal-book of the first years of her child's life, HCL, for an example from the 1820s.

46. Susan Mansfield Huntington diary, Feb. 7, 1813—see also May 21, 1812; diary of Mercy Flynt Morris, Aug. 2, 1828, CHS.

of Cambridge, Massachusetts, wrote to her absent husband about their young son, "At times, my heart would sink without him. I have a feeling that he is to me the medium & representative of 'the Comforter' promised to the Church by Her Bridegroom when He left her. I thank God for him. ... For the most part Mother's Love is the predominant spirit in our little household." Mother's love had to be self-limiting, however, for religious women who believed that "love of the creature" should never surpass respect for God's will. Susan Huntington's diary reflected her continual struggle between longing to be free of earthly attachments in order to seek God, and "idolatrous" clinging to her children. Children's deaths became the proving ground of women's religious faith. "I cannot steadily contemplate the idea of losing him," one mother wrote in a letter, regarding her ill child, "but My Dear Sister do you think this inconsistent with a christian spirit. ... I have never expected strength to be resigned to the death of a dear child."[47]

Contradictions inhered within the formulation of motherhood as a vocation. First, women could not control conception with certainty, except by abstinence from sexual relations. Perhaps many echoed the private feelings of Millicent Leib Hunt (who generally conformed to the model of a pious and dutiful wife) when she realized that she was pregnant for the fifth time: "yes, even now the frail foetus within me is the abode of an immortal spirit, and this has caused thoughts of discontent. I would it were

47. Elizabeth Graeter, Cambridge, Mass., to Francis Graeter, Eastport, Maine, Aug. 14, 1836, Hooker Collection, SL; Susan Mansfield Huntington diary, 1812–23, passim; Mary Irwin to Eliza W. Pitkin, Dresden, Ohio, March 13, 1835, Hooker Collection, SL. Cf. Mary Orne Tucker's record of the remarks of a friend, respecting the death of a Haverhill child: "that 'God to save the parent took the child' for he was quite the idol of his mother; she seemed almost to forget the first great command, 'Thou shalt have no *other* Gods before me.'" Mary Orne Tucker diary, April 13, 1802.

not thus, I love my liberty, my ease, my comfort and do not willingly endure the inconvenience and sufferings of pregnancy and childbirth." For one who took seriously the responsibilities of motherhood, the arrival of another child posed anxieties. Susan Huntington became "rather desponding" during her pregnancy in 1813. "The idea of soon giving birth to my 3d child & the consequent duties I shall be called to discharge distresses me so I feel as if I should sink," she admitted. "[I] see so many defects in my conduct to my offspring *now,* that I know not how it will be *possible* for me to do my duty then. Oh God! strengthen me."[48]

Portrayed as women's self-fulfillment, motherhood manifested itself in self-denial. The correct rearing of children required "habitual command over one's own passions," warned Lydia Maria Child in her *Mother's Book.* "The care of children requires a great many sacrifices, and a great deal of self-denial, but the woman who is not willing to sacrifice a good deal in such a cause, does not deserve to be a mother." Furthermore, child-rearing literature of the day advised that the child should quickly become self-governing. The mother-child relationship was a vehicle for the child's growth, not for maternal satisfaction. Fragments of evidence suggest that mothers tried to follow this model. Elizabeth Ellery Sedgwick, who kept a journal of her daughter's first five years, recorded when the child was twenty months old, "now . . . I felt desirous to cultivate in you habits of independence, that you might seek your own employments and not depend entirely on others for your pleasures." She noted subsequent incidents that seemed to reveal the dawn of conscience and self-control in her daughter. Mary Lee felt that her daughter was "getting to

48. Quotation from diary of Milicent Leib Hunt in Horace Adams, "A Puritan Wife on the Frontier," *MVHR* 27 (1940):81; Susan Mansfield Huntington diary, March 24, 1813.

an age that will suffer from too much attention" when she was not yet two. In reference to a three-and-a-half-year-old son she also noted, "I hope his own *reason,* aided by my *judicious* correction, will soon enable him to gain some control over his own *selfwill.*"[49]

The perceived dichotomy between home and world also made the mother's task perplexing. One mother acknowledged that, in the course of informing a friend how she was acting on her "theory about home education" by teaching her own and two other small children at home every morning. Aware that opinion was divided—that some authorities maintained "the world must be met" the sooner the better—she nonetheless followed "the principle that temptations & trials would come to my children soon enough, . . . & the longer I keep them under my own eye, the better I hope they will be fortified by good principles & good habits—to resist the evils which they must necessarily meet by & by." But she was unsure that her course was the best, "even if mothers have sufficient time to devote to the instruction of their children."[50]

The canon of domesticity expressed the dominance of what may be designated a middle-class ideal, a cultural preference for domestic retirement and conjugal-family intimacy over both the "vain" and fashionable sociability of the rich and the promiscuous sociability of the poor.

49. Lydia Maria Child, *The Mother's Book* (2d ed., Boston, 1833), pp. 15-16 (Lydia Maria Child, though married, bore no offspring); Elizabeth Ellery Sedgwick's journal-book of the first years of her child's life, 1824-29, pp. 21, 66, 82; Mary Lee to Henry Lee, Sept. 1, 1813, and May 20, 1821, in Morse, *Henry and Mary Lee,* pp. 202, 239. In a review of the early nineteenth-century child-rearing literature, Robert Sunley concludes, "it was not considered desirable for the child to remain protractedly dependent on adult authority. Rather he was to become at an early age a self-maintaining moral being." "Early Nineteenth-Century American Literature on Child Rearing," in Margaret Mead and Martha Wolfenstein, eds., *Childhood in Contemporary Cultures* (Chicago: University of Chicago Press, 1955), p. 162.

50. C. L. Coe to Elizabeth Lyman Mills, c. 1837-38, Elizabeth Lyman Correspondence, CSL.

Many women— and, strikingly, often the wealthier ones—
articulated such an ideal before 1830. A merchant's wife
of Portland, Maine, recorded the prosaic details of rising
and breakfasting with her husband and concluded with the
exclamation, "Oh ye Voluptious [*sic*] and idle disapated
[*sic*] people I pity you because ye know not the pleasure
of domestic happiness. My God, I thank thee that thou
hast given me a mind capable of enjoying this kind of
bliss." The daughter of a prominent Portsmouth (New
Hampshire) family thought a local acquaintance's shift
from "fashionable follies" to "domestic retirement" important enough to mention in a letter to her father, who
was in Congress in Washington. Similarly, a young wife in
Boston scorned frivolous social life and criticized her
peers, "I am quite at a loss to know how people w/ the
power of thought & reflection & the various resources
within the sphere of intellect & the *hands'* employ can so
often complain of the tediousness of time—or think it
'misery to be alone'—'to talk with our past hours is surely
well' & how can this be done if never in retirement?" With
good fortune, experience confirmed the ideal. Elizabeth
Sedgwick reflected in her diary on the winter of 1827-28,
"Indeed, my home was so happy a one, that I found my
interest in general society constantly lessening." A daughter of the seaboard elite noted that her sister, whose marriage had removed her (geographically) from urban polite
society, had lost "nothing of her warm affections by being
in society she cannot love"; "she has that in her own family that makes general society of little consequence to her
—with a husband she loves so tenderly & such a sweet
blue-eyed boy, I should wonder if she were not happy."[51]
   The reign of this ideal implied a repudiation of aristocratic models. It assigned the domestic vocation as a level-

51. Anna Bryant Smith diary, Aug. 6, 1802, quoted in typescript "Notes on
Anna Bryant Smith," MeHS; Sarah Parrott to John Fabyan Parrott, Jan. 16,
1819, Parrott Family Papers, NHHS; diary of Sophia Munroe, Dec. 22, 1815,

ing vocation for all women. While reaffirming the importance of family sentiment, domesticity ultimately was
intended to implant, in the family, social control of a kind
that seemed necessary and appropriate in a democratic
republic. Frequent biographies of "mothers of the wise
and good" in the domestic literature connoted that the
chief aim of women's vocation was the rearing of moral,
trustworthy, statesmanlike citizens. George Washington's
mother became a favored model. The story of her training
George to be "a good boy" showed in a stroke that mothers were crucial influences, that women's social and political contribution consisted purely in their domestic vocation,
and that the nation could not do without their service.[52]

CHS; Elizabeth Ellery Sedgwick journal-book, 1827-28; diary of Margaret
Searle (Curson), Jan. 1812, Curson Family Papers, HCL.

Cf. also the remarks of twenty-one-year-old Abigail May, on a visit to Portland, Maine, about her hostess: "Mary treats me like a sister; and really I feel
proud of the Honor—her character rises upon me every day—her excellence
appears in domestic affairs: she superintends every thing up early and late; and
what makes this trait a great virtue there is no necessity for her doing it—four
domestics and quite a small family—but she chuses [sic] to make all the Pastry
cakes preserves &c and gives orders in all branches of business—few people that
see the beautiful and elegant Mary Kent in a large company superbly dressed
and informed she was the only child of a man of fortune would expect these
useful acquirements—as Beauty and fortune are in general sufficient without
even intellectual endowments to command respect and admiration. Mary's
mind is equal to her person— . . . in short I say with sincerity and belief—
'happy is the Man who calls her his wife—happy the Child who calls her
mother.'" Journal of residence in Portland, Maine, 1796, MeHS.

52. See "The Mother of Washington," *Ladies' Magazine* 4 (Sept. 1831):
385-94; "Influence of Woman—Past and Present," *Ladies' Companion* 13
(Sept. 1840):245-46; J. S. C. Abbott, *The Mother at Home,* pp. 10-11; Joseph
Emerson, *Female Education* (Boston and New York, 1822), pp. 4-6. Anne L.
Kuhn reviews this theme in *The Mother's Role in Childhood Education: New
England Concepts 1830-1860* (New Haven: Yale University Press, 1947), pp.
76-79. The model did not wholly coincide with the reality; in later years, at
least, Washington's mother was a querulous, demanding, mercenary woman
who embarrassed her son. See Julia C. Spruill, *Women's Life and Work in the
Southern Colonies* (New York: Norton, 1972), pp. 60-61. There was in the
post-Revolutionary years, a corresponding deification of Washington himself

Since the Revolutionary era it had been a commonplace theme in American republican ideology that the government's success depended on the stability of virtue among its citizens.[53] When social developments of the early nineteenth century unsettled known order and known virtue, some New Englanders began to dwell on the foreboding side of that theme. Ethnic, religious, and wealth characteristics among Americans were diversifying at the same time that technological improvements facilitated communication from region to region, people moved to the "uncivilized" West, and the suffrage was extended to almost all white adult males; the lack of control seemed ominous.[54] "The licentiousness of a lawless democracy, without virtue or intelligence, is, we learn from history, . . . more terrible than the oppressions of despotism," warned Sarah Hale. Once early childhood was seen as the training ground of individual virtue, and the mother as its commander, women's role seemed obvious. The *Ladies' Magazine* editor chose the domestic vocation for women purposely. "We do

as an exemplary citizen, a model to which men should aspire. See Marcus Cunliffe, *George Washington: Man and Monument* (Boston: Little-Brown, 1958), vol. 1.

53. See Gordon S. Wood, *The Creation of the American Republic 1776–1787* (New York: Norton, 1972), esp. pp. 65-70, 123-24.

54. See Clifford S. Griffin, "Religious Benevolence as Social Control," *MVHR* 44 (Dec. 1957):423-44. Cf. the comments recorded in the private journals of Henry Clarke Wright, when he was a trinitarian Congregationalist minister (before his conversion to radical abolitionism): "I have no doubt that the enemies of free institutions in Europe are trying to overthrow the institutions of this Country through the means of the Catholic Religion. . . . If the Catholics get the ascendancy in the Western Valley they will rule the Country"; and "I fear the facilities of intercourse in this Country—while increasing the business & moneyed interests of the Nation it will by spreading vice & irreligion prove its ruin. Those very things which all regard as improvements will be our destruction—by inflaming the passion for prosperity & giving to it tenfold more activity & power." Jan. 21, and Feb. 21, 1834, journal 4, HCL.

not, in our country, at least, want . . . those talents and acquirements, which have fitted women to rule empires and manage state intrigues", she wrote, "we want patterns of virtue, of intelligence, of piety and usefulness in private life." The success of self-government in a nation of diverse characters, dependent on majority rule, required "the culture of the heart, the discipline of the passions, the regulation of the feelings and affections."[55] Here was woman's part.

A discernible social theory, which supported such an appraisal of women's domestic value, prevailed at the time in many New England minds. Essentially a secularization of the evangelical Christian view that society improved as more people professed faith, it said that individual moral qualities determined (not only measured) social gain or failure. Consequently, the only reliable means of initiating social progress appeared to be by strengthening individual character (rather than, for instance, reconstructing institutions). The Reverend Joseph Tuckerman of Boston, who exposed the plight of underpaid working women, in 1830, reminded his readers "that while it is the duty of all . . . to minister to the *temporal wants* of their suffering fellow creatures, it is yet never to be forgotten by any who can serve them, that the most effectual means by which we may improve their condition is, by *improving their characters.*"[56] In response to conditions of rapid change, people looked to individual initiative and to the resurrection of strength of character for their rescue.[57] That accent was pronounced in the rhetoric of educational reformers, among others. Advocates of common school education in

55. *Ladies' Magazine* 2 (Jan. 1829):31-32, 393-95; see also 4 (Jan. 1831):3 and 4 (June 1831):247.

56. Joseph Tuckerman, *An Essay on the Wages Paid to Females for their Labour* (Philadelphia, 1830), p. 42. Cf. Hale's favorable review of Tuckerman's book, *Ladies' Magazine* 3 (July 1830):329-32.

57. See William R. Taylor, *Cavalier and Yankee* (Garden City, N.Y.: Anchor Books, 1963), pp. 74-77, 100-04.

the 1830s and 1840s equated their goal with a universal improvement of character, to be accomplished by inculcating ethical standards and self-restraint during "the docile and teachable years of childhood." (The schoolmen's anxiety may suggest that they doubted the competence of the domestic sphere to accomplish the job, but such educators as Horace Mann and Henry Barnard both claimed to believe that if only one sex could be educated, it should be the female, because of mothers' educational influence.[58])

The purpose of women's vocation was to stabilize society by generating and regenerating moral character. This goal reflected an awareness, also apparent in other social commentary and reform efforts of the time, that the impersonal world of money-making lacked institutions to effect moral restraint. New England reformers seemed to discern what Max Weber later elucidated, that "a rational economy is a functional organization oriented to money-prices which originate in the interest-struggles of men in the *market*. . . . Money is the most abstract and 'impersonal' element that exists in human life. . . . In the past it was possible to regulate ethically the personal relations between master and slave precisely because they were personal relations. But it is not possible to regulate—at least not in the same sense or with the same success—the relations between the shifting holders of mortgages and the shifting debtors of the banks that issue these mortgages: for in this case, no personal bonds of any sort exist."[59] The question was how

58. Quotation from Horace Mann, "The Necessity of Education in a Republican Government" (1838), reprinted in Edwin C. Roswenc, ed., *Ideology and Power in the Age of Jackson* (Garden City, N.Y.: Anchor Books, 1964), p. 151. See Merle Curti, *The Social Ideas of American Educators* (Paterson, N.J.: Pageant Books, 1959), pp. 177-78; and Michael B. Katz, *The Irony of Early School Reform: Educational Innovation in Mid-Nineteenth Century Massachusetts* (Cambridge, Mass.: Harvard University Press, 1968), pp. 117-24.

59. "Religious Rejections of the World and their Directions," part 4, "The Economic Sphere," in H.C. Gerth and C. Wright Mills, eds., *From Max Weber: Essays in Sociology* (New York: Oxford University Press, 1958), p. 331.

to regulate personal relations—how to regulate morality—if "the world" had become an arena of amoral market struggles.

The canon of domesticity answered by constituting the home as a redemptive counterpart to the world. Yet the ultimate function of the home was *in* the world. It was to fit men to pursue their wordly aims in a regulated way. The accent on individual character and self-control in the canon of domesticity simulated—and underpinned—individual economic struggle, just as women's vocations simulated men's.

By giving all women the same natural vocation, the canon of domesticity classed them all together. This definition had a dual function in the national culture. Understanding the rupture between home and the world in terms of gender did more than effect reconciliation to the changing organization of work. The demarcation of women's sphere from men's provided a secure, primary, social classification for a population who refused to admit ascribed statuses, for the most part, but required determinants of social order. "There can be no human culture without classification," in the succinct phrase of a modern linguist.[60] But in the attempt to raise a democratic culture almost all types of classification had to be rejected, except the "natural" ones such as sex (and race) and the achieved ones such as "self-made" wealth. The division of spheres supplied an acceptable kind of social distinction. Sex, not class, was the basic category. On that basis an order consistent with democratic culture could be maintained. Furthermore, the emphasis on women's shared purpose in their vocation positively disputed the idea that

60. Roland Barthes, "Historical Discourse," in Michael Lane, ed., *Structuralism: A Reader* (London: Jonathan Cape, 1970), p. 412.

class divisions existed in America. Sarah Hale maintained that every lady *must* be interested in the poor and miserable members of her own sex.[61] In the process of constructing women's vocation, the canon of domesticity enshrined the unifying, leveling, common identity of the domestic "American lady" (not the aristocratic lady) for all.

Because it included "all" women, and was endowed with social and political meaning, the domestic vocation gained enormous persuasive strength. It gave many women a sense of satisfaction as well as solidarity with their sex. "What an important sphere a woman fills!" an eighteen-year-old in Massachusetts responded to her reading of Hannah More's *Strictures on the Modern System of Female Education,* a weighty English progenitor of the American canon of domesticity, "how thoroughly she ought to be qualified for it—but I think hers the more honourable employment than a man's—for all men feel so grand and boast so much —and make such a pother [*sic*] about their being lords of the world below—if their mothers had not taken such good care of them when they were babies, and instilled good principles into them as they grew up, what think you would have become of the mighty animals—oh every man of sense must humbly bow before woman. She bears the sway, not man as he presumptuously supposes."[62]

"Womanhood" itself summed up the vocation. "I am a *woman,*" a correspondent to the *Ladies' Magazine* prefaced her letter, "of course I feel as a woman, I speak as a wo-

61. *Ladies' Magazine* 4 (Feb. 1831):81-85 (Hale's review of Mathew Carey's investigation of the wages of urban seamstresses). Catharine Beecher's antebellum writings exemplified the view that gender identity, rather than class, regional, or religious identification, was the appropriate means to create personal order in a democratic society. See Kathryn Kish Sklar's cogent discussion of this theme in *Catharine Beecher: A Study in American Domesticity* (New Haven: Yale University Press, 1973), pp. 156-61.

62. Mehitable May Dawes (Goddard) diary, June 12, 1815.

man, and I hope, I *understand* as a woman." Sarah Hale
propagated this kind of identification in her journalism; as
she wrote early in her career, "If we may only obtain for
our work the credit of judiciously directing the attention
of females to those subjects which concern them as women; if we can awaken them to a sense of their importance
as women; if we can, by our reflections, aid them in their
endeavors to perform their duties as women, our purpose
is answered, our ambition gratified."[63] In aspects such as
this the canon of domesticity intensified women's gender-
group identification, by assimilating diverse personalities
to one work-role that was also a sex-role signifying a
shared and special destiny.

63. "Cordelia," *Ladies' Magazine* 3 (Oct. 1830):458; 2 (June 1829):282.

3

EDUCATION

Literacy was virtually universal among New Englanders—both men and women—in 1840, whereas sixty years earlier, in Revolutionary times, only about half of New England women could sign their names.[1] That one hundred percent increase in women's literacy played an essential part in the evolution of their status during the intervening years. Equally remarkable, in the same period a cohesive rationale for schooling women beyond basic literacy was developed. The particular justification that triumphed, amid contemporary arguments for and against women's education, illuminated the contours of women's lives while further shaping them.

Seventeenth-century New Englanders paid slight attention to the education of women. Since women's intellect was considered inferior to men's, extensive learning for women was considered inappropriate or, at worst, dangerous. Isolated examples of piously learned women vied with more frequent examples of men's hostility to, or

1. See Kenneth A. Lockridge, *Literacy in Colonial New England* (New York: Norton, 1974), esp. pp. 38-42, 57-58, on eighteenth-century women's literacy; and Maris Vinovskis and Richard M. Bernard, "Women in Education in Ante-Bellum America," unpublished Working Paper 73-7, Center for Demography and Ecology, University of Wisconsin, Madison, June 1973, table 7, showing U.S. census data for 1850. Since, as the latter points out (p. 6), adult literacy measures past schooling, the census data suggest that the new opportunities for schooling for women occurred before 1830.

disgust with, such creatures. John Winthrop wrote in 1645 of the "sad infirmity, the loss of her understanding and reason," that beset the wife of Governor Hopkins of Hartford, "by occasion of her giving herself wholly to reading and writing, and had written many books." "If she had attended her household affairs, and such things as belong to women," he continued, "and not gone out of her way and calling to meddle in such things as are proper for men, whose minds are stronger, etc., she had kept her wits, and might have improved them usefully and honorably in the place God had set her." Anne Bradstreet, who was a poet as well as a devoted wife and mother, acknowledged in 1642, "I am obnoxious to each carping tongue,/ Who sayes, my hand a needle better fits,/A Poets Pen, all scorne, I should thus wrong;/For such despight they cast on females wits. . . ."[2]

It is unlikely that girls attended public schools as did boys during the seventeenth century. In Dedham, Massachusetts, for example, the usual seventeenth-century school assessment on each householder was based exclusively on the number of boys in his family between the ages of four and fourteen.[3] Girls who learned to read, write, or cipher probably were taught within their own family circle, or by older women in "dame schools," which were extensions of mothers' teaching. According to a recent study, the public schools' discrimination against girls was responsible for widening the gap between male and female literacy rates during the colonial period. About

2. Winthrop and Bradstreet are quoted in Aileen S. Kraditor, ed., *Up from the Pedestal* (Chicago: Quadrangle Books, 1970), pp. 30, 29. In "Vertuous Women Found: New England Ministerial Literature, 1668-1735," *AQ* 28 (1976): Laurel Thatcher Ulrich tries to make a case for Puritan approval of women's scholarly pursuits (pp. 24-25) but comes up with contradictory evidence herself (pp. 33-40).

3. Lawrence Cremin, *American Education: The Colonial Experience* (New York: Harper Torchbooks, 1970), p. 524.

half of the men and a third of the women in the first generation of New England settlers could sign their names, but by the end of the colonial period the proportion of men had advanced to 80 percent or more, while female literacy (judged by signatures) stagnated during the eighteenth century at the level of 40 to 45 percent.[4]

Because of the summer session in which reading and sewing were taught by young women, the proportion of girls learning to read may have increased during the latter half of the eighteenth century, without becoming visible in a larger proportion of women able to sign their names.[5] A consensus on the desirability of female literacy seems to have emerged during these years; after the attainment of American independence, educational plans intended to serve American nationalism and republicanism provided for the primary education of girls as well as boys. Every submission to the American Philosophical Society's prize essay contest in 1795, on the topic of an American system of education, proposed universal free schools open to both sexes.[6] As summer sessions open to girls became increasingly regular after 1790—and the curriculum included writing by that time, it seems—full literacy came within the grasp of greater numbers.[7]

4. Lockridge, *Literacy in Colonial New England*, pp. 38-42, 57-58. The proportion of females able to sign rose to about 40 percent by 1700 and then advanced little further during the eighteenth century.

5. See chapter 1, note 15. Using data from Dedham, Massachusetts, and the method (also employed by Lockridge) of counting the number of signatures and the number of "marks" on legal documents, Cremin finds an increase in female literacy during the eighteenth century. *American Education*, pp. 526, 526-27n. Dedham was one of the earliest towns to provide summer sessions for girls, doing so in 1760.

6. Merle Curti, *The Social Ideas of American Educators* (Paterson, N.J.: Pageant Books, 1959), p. 47. See also Allen Oscar Hansen, *Liberalism and American Education in the Eighteenth Century* (New York: Octagon Books, 1965; orig. 1926).

7. The precise dating of the inclusion of writing in the curriculum of summer sessions remains unclear; it likely varied from town to town. Cf. this diary

Education for girls beyond the primary level required more explicit justification. Benjamin Rush's *Thoughts on Female Education,* an address delivered at the opening of the Young Ladies' Academy in Philadelphia in 1787, epitomized the progressive republican attitude on the subject. In good Revolutionary style, Rush wished to erase British models of fashionable womanhood—which he saw as ornamental at best and, at worst, corrupting—and replace them with an ideal "accomodated [*sic*] to the state of society, manners and government" in the United States. Several characteristics of American women's lives seemed to him to demand a new kind of education. He assumed (accurately) that American women married earlier than British; having limited time for education, they needed to concentrate on the "more useful" branches. The "uses" for their education appeared in their obligations as wives and mothers in an expanding republic, in Rush's view. Where men were occupied in seeking fortunes, their wives had to learn to be effective "stewards, and guardians" of the family's assets. Where men were occupied with business to the extent that "a principal share of the instruction of children naturally devolves upon the women," the latter had to be educated to be good mothers. And in a republic dependent on citizens' understanding of principles of liberty and representation, mothers had to

---

entry written in 1828 by Lavinia Bailey Kelly (Cilly), who was born on April 30, 1818, in Northwood, N.H.: "The first school that I attended was kept by Miss Mary Frost, of Andover, Mass. . . . in the summer of 1822. In the summers of the following years I attended school kept by Miss Frost, 1823, Miss Matilda Prentice 1824, Miss Martha Mead 1825, Miss Prentice 1826, Miss Harriet Nealey 1827. In the winters I never attended school. In the spring of this year I was at Warner, and attended a school kept by Miss Sally Lyman about a fortnight." In the summer of 1828 she attended "the young ladies school kept at Mr Hills in this town [Northwood] , by Miss Mary Hiddes and Miss Caroline Boynton of Dunstable." There were twenty-four pupils, all but two from Northwood; Lavinia and her two sisters were the youngest; they were studying geography and writing, and learning to work lace. Diary, NHHS.

be especially suitably educated. Furthermore, because servants were neither so numerous, permanent, competent, nor readily subordinate as in Great Britain, "ladies" had to be prepared to attend personally to household duties.[8]

Rush justified female education for its social utility: an American woman required education to form her into "an agreeable companion for a sensible man," an efficient household economist, a proponent and example of Christian morals, and a capable mother of liberty-loving sons. His plan addressed women in the presumptive roles of man's companion, wife, mother, wielder not of public power but of private influence and morality. Clearly, Rush argued neither for justice with regard to women's opportunities for learning nor for women's participation in the advancement of knowledge. His reasoning was utilitarian; his plan for female education was functional. Suitable education of women would protect the republic from that artificiality and luxury that he believed had decayed British society and threatened the upper classes of America. It would preserve the family as an agency of moral instruction, facilitate male entrepreneurship, and generalize frugality and economic discipline. Without threatening male dominance, it would make women more capable adjuncts of their husbands and families.

The chief alternative to Rush's approach, at the time, was hostility to the notion of educating women. Women interested in intellectual advancement found that they were "so degraded, as to be allowed no other ideas, than

8. Benjamin Rush, *Thoughts upon Female Education, Accomodated to the Present State of Society, Manners, and Government in the U.S.A.* (Philadelphia: Prichard and Hall, 1787). The curriculum Rush advised included English reading, spelling, grammar, and pronunciation; clear handwriting; arithmetic and bookkeeping; an acquaintance with geography and historical chronology; sufficient science to prevent superstition and to aid in sickroom and kitchen; vocal music and perhaps dancing; guidance of reading toward history, travels, poetry, and moral essays (to prevent reading of novels); and regular instruction in Christianity and the Bible.

those which are suggested by the mechanism of a pudding, or the sewing the seams of a garment"; or, that "the mind of a female, if such a thing existed, was thought not worth cultivating."[9] During the Revolution Abigail Adams confided to her husband, whose own more "generous" and "liberal" sentiments she trusted, "in this country you need not be told how much female education is neglected, nor how fashionable it has been to ridicule female learning." The few who protested that it was *unjust* to denigrate and deny women's mental capacities also stressed that it was socially detrimental. Abigail Adams's defense of female education rested on her belief that "much depends . . . upon the early education of youth, and the first principles which are instilled take the deepest root"; like Rush, she reasoned that "if we mean to have heroes, statesmen, and philosophers, we should have learned women." Judith Sargent Murray, a truer feminist partisan than Abigail Adams, declared that women were the intellectual equals of men and had the right to cultivate their minds; but she also argued, in favor of women's education, that women suitably educated would forsake trifles, gossip, and fashions and would be more valuable wives. Far from denying that domestic affairs were their business, Murray claimed that some intellectual freedom and opportunity would allow women to find more satisfaction in their domestic occupations.[10]

9. Judith Sargent Murray, from "On the Equality of the Sexes" (1790), quoted in Kraditor, *Up from the Pedestal,* p. 34; Eliza Southgate, letter to her cousin Moses Porter, 1801, quoted in Nancy F. Cott, ed., *Root of Bitterness: Documents of the Social History of American Women* (New York: Dutton, 1972), p. 105. See the further discussion of late-eighteenth-century opposition to "learned women" in Linda K. Kerber, "Daughters of Columbia: Educating Women for the Republic, 1787-1805," *The Hofstadter Aegis,* Eric L. McKitrick and Stanley M. Elkins, eds. (New York: Knopf, 1974).

10. Abigail Adams to John Adams, June 30, 1778, and Aug. 14, 1776, in Charles Francis Adams, ed., *Familiar Letters of John Adams and his Wife Abigail Adams, during the Revolution* (New York, 1876), pp. 339, 212-13; Judith Sargent Murray, in Kraditor, *Up from the Pedestal,* pp. 31-34.

Eliza Southgate, a young woman who had an academy education at the turn of the century, echoed Judith Murray's defense. Women's capacities of discernment and judgment declined for lack of use, she objected; was "the mind of woman the only work of God that was 'made in vain?'" Yet she also believed that cultivation of women's mental powers would not threaten men's prerogatives. "Far from destroying the harmony [between the sexes] that ought to subsist," she asserted, in debate with a male cousin about the propriety of educating women, the improvement of women's minds "would fix it on a foundation that would not totter at every jar. Women would be under the same degree of subordination that they now are; enlighten and expand their minds, and they would perceive the necessity of such a regulation to preserve the order and happiness of society." When her cousin retorted with "a kind of fury" and claimed that education of women "will inevitably produce superciliousness and a desire of ascendancy," Southgate disagreed. "You ask if this plan will render one a more dutiful child, a more affectionate wife, &c, &c, surely it will," she wrote. "Those virtues which now are merely practised from the momentary impulse of the heart, will then be adhered to from principle, a sense of duty, and a mind sufficiently strengthened not to yield implicitly to every impulse."[11]

A scholar in a Boston public school in 1791 summed up the contemporary argument for female enlightenment in an "Oration upon Female Education," then recorded for posterity in Caleb Bingham's *American Preceptor,* a textbook that remained in use for subsequent decades. The speaker hailed the disappearance of "mists of superstition and bigotry" that had prevented the education of daughters along with sons. The "political fathers, and all patrons of science" in America had recognized that all were "indebt-

11. Eliza Southgate, in Cott, *Root of Bitterness,* pp. 107, 109.

ed to their *mothers* for the seeds of virtue and knowledge; that schools and colleges can but cultivate and mature the plants, which owe their origin to the seeds sown in infancy." Here was the primary justification, "that *they* should well be taught, from whom our virtues *are* and from whom our vices *may* be derived!" The prospect of educating both sexes meant that "our young men will be emulous to exceed the geniuses of the east; our daughters will shine as bright constellations in the sphere where nature has placed them."[12]

If the argument for women's education centered on their social usefulness as daughters, wives and mothers, the contemporary view of men's education was equally pragmatic. Beginning in the seventeenth century, John Locke and others had popularized several new ideas: that learning was a means to fit oneself for employment and citizenship; that it was not the preserve of the cleric or scholar but significant mainly for its use in the conduct of life; that its purpose was to promote practical success as well as to expand higher knowledge. That perspective on education, propagated by British writers, was congenial to eighteenth-century America. Benjamin Franklin's learning through his early life—to take the best-known example—furnished a prototype of education conceived as a utilitarian venture. His educational proposals reflected that conception; his model of an "English school" of 1751 intended to produce not scientists or poets but

12. The speaker argued that "while the *sons* of our citizens are cultivating their minds, and preparing them for the arduous, important, and manly employments which America offers to the industrious, their *daughters* are gaining that knowledge, which will enable them to become amiable sisters, virtuous children; and, in the event, to assume characters [i.e., as mothers], more interesting to the public, and more endearing to themselves." "Oration upon Female Education, Pronounced by a Member of One of the Public Schools in Boston, September, 1791," reprinted in Caleb Bingham, *The American Preceptor* (44th ed., Boston, 1813), pp. 48–49, 51.

competent practical men. "Youth will come out of this school fitted for learning any business, calling or profession, except such wherein languages are required," he claimed, "[qualified] to pass through and execute the several offices of civil life, with advantage and reputation to themselves and country."[13]

So far as women's learning commanded any assent in eighteenth-century America, the prevalent utilitarian emphasis deserved the credit. Not until education was accepted as a way of getting on in the world as well as advancing knowledge could there be a widely acceptable reason for schooling women, whose intellects were demeaned, whose acquaintance with new ideas was feared, and whose pedantry was ridiculed. Basing education on its usefulness in life had different ramifications for men and for women, however. Education for men in America had to increase in scope—had to be open-ended—in order to be functional. The Boston school orator hoped to see sons educated for *all* "the arduous, important and manly employments which America offers to the industrious." Franklin proposed to fit youth for "any business, calling or profession." Utilitarian education for women in America *narrowed* their prospects because it was based on a limited conception of woman's role. "Every man, by the Constitution, is born with an equal right to be elected to the highest office," the Reverend John Ogden of Portsmouth reminded his readers, as he made his case for appropriate education for both sexes in republican America. "And every woman, is born with an equal right to be the wife of the most eminent man."[14]

13. Franklin quoted in Lawrence Cremin, *American Education,* p. 376. On utilitarianism in American education, see Cremin, pp. 359, 412, and Russell B. Nye, *The Cultural Life of the New Nation* (New York: Harper Torchbooks, 1963), p. 154.

14. See notes 12 and 13 and John Cosens Ogden, *The Female Guide* (Concord, N.H., 1793), p. 26.

—◦◖◗◦—

Despite the inchoate educational theory of the post-Revolutionary period, strong prejudice against "learned women" persisted, and opportunities for advanced education were marginal. One kind of objection, traceable to Rousseau, was that serious education robbed women of their charms and disrupted their contentment. "Born for a life of uniformity and dependence," women had occasion for "reason, sweetness and sensibility, resources against idleness and languor, moderate desires and no passions"—and no genius, declared an anonymous work reprinted in several American editions. Genius would, it went on, "make them regret the station which Providence has assigned them, or have recourse to unjustifiable ways to get from it. The best taste for science only contributes to make them particular. It takes them away from the simplicity of their domestic duties, and from general society, of which they are the loveliest ornament."[15]

A particularly middle-class version of this reasoning stressed that education would introduce false gentility. Sally Ripley's schoolmates at a coeducational school in Greenfield, Massachusetts, put on a play in 1799 which treated this problem. One female character tried to persuade a reluctant friend to attend an academy. "Uncle Tristam says he hates to have girls go to school, it makes them so dam'd uppish & so deuced proud that they won't work," the latter protested. More important, "How will the young fellows take it if we shine away & don't like their humdrum ways—Wont they be as mad as vengeance—& associate with the girls that don't go to school?" Eventually, her friend's reasoning that education might help her

15. *Sketches of the History, Genius and Disposition of the Fair Sex* (Gettysburg, Pa., 1812), quoted in Thomas Woody, *A History of Women's Education in the United States* (New York: Science Press, 1929), 1:107.

acquire a better husband, rather than frighten the boys away, persuaded her.[16]

Such arguments recurred through the decades in more and less sophisticated forms. To oppose Catharine Beecher's introduction of a course in moral philosophy at her Hartford school for girls in 1829, an editorial writer in the *Connecticut Courant* declared, "I had rather my daughters would go to school and sit down and do nothing, than to study philosophy, etc. These branches fill young Misses with *vanity* to the degree that they are above attending to the more useful parts of an education." Whether the acquisition of knowledge conflicted with the performance of domestic duties was a matter of continuing debate. Sarah Alden Bradford and Abba Allyn were two young Massachusetts women who had exceptional opportunities for intellectual pursuits at home. "We are [both] blest with parents who are desirous of our improvement in useful knowledge," Bradford wrote to Allyn in 1806. "How thankful should we be for their kindness, and endeavour to repay it in some measure, by industrious attention to our studies." She continued,

> I am acquainted with a sensible girl who is anxious to improve her mind, but her father, instead of commending her design, endeavours to convince her that all knowledge, except that of domestic affairs, appears unbecoming in a female. An acquaintance with domestic affairs is certainly of the highest importance, but are females in general so totally engaged by the business of the family, as to find no time for cultivating the mind?[17]

16. Diary of Sally Ripley, 1799, AAS (play script is copied into back of volume).

17. *Connecticut Courant* quoted in Kathryn Kish Sklar, *Catharine Beecher: A Study in American Domesticity* (New Haven: Yale University Press, 1973), p. 94; Sarah Bradford (Ripley) to Abba Allyn, c. 1809, SL.

The improvement of women's higher education in the
half-century after the Revolution was an uphill battle.
The best-educated women in those years were self-taught,
or tutored at home by teachers or relatives, although
institutions offering secondary education for girls began
to be founded. Philadelphia led in the founding of girls'
academies, with Dove's and Benezet's schools in the 1750s,
and Brown's and Poor's in the 1780s.[18] In New England,
private secondary schooling for girls initially appeared on
the margins of increased opportunities for boys, in an
idiosyncratic process of development. Early academy
education of girls took place at male—or, to be accurate,
at *de facto* coeducational—institutions. Diverse causes
contributed, including the social aims of certain educators
and ministers, the motives of elite or enterprising families
to distinguish their daughters by education, and the
financial needs of new private schools and academies. In
the 1780s and 1790s some male schoolteachers (often
college students or ministers) opened private schools for
boys but were willing to teach girls as well, and attracted
parents who wanted to give their daughters the privilege
of education. The first men to become known as instructors of girls, among them Caleb Bingham in Boston,
Timothy Dwight in Northampton, Massachusetts, and
William Woodbridge in New Haven, Connecticut, were not
instructors of girls only.[19]

18. Mary Sumner Benson, *Women in Eighteenth-Century America: A Study
of Opinion and Social Usage* (New York: Columbia University Press, 1935),
pp. 139–41.

19. Caleb Bingham opened a private school for girls in Boston in 1784, but
kept it for only a few years. When the selectmen realized that their daughters'
education would be less expensive if incorporated into the public schools, they
empowered Bingham to keep a "double-headed" system in the Boston writing
school. On this system girls attended from April to October, for half a day.
Timothy Dwight admitted girls to his academy in Greenfield, Connecticut, in
the mid-1780s, and operated a day school for both sexes in Northampton,
Massachusetts, between 1795 and 1817. William Woodbridge taught school in

The important question respecting girls' secondary education in New England at the turn of the century is not how many "female academies" there were, but how many academies for boys admitted girls too. In Connecticut several—at Waterbury, Hartford, Norwich, Sharon, and Litchfield—did so, in addition to William Woodbridge's. In Massachusetts, New Hampshire, and Maine the historian of Bradford Academy has found thirty-four academies begun between 1783 and 1805 which seem to have admitted girls as well as boys. These schools ordinarily kept the girls' instruction distinct by teaching them in a separate room or part of a room, or during different (and shorter) hours, or exclusively during the summer. [20]

The diaries and correspondence of young men and women reveal a vaster array of schools than the histories have recognized. Many of these must have been ephemeral establishments, lasting only as long as a teacher's need for money, and ability to find students, complemented each other. The manuscript memoirs of Samuel D. King of the small town of Sutton, Massachusetts, for example, show that he kept coeducational schools there, enrolling about twice as many boys as girls, from 1779 through the early 1780s. At her school in Greenfield, taught by Mr. Proctor Pierce, Sally Ripley studied English and geography and several other subjects between 1799 and 1801, when she was in her early teens. She moved on to a summer session

---

New Haven during his last year at Yale, 1779-80, and offered arithmetic, geography, and composition to girls. He later taught at Exeter Academy (boys only), and then opened an academy in Medford, Massachusetts which had about twice as many female as male pupils. See ibid., pp. 148-51, and Jean Pond, *Bradford: A New England Academy* (Bradford, Mass.: Alumnae Assoc., 1930), pp. 23-27.

20. Benson, *Women in Eighteenth-Century America*, pp. 150-53; Woody, *A History of Women's Education*, 1:339-42; Pond, *Bradford*, pp. 34-53 (list of academies, pp. 37-38). Pond's book has the best treatment of academies admitting girls in this period.

at Dorchester Female Academy in 1804. Her three younger sisters, meanwhile, attended a school opened in Greenfield by "Miss Banister of Conway" in 1801. Mehitable May Dawes, an orphan who lived with her well-to-do aunt and uncle in Brookline, Massachusetts, began at Woburn Young Ladies Academy in July 1802, when she was five years old (and triumphed over the eight- and ten-year-olds in a spelling contest!). In 1807 she attended Jamaica Plain Academy; in 1808, "Mrs. Cranch's"; and in 1810, she boarded at the Misses' Martin's Academy in Portland, Maine, where her uncle felt her "opportunities for valuable acquirements are excellent." Zeloda Barrett, who lived on a farm, went to school in New Hartford, Connecticut, in the winter of 1804, when she was eighteen, but what kind of school it was is uncertain. Sarah Connell of Newburyport spent winter terms at "Mrs. Brown's" in her hometown and summer terms in 1806–07 at school in Andover, Massachusetts—this could have been at Franklin Academy, which was coeducational. She attended Newburyport Academy, a coeducational institution, for the winter term 1807–08, and then returned to "Mrs. B's" in March. Farther west in Massachusetts, Hannah Bliss went to school for winter terms from 1814 to 1818, learning reading, writing, spelling, grammar, rhetoric, geography, and arithmetic under the tutelage of first the Reverend C. B. Storrs and then Mr. A. Bolles.[21]

The schools or academies that began in this period to

21. Memoirs of Samuel D. King of Sutton, Mass., HD; Sally Ripley diary, July 1799, April, June, 1801; diary of Sarah Ripley (Stearns), May 19, 1804, Stearns Collection, SL; school prizes and certificates of Mehitable May Dawes, and Benjamin Goddard to Mehitable May Dawes, Aug. 21, 1810, May-Goddard Collection, SL; diary of Zeloda Barrett, 1804, CHS; *Diary of Sarah Connell Ayer* (Portland, Me., 1910), pp. 12-17, 26—on Newburyport Academy see Pond, *Bradford*, p. 26; diary of Hannah A. Bliss, Nov. 8, 1814, April 9, 1815, Dec. 6, 1816, Jan. 25, 1818, MHS. This list of schools mentioned in women's diaries is indicative only, not exhaustive.

educate girls exclusively were almost always conducted *by women.* Susanna Rowson and Sarah Pierce originated two of the most notable. Mrs. Rowson, a native of Britain, made a name for herself there as a stage actress. After emigrating she attained greater fame as the author of *Charlotte Temple,* one of the first "best-selling" American novels. Students at the school she founded in Boston (1797) and then moved to nearby Medford admired her greatly but apparently received only slight intellectual guidance. Sarah Pierce opened a school in the dining room of her home in Litchfield, Connecticut, in 1792 and continued it there in one room until 1827, when the school was incorporated as Litchfield Female Academy and moved into a new building. During the early years she offered a basic literary education and some "elegant accomplishments." Catharine Beecher, who attended in 1810, found grammar, arithmetic, geography, history, and the "accomplishments" of map-drawing, painting, embroidery, and piano available.[22]

Contradicting the emergent ideology of functional education for women, most all-female schools around the turn of the century provided "accomplishments" to adorn the daughters of the wealthy. An advertisement in the New-buryport *Impartial Herald* in 1791 was typical: "Mrs. Woodbury announces that she will open a boarding school for young ladies at her house on Market St. where instruction will be given in the French and English languages, drawing, embroidery, etc."[23] The likeliest way for a woman to earn money in private teaching at the time was to offer "accomplishments" to girls. Nancy Maria Hyde, of

22. Pond, *Bradford,* p. 30. On Mrs. Rowson, see biography in E. T. James and J. W. James, eds., *Notable American Women* (Cambridge, Mass.: Harvard University Press, 1971). Eliza Southgate said of her education at Mrs. Rowson's academy (see Cott, *Root of Bitterness,* p. 106), "I left school with a head full of something, tumbled in without order or connection."

23. Quoted in Pond, *Bradford,* p. 26.

Norwich, Connecticut, suddenly faced with supporting her widowed sister and family in 1810, decided to equip herself to be a painting teacher. She taught, apparently, at the school for young ladies run by Lydia Huntley in Hartford. Although she accommodated herself to ornamental education, this pious young woman objected to the emphasis on it. "Usefulness should be the result of education, the great object of future life," she urged in lectures to her students. Education was to "inspire virtuous sentiments" in women, teach them to think, reason, and discriminate, and sustain them when the "charms of youth" had gone. "Though women are not destined to the commotions of public life, or to act in those professions, which hold forth a stimulus to the exertions of the other sex, it is still necessary that they be taught the value of knowledge, and instructed in a taste for literary pursuits."[24]

By the 1810s, a growing number of all-female secondary schools could benefit from an educational philosophy regarding the special needs of the female sex. An academy for girls in Pittsfield, Massachusetts, was incorporated in 1807, and one in Bath, Maine, in 1808. In Keene, New Hampshire, in 1814 Catharine Fiske opened a school for girls that operated until 1837. Emma Hart Willard, who taught at the Middlebury (Vermont) Female Academy between 1807 and 1809, founded the Middlebury Female Seminary in 1814. She moved to New York in 1821 and founded her Troy Seminary. The Reverend Joseph Emerson retired from his pulpit in Beverly, Massachusetts, in

24. *Writings of Nancy Maria Hyde of Norwich, Conn., Connected with a Sketch of her Life* (Norwich, 1816), pp. 156, 157. Hyde does not mention the name of the academy at which she taught, but it was Lydia Huntley who edited her memoirs.

When ,Emma Willard proposed *A Plan for Improving Female Education* (Middlebury, Vt., 1918; reprint ed.) in 1819, she objected that existing schools were usually unequipped, impermanent, poorly staffed, and unstandardized, and that preceptresses devised their curricula on the basis of what would bring in the most money, which usually meant concentrating on "accomplishments."

1818 and opened a female seminary in Byfield, Massachusetts, where both he and his wife Rebeccah Hasseltine taught, introducing such innovative pedagogical techniques as topical study and discussion in place of learning by rote. Zilpah Grant, a young woman who was influenced by Emerson's methods, opened Adams Academy for girls in Derry, New Hampshire, in 1822. Six years later she and her colleague Mary Lyon moved to Ipswich, Massachusetts, and opened a female academy there. An ambitious curriculum was offered at Miss Prescott's girls' school in Groton, Massachusetts, from 1820 to 1830. Catharine Beecher, who would equal and surpass Emma Willard and Mary Lyon as an advocate of women's education, began in 1823 teaching in a day school that was incorporated as Hartford Female Seminary in 1828. Abbot Academy at Andover, Massachusetts, for girls only, was incorporated in 1829. Bradford Academy in the Massachusetts town of that name, founded as a coeducational institution in 1803, restricted its aim to women's education in 1830.[25]

The movement to found separate institutions for women resolved a dilemma in women's education in the early nineteenth century. Coeducational academies could serve as an interim measure only; common education had to seem either absurd or threatening, if education was valued pragmatically and the differences between the expected life patterns of men and of women were extreme. Allowing women in institutions for men appeared less and less reasonable as the canon of domesticity froze the contrast between the occupations of the two sexes. The education of women required a separate rationale. Ornamental education was the first specialized education offered; but because it connoted aristocratic vanity and

25. Woody, *A History of Women's Education*, 1:342-43; Pond, *Bradford*, pp. 112, 118-19, 130-31; on Miss Prescott's, *Groton Historical Series*, 1:5 (1887), pp. 8-11, 3:9 (1893), p. 405. Again, I have not attempted here a *complete* listing of female academies known to have existed before 1835.

subservience to European mores, and contravened the utilitarian bent of education and culture in the early United States, it had class-limited appeal and approval. The rise of ambitious female academies implied that both the education of girls at boys' academies and the education of girls in decorative accomplishments were dead ends. What was needed was education that recognized women's mental capacities *and* recognized their separate destiny.

In a lecture to the Boston Female Asylum in 1809, John S.C. Gardiner, an Episcopalian minister, presented the view that was taking the lead. He blamed superficial or ornamental instruction for creating a disparity between men's and women's reason and intellectual strength. Failings in women's education were more dangerous than failings in men's, he asserted, because of women's "most powerful influence on society, as wives, as mistresses of families, and as mothers." Women needed education to supply them with discipline and good sense for their roles "as beings, who are to be wives, and mothers, the first and most important guardians and instructors of the rising generation, as being endued [*sic*] with reason, and designed for immortality."

Such a rationale, while it elevated women's intellectual status, defined them wholly with reference to sex-specific duties. Now, in this view, it was appropriate to educate women because of their sex, not despite it. The educational reform journals, such as the *Common School Journal,* the *American Journal of Education,* and the *Annals of Education,* which began publication between 1819 and 1825, disseminated this attitude, carrying numerous articles that deduced the need for educating women from the importance of their maternal and domestic roles.[26] By

26. John S.C. Gardiner, *A Sermon, Delivered . . . before the Members of the Boston Female Asylum* (Boston, 1809), pp. 19–20. On the educational journals, see Woody, *A History of Women's Education,* 1:96–97.

intending education to fit women better for wifehood and
motherhood, such a rationale allayed fears about the conflict between learning and domestic duties. The founders
of secondary schools for girls adopted it with increasing
unanimity.

These educators could avoid comparing women's mental
abilities with men's because they assumed that "the circumstances of life require a different exercise of those
abilities," in Sarah Pierce's words. "The employments of
man and woman are so dissimilar," she said, "that no one
will pretend to say that an education for these employments must be conducted on the same plan; but the discipline of the mind, the formation of those intellectual
habits which are necessary to one sex are equally so to
the other." When Emma Hart Willard submitted a proposal
for a state-sponsored female seminary to the New York
legislature in 1819, she said that the school would differ as
much from a school for men as women's character and
duties differed from men's. Her belief in education for
usefulness dictated that plan. The cardinal purpose of
education was, in Willard's view, to "bring its subjects to
the perfection of their moral, intellectual and physical
nature: in order, that they may be of the greatest possible
use to themselves and others." Many other sponsors of
female education echoed her. Charles Burroughs, a minister of Portsmouth, assured those who listened to his address on female education in 1827 that the purpose of
educating women was not to make them philosophers or
scientific lecturers. "When we speak of the extent of
female education," he said, "we speak only in relation to
its practical utility, and to its importance, as connected
with the virtues and happiness of females, and with the
general interests of society." This beacon illuminated the
course of lectures that Almira Hart Phelps gave at her
sister's Troy Seminary in 1830–31. She exhorted the
students to "prove by your own example, that knowledge

is not to be a curse to your sex, that it is to lead them in the path of duty, not *out* of it; that it is to make them better daughters, wives and mothers; better qualified for usefulness in every path within the sphere of female exertions."[27]

As Benjamin Rush had announced decades before, the strongest justification for educating women lay in the social utility and political value of well-instructed mothers. "Most men are so entirely engrossed by business as to have but little opportunity of fully understanding the characters of their children," Sarah Pierce observed, and went on to stress mothers' responsibility for maintaining republican virtue and morality. At the dedication of his seminary in Saugus in 1822 Joseph Emerson used striking imagery to emphasize the link between motherhood and the need to educate women. "If I could for a moment believe the horrible idea, that females have no immortal souls," he declaimed "even at that moment, I would say, Let the female character be raised, that she may elevate her sons." Thomas Gallaudet, the educational reformer best known for his efforts with the deaf, advocated education for women because he believed a mother's impact on her child was "inferior only to that of God; and she is the instrument whom He employs." In the words of George B. Emerson, who was affiliated with the American Institute of Instruction and taught the high school for girls in Boston in the early 1820s, the importance of a mother's duties signified that "every woman should therefore be educated with reference to these duties." Women's service as moth-

27. Sarah Pierce, address of Oct. 29, 1818, quoted in Emily N. Vanderpoel, ed., *Chronicles of a Pioneer School* (Cambridge, Mass.: University Press, 1903), pp. 176-77—see also her *More Chronicles of a Pioneer School* (New York: Cadmus Bookshop, 1927), pp. 202-10; Willard, *A Plan*, pp. 5-6, 13; Charles Burroughs, *An Address on Female Education, Delivered in Portsmouth, N.H., Oct. 26, 1827* (Portsmouth, 1827), pp. 38-39; Almira Hart Phelps, *Lectures to Young Ladies* (Boston, 1833), p. 247.

ers was the lynchpin of Emma Willard's argument before the New York legislature: she reasoned that government-sponsored education of women would assure to the state the reproduction of virtuous citizens.[28]

Advocates of women's education also gave prominence to women's general influence over men, apart from motherhood. Charles Burroughs saw in female education a means to create "a wonderful and an accumulating mass of moral energy," which would propel society toward reform. Female education encompassed "all that relates to the highest interests of man," Thomas Gallaudet said, "for what is there affecting his temporal welfare, or his eternal destiny, on which is not brought to bear, in one form or another, the influence of woman." Another of its conspicuous social benefits was its production of female teachers. Women's maternal destiny now seemed to educators' satisfaction to prove their fitness as instructors and influencers of youth. Emma Willard argued not only that women were "naturally" suited to teach but that they could be hired at lower salaries in the common schools and that their employment would free more men to increase the wealth of the nation. In Joseph Emerson's estimation, the schoolroom ranked next to the home as a sphere of women's work. He "suspected" that nature had designed the teaching profession to be women's, since the law, medicine, religion, and politics were exclusively (and appropriately) men's. Catharine Beecher drew tighter the link between motherhood and schoolteaching by asserting that "woman's profession,"

28. Fragment of Sarah Pierce's writing, c. 1820, quoted in Vanderpoel, *Chronicles of a Pioneer School*, p. 214; Joseph Emerson, *Female Education; A Discourse Delivered at the Dedication of the Seminary Hall in Saugus, Jan. 15, 1822* (Boston and New York, 1822), pp. 8-9; Thomas Gallaudet, *An Address on Female Education, Delivered . . . at the opening . . . of the Hartford Female Seminary* (Hartford, 1828), p. 14; George B. Emerson, *Lecture on the Education of Females, Delivered before the American Institute of Instruction* (Boston, 1831), p. 11; Willard, *A Plan*, pp. 5-6, 16, 29-30, 34.

inside and outside the family, was to form pure minds
and healthy bodies. Along with an increasing host of
educators, Beecher believed that the most direct path to
the regulation of conscience and reason ran through the
"affections," or "heart," the realm in which women's
influence reigned. In these natural facts she discerned the
efficacy of training women to be teachers.[29]

To base women's education on their social usefulness
as wives, mothers, and teachers did not mean to shape
or limit their curriculum precisely. Emma Willard proposed
religious and moral instruction, a literary course that
would include the study of human psychology and natural philosophy (in preparation for child-rearing), a
domestic course that would raise housewifery to a science, and an optional course of ornamental accomplishments. Joseph Emerson attempted to balance intellectual
exercise with physical exercise, domestic philosophy, and
all-important religious study. George Emerson thought
female education should include botany, Latin, chemistry
and natural philosophy (for health purposes), arithmetic,
geometry, and composition. Catharine Beecher justified
the provision of courses on mental and moral philosophy
in her Hartford Female Seminary.[30]

By the second quarter of the nineteenth century the
philosophy of female education seemed to fulfill Eliza
Southgate's affirmation of 1800. It promised to train
women to know their place. The usefulness, scope, and
justification of women's education were linked to their
"stations" of daughter, sister, wife, mother. Educators
looked at women in relation to men, and attuned their

29. Burroughs, *An Address,* p. 23; Gallaudet, *An Address,* p. 4; Willard, *A
Plan,* pp. 27–28; J. Emerson, *Female Education,* pp. 9–10; Catharine E.
Beecher, *Suggestions Respecting Improvements in Education* (Hartford,
Conn., 1829), pp. 7–9, 43–54.

30. Willard, *A Plan;* J. Emerson, *Female Education,* pp. 12–17; G. Emerson,
Lecture, pp. 15–24; Sklar, *Catharine Beecher,* pp. 78–94.

instruction to their presumed interpersonal roles. (In contrast, men's education was never justified on account of their influence on women). Such education would simultaneously arm women with principles for wife-and-motherhood and prepare mothers to instill proper motives in their children; it acted doubly to assure social stability.[31] Whether this consensus on the justification for women's education arose from tactical defensive reasoning in a hostile environment, or ensued from sincere conviction—and whether it was the only possible path on which women's education *could* have advanced, in this period—remain unanswered questions. But certainly, by stressing a certain sexual destiny, the predominant philosophy of female education encouraged women to understand gender as the essential determinant of their lives.

If, as educators said, womanhood prescribed for all the same duty, the same station, and therefore the same kind of education, it united them, dissolving class and regional lines. Advocates of women's education intended it to disregard economic status, and emphasized the advantage in instructing women uniformly so that they could cope with unforeseen changes in wealth. Circumstances in the United States, Catharine Beecher thought, especially demanded standard preparation of women to manage and serve in households and provide moral ballast. "Everything [here] is moving and changing," she wrote. "Persons in poverty, are rising to opulence, and persons of wealth, are sinking

31. Cf. the motives behind the expansion of common schools; see Curti, *Social Ideas of American Educators,* pp. 83-85; Michael B. Katz, *The Irony of Early School Reform: Educational Innovation in Mid-Nineteenth-Century Massachusetts* (Cambridge, Mass.: Harvard University Press, 1968). Contemporary arguments for universal education asserted that "whilst ignorance is the *hot-bed* of vice, imperfections and follies of every sort; its opposite, knowledge, is the parent of *order;* the fosterer of virtue; the tabernacle of truth." B. O'Sullivan, *A Series of Lectures on Female Education, No. 1* (Washington, D.C., 1828), p. 10.

to poverty. There are no distinct classes, as in aristocratic lands, whose bounds are protected by distinct and impassable lines, but all are thrown into promiscuous masses."[32] Before Beecher, a writer in the *Ladies' Magazine* had expressed the same concern that women all be trained for household competence in the several female "relations" in life, because of American vicissitudes of wealth. The servant girl might become the mistress, or vice versa.[33] Such reasoning can be read as a protest against women's powerlessness in the face of changing fortune—since they were economically dependent—and an attempt to equip them to be better mistresses of their fates. Class-blind but sex-specific education for women more loudly affirmed that economic mobility existed in America, while it promised to deter chaos by enforcing a sexual order.

32. Catharine Beecher, *Treatise on Domestic Economy* (rev. ed., New York, 1847), quoted in Cott, *Root of Bitterness,* pp. 175–76. Cf. the remarks of a Philadelphia woman: "The vicissitudes of fortune and the circulation of property, incident to the nature of our laws, are every day reducing proud and wealthy families to want, and elevating the humble to affluence. . . . How necessary is it then, that each one of our daughters, of any class in life, should be prepared for these reverses, and qualified to adorn any situation, or circle in society, by the mobility and the resources of the mind." Mrs. Townshend Stith, *Thoughts on Female Education* (Philadelphia, 1831), p. 29. Stuart Blumin's careful study, "Mobility and Change in Ante-Bellum Philadelphia," in Stephan Thernstrom and Richard Sennett, eds., *Nineteenth-Century Cities: Essays in the New Urban History* (New Haven: Yale University Press, 1969), shows that upward occupational and residential mobility stayed approximately constant between 1820 and 1860 while downward occupational and residential mobility substantially increased; the concerns of advocates of women's education appear to have been well warranted.

33. "N.," in *Ladies' Magazine* 3 (May 1830):198–208. Sarah Josepha Hale was a valiant supporter of women's education on account of her esteem for women's power over the minds of the next generation and she made this a dominant theme in the *Ladies' Magazine* in its first years. The idea that education would unfit women for the domestic sphere, in Hale's view, was as fallacious as was the idea that men were incapable of self-government and must submit to despotism. (This analogy of hers, like others in her writings, served to separate the duties of the two sexes while making them comparable.) See *Ladies' Magazine* 4 (April 1831):146.

The successful rationale for improving women's minds thus was founded on, not opposed to, women's domestic occupation and maternal destiny.[34] But women's schools had important consequences unpredicted by the early advocates. One was to subvert the status quo with respect to women's breadth of interests. As some opponents had correctly feared, education led many women to look beyond their domestic duties. Once guided to serious study and reasoning, some turned to books outside their own curriculum, including works in law, medicine, and philosophy. A few even looked critically and analytically at the Bible. Aware of wider perspectives, some women put their minds to work at other purposes than refining their subordination to men. (Elizabeth Cady's attendance at the Troy Seminary in 1830-31, for instance—in time to hear Almira Phelps's stirring lectures—did not lead her to complacency in marriage to Henry Stanton.)[35] Educated women predominated among the feminists of the mid-nineteenth century who are remembered today. Not only the intellectual exercise but likely their awareness of the justification for their education contributed to their rebellion. The orientation toward gender in their education fostered women's consciousness of themselves as a group united in purpose, duties, and interests. From the sense among women that they shared a collective destiny it was but another step (though a steep one) to sense that they might shape that destiny with their own minds and hands.

34. Cf. also the *First Annual Report from the Executive Committee of the Board of Managers of the Boston and Vicinity Female Improvement Society* (Boston, 1836). This society (composed of men) aimed to improve mothers by establishing a seminary to train female teachers to teach their own sex.

35. See Elizabeth Cady Stanton, *Eighty Years and More: Reminiscences 1815-1897* (New York: Schocken Books, 1971; reprinted from 1898 ed.).

4

RELIGION

Woman was "fitted by nature" for Christian benevolence, announced a Presbyterian minister in Newburyport, Massachusetts, in 1837—"religion seems almost to have been entrusted by its author to her particular custody." As he saw it, Christianity had performed a unique service for women by bringing them social advantages as well as spiritual hope, and women had incurred a corresponding obligation.[1] The numbers and activity of women in New England churches suggest that they found benefits indeed in their religious devotion—but did their perception of the benefits, and the minister's, exactly coincide?

The Puritans who settled Massachusetts Bay worshipped a patriarchal God, but as early as the mid-seventeenth century women outnumbered men in the New England churches. While the church hierarchy remained strictly male the majority of women in their congregations increased, and ministers felt compelled to explain it.[2] "As

1. Jonathan Stearns, *Female Influence, and the True Christian Mode of its Exercise: A Discourse delivered in the 1st Presbyterian Church in Newburyport, July 30, 1837* (Newburyport: John G. Tilton, 1837), p. 11. He had to qualify his assertion with "almost," I assume, in order to encourage male church-goers and also to account for the exclusion of women from the ministry.

2. Women's majority did not increase in a linear fashion from the seventeenth to the nineteenth centuries because during the Great Awakening of the 1740s proportionally more men converted than during nonrevival years. On the sex ratio among church members during the seventeenth century see Ed-

there were three Marys to one John, standing under the Cross of our Dying Lord," Cotton Mather wrote in 1692, "so still there are far more Godly Women in the World, than there are Godly Men; and our Church Communions give us a Little Demonstration of it." Mather offered two explanations for the persistent pattern. Because of Eve's sins God had decreed that woman's lot would include subjection to man, and pain in childbirth; but he had mercifully converted these curses into blessings. The trials that women had to endure made them "tender," made them seek consolation, and thus turned them toward God and piety. Mather also thought that women had more opportunity and time to devote to "soul-service" than men had because they were ordinarily at home and had little "Worldly Business." Two decades later, when the Reverend Benjamin Colman praised women for showing "more of the Life & Power of Religion" than men, he discerned similar causes: women's "natural Tenderness of Spirit & Your Retiredness from the Cares & Snares of the World;

mund S. Morgan, "New England Puritanism: Another Approach," *WMQ* 3d ser., 18 (1961):236–42; Darrett Rutman, "God's Bridge Falling Down—'Another Approach' to New England Puritanism Assayed," *WMQ* 3d ser., 19 (1962):408–21; on the early eighteenth century see Cedric Cowing, "Sex and Preaching in the "Great Awakening," *AQ* 20 (1968):625–34; J. Bumsted, "Religion, Finance and Democracy in Massachusetts: The Town of Norton as a Case Study," *JAH* 57 (1971):817–31; James Walsh, "The Great Awakening in the First Congregational Church of Woodbury, Connecticut, *WMQ* 3d ser., 28 (1971):543–52; Gerald F. Moran, "Conditions of Religious Conversion in the First Society of Norwich, Connecticut, 1718–1744," *JSH* 5 (1972):331–43; Philip J. Greven, Jr., "Youth, Maturity, and Religious Conversion: A Note on the Ages of Converts in Andover, Massachusetts, 1711–1749," *Essex Institute Historical Collections* (April 1972):119–34; on the early nineteenth century see Nancy F. Cott, "Young Women in the Second Great Awakening," *FS* 3 (1975):15–29; Donald Mathews, "The Second Great Awakening as an Organizing Process," *AQ* 21 (1969), esp. p. 42; Whitney R. Cross, *The Burned-Over District* (New York: Harper Torchbooks, 1965), esp. pp. 84–89; and Barbara Welter, "The Feminization of Religion in Nineteenth-Century America," in Mary Hartman and Lois Banner, eds., *Clio's Consciousness Raised* (New York: Harper Torchbooks, 1973).

so more especially in Your Multiplied Sorrows the curse pronounc'd upon our first Mother Eve, turn'd into the greatest blessing to Your Souls." Writers later in the eighteenth century dropped the references to Mother Eve and focused instead on the religious inclination "naturally" present in female temperament. In the British work *A Father's Legacy to his Daughters,* which was widely reprinted in New England after 1775, Dr. John Gregory maintained that women were more "susceptible" to religion because of their "superior delicacy," "modesty," "natural softness and sensibility of . . . dispositions," and "natural warmth of . . . imagination." (Men, he assumed, naturally had harder hearts and stronger passions, and were more dissolute and resistant to religious appeal because of the greater freedom they enjoyed.) Gregory also thought that women needed the consolations of religion, since they suffered great difficulties in life yet could "not plunge into business, or dissipate [them]selves in pleasure and riot" (as men might) for diversion. An influential British Evangelical named Thomas Gisborne made a similar appraisal of women's religious inclinations at the turn of the century, giving more weight, however, to women's distress and fear in childbirth as motivations of their piety.[3]

By the early nineteenth century New England ministers took for granted that women were the majority among Christians. They had assimilated the eighteenth-century argument that "women are happily formed for religion"

3. Cotton Mather, *Ornaments for the Daughters of Zion* (Cambridge, Mass., 1692), pp. 44-45; Benjamin Colman, *The Duty and Honour of Aged Women* (Boston, 1711), pp. ii-iii; Dr. John Gregory, *A Father's Legacy to his Daughters* (London: John Sharpe, 1822), pp. 11-12; Thomas Gisborne, *An Enquiry into the Duties of the Female Sex* (London, reprinted Philadelphia: James Humphreys, 1798), pp. 182-83. I cite these English works because of the evidence that they were read in New England; on this, see Nancy F. Cott, "In the Bonds of Womanhood: Perspectives on Female Experience and Consciousness in New England, 1780-1830" (Ph.D. diss., Brandeis University, 1974), pp. 225-27.

by means of their "natural endowments" of sensibility,
delicacy, imagination, and sympathy.[4] It testified how
far New England Protestantism had become a matter of
"the heart" rather than "the head" between the seventeenth and the nineteenth century—just as it had become a
religion chiefly of women rather than men—that such characteristics manifested a "religious" temperament.[5] Recall-
ing Christ's blessing of the meek and merciful, the Reverend
Joseph Buckminster asked a Boston women's organization
in 1810 if it was "surprising, that the most fond and faithful votaries of such a religion should be found among a sex,
destined by their very constitution, to the exercise of the
passive, the quiet, the secret, the gentle and humble virtues?" Men, the "self-styled lords of Creation," pursued
wealth, politics or pleasure, but "the dependent, solitary
female" sought God. Because of their softheartedness women were attuned to Christianity, Buckminster thought,
and they appreciated Christianity because it valued domestic life. He summed up dramatically, "I believe that if
Christianity should be compelled to flee from the mansions

4. Quotation from Daniel Chaplin, *A Discourse Delivered before the Charitable Female Society in Groton [Massachusetts], October 19, 1814* (Andover,
Mass., 1814), p. 9.

When I speak of "New England ministers' views" in what follows, my opinions primarily derive from my reading of 65 sermons concerning or addressed
to women between 1792 and 1837, of which 54 were written between 1800
and 1820, and 57 were delivered to meetings of female associations in New
England towns and cities. The denomination best represented were the trinitarian Congregationalists, who contributed at least a third of the sermons,
while Unitarian Congregationalists, Presbyterians, Episcopalians, Baptists, and
others together gave the rest. Denominational differences did not percep-
tibly vary ministers' assessments of women's roles, however. But note that I
am not dealing here with the Methodist contribution or the influence of
Charles G. Finney's revivalism, which occurred chiefly after 1835 in New
England. I have presented the ministers' views in greater detail in "In the
Bonds of Womanhood," chap. 3. A complete listing of the sermons appears
at the end of this book.

5. Jonathan Edwards was, of course, a central figure in this transformation.
See chapter 5, "Sisterhood," esp. note 15.

of the great, the academies of the philosophers, the halls of legislators, or the throng of busy men, we should find her last and purest retreat with woman at the fireside; her last altar would be the female heart; her last audience would be the children gathered around the knees of a mother; her last sacrifice, the secret prayer, escaping in silence from her lips, and heard perhaps only at the throne of God."[6] Christianity was essentially female, his pronouns revealed.

Buckminster and his colleagues developed a powerful rationale for women's special obligations to Christianity. They reasoned that women's devotion to the religion was only fair recompense for the gospel's service in elevating them to their "proper" rank. Only Christianity, they claimed, made "men willing to treat females as equals, and in some respects, as superiors"; only Christianity "exalt[ed] woman to an equal rank with man in all the felicities of the soul, in all the advantages of religious attainment, in all the prospects and hopes of immortality"; only Christianity redeemed human nature from the base passions and taught reverence for domestic relations.[7] Drawing comparisons from history and from other cultures (readily at hand because of the foreign-mission movement), ministers affirmed that New England women owed their social rank to the progress of Christian civilization. This was an omnipresent theme.[8]

6. Joseph Buckminster, "A Sermon Preached before the Members of the Boston Female Asylum, September 1810," hand-copied and bound with other printed sermons to the BFA, pp. 7-9, BPL.

7. Chaplin, *A Discourse*, p. 12; Pitt Clarke, *A Discourse Delivered before the Norton Female Christian Association, on . . . June 13, 1818* (Taunton, Mass., 1818), p. 11; Samuel Worcester, *Female Love to Christ* (Salem, Mass., 1809), pp. 12-13.

8. E.g., see Daniel Clark, *The Wise Builder, a Sermon Delivered to the Females of the 1st Parish in Amherst, Mass.* (Boston, 1820), pp. 17-18, 23-24; John Bullard, *A Discourse, delivered at Pepperell, September 19, 1815, before the Charitable Female Society* (Amherst, N.H., 1815), pp. 9-10; Benjamin

Contrasts between the condition of women in New England and in the countries to which missionaries traveled made it plausible that the Christian gospel had "civilized" men's attitudes to women. To appeal to a female charitable society for funds in 1829, the male trustees of the New Hampshire mission society asserted that "heathen" women were "ignorant—degraded—oppressed—enslaved. They are never treated by the other sex as companions and equals. They are in a great measure outcasts from society. They are made to minister to the *pleasures* of man; they are made to do the *work* of men; but, admitted to the enjoyment of equal rights, and raised to the respectability and happiness of free and honourable social intercourse, they are not." New Hampshire women by contrast were respected and free, and had access to knowledge.[9] Rebeccah Lee, wife of the pastor in Marlborough, Connecticut, urged this point of view on the members of several female societies there. "To the Christian religion we owe the rank we hold in society, and we should feel our obligations," she declared.

> It is that, which prevents our being treated like beasts of burden—which secures us the honourable privilege of human companionship in social life, and raises us in the domestic relations to the elevated stations of wives and mothers. Only seriously reflect upon the state of our sex, in those regions of the globe unvisited and unblessed with the light of Christianity; we see them degraded to a level with the brutes, and shut out from the society of lordly *man;* as if they were made by their Crea-

Wadsworth, *Female Charity an Acceptable Offering*... (Andover, Mass., 1817), pp. 27–28; David T. Kimball, *The Obligation and Disposition of Females to Promote Christianity* ... (Newburyport, 1819), p. 4.

9. *16th Annual Report on the concerns of the Female Cent Institution, New Hampshire* (Concord, N.H., 1829), pp. 3–4 (quotation), 4–6.

tor, not as the companions, but as the slaves and
drudges of domineering masters. . . . Let each one then
ask herself, how much do I owe?[10]

The "feminization" of Protestantism in the early nineteenth century was conspicuous.[11] Women flocked into
churches and church-related organizations, repopulating
religious institutions. Female converts in the New England
Great Awakening between 1798 and 1826 (before the
Methodist impact) outnumbered males by three to two.[12]
Women's prayer groups, charitable institutions, missionary
and education societies, Sabbath School organizations, and
moral reform and maternal associations all multiplied phe-
nomenally after 1800, and all of these had religious motives.
Women thus exercised as fully as men the American pen-
chant for voluntary association noted by Tocqueville in
the 1830s, but women's associations before 1835 were *all*

10. Mrs. Rebeccah Lee, *An Address, Delivered in Marlborough, Connecticut,
September 7, 1831* (Hartford, 1831), p. 4. She also noted, "There is not a
town or village in our country, perhaps, where females are not actively engaged
in this good cause, and from us much is expected in the present day."

11. The term is Barbara Welter's, in "The Feminization of Religion."

12. See Ebenezer Porter, *Letters on Revivals of Religion* (Andover, Mass.:
The Revival Association, 1832), p. 5; and Cott, "Young Women in the Second
Great Awakening." Beginning in 1830 Methodist evangelism under Charles G.
Finney encouraged women's religious activity, particularly their public pray-
ing, more vigorously than other denominations. On the contribution of Methodist practice to Congregational and Presbyterian revival measures in the
northeast before Finney, see Richard Carwardine, "The Second Great Awakening in the Urban Centers: An Examination of Methodism and the 'New Measures'," *JAH* 59 (1972):327–41.

Studies of many individual communities will be necessary before the precise
impact of the revivals on the sex ratio among church members can be ascer-
tained. Recent historical research on the Second Great Awakening suggests
that the proportion of men among the converts was greater during revival
years than ordinary years, but only large enough to reduce the female majority
somewhat, not to undermine it. See Mary P. Ryan, "A Woman's Awakening:
Revivalist Religion in Utica, New York, 1800–1835," paper delivered at the
Third Berkshire Conference on the History of Women, Bryn Mawr, Pa., June
10, 1976, and Paul E. Johnson, "A Shopkeeper's Millennium: Society and
Revivals in Rochester, N.Y., 1815–1837" (Ph.D. diss., University of California
at Los Angeles, 1975).

allied with the church, whereas men's also expressed a variety of secular, civic, political, and vocational concerns.[13]

This flowering of women's associational activities was part of the revival movement of the early nineteenth century in which Protestants tried to counteract religious indifference, rationalsim, and Catholicism and to create an enduring and moral social order. Ministers were joined by lay persons, often (not always) of wealthy and conservative background, in giving the Awakening its momentum. They interpreted the aftermath of the French Revolution in the 1790s as proof of the dangers of a "godless" society, and feared that the American republic, with its growing urban populations, its Catholic immigrants, its Western inhabitants far from New England culture and clergy, might fall victim to similar "godless' influence. They saw religious education not only as a means to inculcate true faith but as a route to salvation on this earth, since it could teach the restraints demanded for an orderly society. The lay activites of the revival intended education, religious conversion, and the reformation of individual character whether they took the form of distributing bibles and tracts among the urban poor and Western frontier residents, raising money to train ministers or missionaries to evangelize the unchurched, setting up Sabbath schools for children to begin the business of Christian training early, or other myriad forms.[14]

Ministers' religious and denominational aims, conserva-

13. See Alexis de Tocqueville, *Democracy in America,* ed. Phillips Bradley (New York: Vintage Books, 1945), 1:198-205, 2:114-18, 123-28. Cf. Richard D. Brown, "The Emergence of Voluntary Associations in Massachusetts, 1760-1830," *Journal of Voluntary Action Research* 2 (1973), esp. 68-70.

14. See Clifford S. Griffin, "Religious Benevolence as Social Control, 1815-1860," *MVHR* 44 (1957), esp. 440-42; Charles I. Foster, *An Errand of Mercy: The Evangelical United Front, 1790-1837* (Chapel Hill, N.C.: University of North Carolina Press, 1960). A recent critique by Lois Banner, "Religious Benevolence as Social Control: A Critique of an Interpretation," *JAH* 60 (1973): 23-41, stresses the organizational dynamics of the Protestant denominations and the sincere educational and humanitarian aims of proponents.

tives' manipulation of religious benevolence for social control, humanitarians' perceptions of the needs of the poor, and women's orientation toward religious and gender-group expression all contributed to the proliferation of Christian women's societies. Since the prayer meetings called during religious revivals were often sex-segregated, they could serve as prototypes of religious organizations exclusively for women. The British Evangelical movement also supplied explicit models of charitable and humanitarian efforts by women.[15] These several motives and predispositions help to explain the extraordinarily swift rise and geographical dispersion of women's religious benevolent associations. Under the combined forces of local ministers, agents of national benevolent organizations and individual women who took to heart their obligations, female religious and charitable societies were established in all the larger cities of New England shortly after the turn of the century—in Middlebury and Montpelier, Concord and Portsmouth, Portland and Eastport, Providence and Newport, Hartford and New Haven, Boston, Salem, and Newburyport. Small towns in Vermont such as Jericho Center, Danville, Cornwall, Thetford, and Castleton had female religious and missionary societies before 1816. Scores of religious charitable societies were formed among New Hampshire women in rural towns between 1804 and 1814. With the encouragement of agents of the New Hampshire Bible Society, women founded local affiliates in 138 towns between 1820 and 1828. Women belonged to dozens of female charitable societies and "education" societies (which raised funds to educate ministers) in Connecticut towns by 1815; and societies for prayer, for propagation

15. Merle Curti, "American Philanthropy and the National Character," *AQ* 10 (1958):425. The first female charitable institution in the United States, the Society for the Relief of Poor Widows and Small Children, was founded in 1796 in New York by a newly arrived Scotswoman, Isabella M. Graham, on the model of a London institution for poor relief.

of the gospel, for missionaary and charitable purposes were even more numerous in Massachusetts. The Boston Female Society for Missionary Purposes corresponded with 109 similar societies in 1817-18.[16]

Why did women support religion so faithfully? Perhaps

16. The formation of the national benevolent societies, such as the American Bible Society, the American Sabbath School Association, etc., did not occur until 1815 and after. Documentation of the existence of women's associations occurs in the titles of ministers' sermons, in printed constitutions and reports and manuscript records of the societies themselves, in women's diaries and letters, and in local histories. In addition to titles listed in the back of this book, see documents from the Jericho Center Female Religious Society, Cent Society, and Maternal Association, and constitution and rules of the Maternal Association in Dorchester, Mass., Dec. 25, 1816, CL; documents of the Charitable Female Society in the 2d parish in Bradford, 1815-21, of the West Bradford Female Temperance Society, 1829-34, of the Female Religious, Biographical, Reading Society (Berean Circle), 1826-32, of the Belleville Female Benevolent Society, or Dorcas Society, 1839-40, and of the Hamilton Maternal Association, 1834-35, EI; *Report on the Concerns of the New Hampshire Cent Institution* (Concord, 1814, 1815, 1816); *The Rules, Regulations, &c of the Portsmouth Female Asylum* (Portsmouth, 1815); Edward Aiken, *The First Hundred Years of the New Hampshire Bible Society* (Concord, 1912), p. 66; Mrs. L. H. Daggett, ed., *Historical Sketches of Women's Missionary Societies in America and England* (Boston, n.d.), p. 50; *Annual Reports of the Education Society of Connecticut and the Female Education Society of New Haven* (New Haven, 1816-26); *An Account of the Rise, Progress, and Present State of the Boston Female Asylum* (Boston, 1803); *Constitution of the Salem Female Charitable Society, Instituted July 1st, 1801* (printed circular, 1801); *Reminiscences of the Boston Female Asylum* (printed, Boston, 1844); *Account of the Plan and Regulations of the Female Charitable Society of Newburyport* (Newburyport, 1803); *A Brief Account of the Origin and Progress of the Boston Female Society for Missionary Purposes, with extracts from the reports of the society in May 1817 and 1818* (Boston, 1818); *Report of the Boston Female Society for Missionary Purposes* (Boston, 1825); *Constitution of the Female Samaritan Society instituted in Boston, Nov. 19, 1817 and revised 1825* (Boston, 1833); *Constitution of the Female Society of Boston and the Vicinity for Promoting Christianity among the Jews, instituted June 5, 1816* (Boston, n.d.); *Constitution of the Fragment Society, Boston, founded 1817* (Boston, 1825); *Constitution of the Female Philanthropick Society, instituted Dec. 1822* (Boston, 1823); *Boston Fatherless and Widows Society, founded 1817, Annual Report* (Boston, 1836); *Second Annual Report, Third Annual Report, of the Boston Female Moral Reform Society* (Boston, 1837, 1838); *Constitution of the Maternal Association of Newburyport* (printed, 1815); *Constitution of the Maternal Association of the 2d Parish in*

Cotton Mather's and Benjamin Colman's reasoning deserves some credence. The specter of death in childbirth repeatedly forced women to think on the state of their souls. And women's domestic occupations may have diverted them from piety less than the "snares" of the world did men; besides, ministers and pious women made every effort to conflate domestic values with religious values. Domestic occupations offered women little likelihood of finding a set of values and symbols to rival the ones proposed by evangelical Christianity. For women at home in New England society, Christian belief had a self-perpetuating force that was not likely to be disrupted by experience that would provide alternative and equally satisfying explanations.[17] Yet women whose occupations took them outside the home, and single women generally, were prominent in the female religious community. Early factory workers participated in revivals, as Catherine Sedgwick, a Unitarian opposed to evangelical fervor, reported to her brother in 1833: "We have had the religious agitators among us lately—They have produced some effect on the factory girls & such light & combustible materials."[18] Per-

West-Newbury, adopted Sept. 1834 (printed, n.d.); Constitution of the Maternal Association (Dedham, Mass., n.d.); Constitution of the Maternal Association of the New Congregational Church in Boston, Mass., organized Oct. 6, 1842 (Boston, 1843); Diary of Sarah Connell Ayer (Portland, Me., 1910), pp. 213-15, 226, 228, 237, 285-307; diary of Mary Hurlbut, Feb. 10, 1833, CHS. See also Keith Melder, "'Ladies Bountiful': Organized Women's Benevolence in Early Nineteenth-Century America," New York History 48 (1967):231-54; Mary B. Treudley, "The Benevolent Fair: A Study of Charitable Organizations Among Women in the First Third of the Nineteenth Century," Social Service Review 14 (1940):506-22.

17. This line of argument was suggested to me by Gordon Schochet's reasoning about patriarchalism in the seventeenth century in "Patriarchalism, Politics, and Mass Attitudes in Stuart England," Historical Journal 12 (1969), esp. 421-25.

18. Catherine Sedgwick to Robert Sedgwick, Sept. 15, 1833, Sedgwick Collection, MHS. See also the diary of Mary Hall, a Lowell operative, NHHS; and Almond H. Davis, ed., The Female Preacher, or Memoir of Salome Lincoln (Providence, R.I., 1843).

haps the eighteenth-century reasoning about women's temperament suiting them for Christian faith had a deeper truth. Characteristics expected in women and in Christians —those of the "tender heart"—increasingly coincided during the eighteenth century, because women supported Christianity more consistently than men, and became ministers' major constituency.[19] By the early nineteenth century, the clergy claimed that women supported (or should support) Christianity because it was in the interest of their sex to do so; that reassured the faithful, whether or not it accurately described their motives.

It is less than satisfying, however, to attribute New England women's religiosity to their mortal risks in childbirth or to a socialization process that inculcated domestic piety and "Christian" temperament in them. Skeptics at the time suggested other reasons. Harriet Martineau, a witty and politically astute British visitor who criticized hypocrisies in American women's expected roles, noticed that "in New England, a vast deal of [women's] time is spent in attending preachings, and other religious meetings: and in paying visits, for religious purposes, to the poor and sorrowful." She even found it plausible "that they could not exist without religion," but considered that an unhealthy circumstance. Women were "driven back upon religion as a resource against vacuity," in her view.[20]

(Although Martineau seems to have meant vacuity of *mind* rather than *time,* some evidence suggests that women without pressing demands on their time were indeed the

19. Lonna Malmsheimer suggests that the numerical predominance of women in New England churches forced adjustments in ministers' views of their character during the eighteenth century, in "New England Funeral Sermons and Changing Attitudes toward Women, 1672-1792" (Ph.D. diss., University of Minnesota, 1973).

20. Harriet Martineau, *Society in America* (New York: Saunders and Otley, 1837), 2:255-57, 229, 363. Martineau strenuously objected to women working to raise money to educate young clerics (as they did in "education" societies); see pp. 363, 415-20.

most devoted to religion. Single women or childless wives not responsible for the whole of their own support were the most likely to record their religous musings unfailingly. Abigail Brackett Lyman began a journal of that sort in her teens when she made a public profession of faith, and continued, as she reflected several years later, "to inscribe nothing in my journal but devotional exercises from the period abovementioned till some time after my marriage when cares increasing & being obliged to entertain considerable company I found it impossible to continue this laudable practice." Another ardent convert remarked plaintively, while she was still single, "Most of my associates were settled in life but I saw that those who had been zealous and devoted before their marriage had mostly declined in piety when pressed with the domestic cares of a family. I said to myself Why is it so? It cannot be because there is anything in that state subversive of piety for it is of Divine appointment."[21])

Martineau's insight was still more piercing. She said women "pursue[d] religion as an occupation" because they were constrained from exercising their full range of moral, intellectual, and physical powers in other ways. With an extension of her allusion religious activities can be seen as a means used by New England women to define self and find community, two functions that wordly occupations more likely performed for men. Traditionally, of course, religion had enlightened individuals of both sexes about their identity and placed them in a like-minded community; but women's particular needs and the configuration of religious institutions at this time enhanced those social

21. Journal of Abigail Brackett Lyman, Jan. 1, 1800, in Helen Roelker Kessler, "The Worlds of Abigail Brackett Lyman" (M.A. thesis, Tufts Univ., 1976), appendix A; "A Short Sketch of the life of Nancy Thomson [*sic*]," autobiographical fragment in the diary of Nancy Thompson (Hunt), c. 1813, CHS. See also the journal of Mary Treadwell Hooker, 1795–1812, CSL.

functions. In an era when Protestantism was a "crusade," when ministers presented evangelical Christianity as embattled and yet triumphant, religious affiliation announced one's identity and purpose. "I made religion the principal business of my life," Nancy Thompson summarized the effect of her conversion at nineteen. Abigail Lyman exhorted herself in 1800 (before the Second Great Awakening had progressed widely) "to Live up to the Professions of Religion I had made—to dare to be singular in this day when iniquity abounds."[22]

Religion stretched before the convert a lifetime of purposeful struggle holding out heartening rewards. It provided a way to order one's life and priorities. The evangelical theology of the early nineteenth century made that process of ordering amenable to personal choice. "The salvation of our precious souls is not to be effected independent of our exertions," Lyman wrote in her journal, "—we are free agents and as such should work out our salvation with fear and trembling. . . . We may believe and rely on the faith of Revelation—and form our actions and tempers by its pure and perfect precepts—or we may resist the truth—appose [sic] its influence & harden our hearts in sin—either the one or the other all are constantly doing." Yet an individual made the religious choice in submission to God's will rather than through personal initiative. The morphology of religious conversion echoed women's expected self-resignation and submissiveness while it offered enormously satisfying assurance to converts. Nancy Meriam, a devout young woman of Oxford, Massachusetts, recorded in her religious notes of 1815, "There is sweetness in committing ourselves to God which the world knows nothing of. The idea that I am intirely [sic] in the hands

22. "Short Sketch," diary of Nancy Thompson, c. 1808; journal of Abigail Brackett Lyman, Jan. 30, 1800; see also diary of Lucinda Read, March 30, 1816, MHS.

of God fills my mind with a secret pleasure which I cannot describe."[23]

Yet religious identity also allowed women to assert themselves, both in private and in public ways. It enabled them to rely on an authority beyond the world of men and provided a crucial support to those who stepped beyond accepted bounds—reformers, for example. Women dissenters from Ann Hutchinson to Sarah Grimké displayed the subversive potential of religious belief. Religious faith also allowed women a sort of holy selfishness, or self-absorption, the result of the self-examination intrinsic to the Calvinist tradition. In contrast to the self-abnegation required of women in their domestic vocation, religious commitment required attention to one's own thoughts, actions, and prospects. By recording their religious meditations women expressed their literacy and rising self-consciousness in a sanctioned mode. Vigilance for their souls and their conformity to God's requirements compelled them to scrutinize their lives. And the more distinctly Christianity appeared a preserve of *female* values, the more legitimate (and likely) it became for religious women to scrutinize their gender-role. If the popular sales of the published memoirs of female missionaries are any guide, that model of religious commitment, which proposed a submission of self that was simultaneously a pronounced form

23. Journal of Abigail Brackett Lyman, Oct. 3, 1802; Nancy Meriam, "Religious Notes, 1811–1815," April 9, 1815, WHS; also see Cott, "Young Women in the Second Great Awakening," on this theme. William McLoughlin summarizes the idea of "compliance with the terms of salvation" thus: "The process of conversion . . . became a shared act, a complementary relationship. Man striving and yearning; God benevolent and eager to save; the sinner stretching out his hands to receive the gift of grace held out by a loving God. This belief in man's free will or his partial power to effect his own salvation had in earlier Calvinist days been condemned as the heresy of Arminianism. For this reason most nineteenth-century ministers preferred to call themselves Evangelicals." *The American Evangelicals 1800–1900* (New York: Harper Torchbooks, 1968), p. 10.

of self-assertion, had wide appeal. Time and again women who made note of little reading except the Bible read the memoirs of Mrs. Newell, missionary to Burma (1814), and responded perhaps as a young matron of Woodmont, Connecticut, did: "O that I could feel as she did . . . , it appears to me as though I had ought to feel willing to contribute freely to spread the gospel among the heathen."[24]

No other avenue of self-expression besides religion at once offered women social approbation, the encouragement of male leaders (ministers), and, most important, the community of their peers. Conversion and church membership in the era of the Second Great Awakening implied joining a community of Christians. As historians have noted, the individual convert in the revival entered "a community of belief in which he [or she] was encouraged to make a decision that would be a positive organizing principle for his [or her] own life." During these decades the sacramental dimension of the church faded in the light of a new conception, "a voluntary association of explicitly convinced Christians for the purpose of mutual edification in the worship of God and the propagandization of the Christian faith as the group defined it." Because the vigor of religion had sunk during the late eighteenth century, the "awakened" Christian community defined itself to an unusual extent by its adversary and evangelical relation to the outside world, as well as by its intramural purposes. "He that is not with us said the Saviour is against us," Abigail Lyman reiterated.[25]

24. Diary of Mrs. S. Smith, March 29, 1825, CSL. See also the diary of Mary Treadwell Hooker; diary of Sarah Ripley Stearns, May 1, 1814, and March 19, 1815, Stearns Collection, SL; correspondence between Almira Eaton and Weltha Brown, 1812–22, Hooker Collection, SL.

25. Richard D. Birdsall, "The Second Great Awakening and the New England Social Order," *Church History* 39 (1970):357; Sidney E. Mead, "The Rise of the Evangelical Conception of the Ministry in America, 1607–1850," in H. Richard Niebuhr and Daniel L. Williams, eds., *The Ministry in Historical Per-*

Being a Christian in this period meant becoming a member of a voluntary community not only in a psychological but in a literal sense, for piety implied group evangelical activity. Associative activity flowed naturally from church membership. The motive to advance personal piety and the cause of Christianity, together with the desire to act cooperatively, and (often) the local minister's support, influenced women to form associations even before they had specific aims. The process of organization of the Female Religious and Cent Society in Jericho Center, Vermont, seems to have been typical. In 1805 a number of women joined together because they wished to "do good" and aid the cause of religion, but they did not know what path to take. They began meeting for prayer. (This was the simplest form religious association took, and probably the most widespread, but also the most difficult to find record of.[26]) With their minister's assistance they formed a society and began to raise money for the missionary movement. The articles of their society proclaimed in 1806 that they would meet fortnightly "for social prayer and praise

spective (New York: Harper and Bros., 1956), p. 224; journal of Abigail Brackett Lyman, Oct. 3, 1802. Historians of religion consistently maintain that during the last two decades of the eighteenth century American churches "reached a lower ebb of vitality . . . than at any other time in the country's religious history," in the words of Sydney E. Ahlstrom, A Religious History of the American People (New Haven: Yale University Press. 1972), p. 365. Douglas Sweet protests that consensus in "Church Vitality and the American Revolution," Church History 45 (1976):341-57. The Second Great Awakening, beginning in the late 1790s, decisively changed the religious climate. Estimates for New England, which generally was the region of highest church affiliation, are unavailable, but Winthrop S. Hudson estimates that church members in the United States as a whole increased from 1 out of 15 in the population in 1800, to 1 our of 8, in 1835, raising the churches' "constituency" from 40 percent to 75 percent of the population; Religion in America: An Historical Account (2d ed., New York: Scribners, 1973), pp. 129-30.

26. Mary Orne Tucker mentions her attendance at such a meeting in her diary, April 12, 1802, EI; see also The Writings of Nancy Maria Hyde of Norwich, Conn. (Norwich, 1816), pp. 182-83, 189-90, 192-93, 201-02, 203-05.

and religious instruction and edification." They also pledged mutual support and group intimacy, resolving that "all persons attending the meeting shall conduct themselves with seriousness and solemnity dureing [*sic*] the Exercises nor shall an Illiberal remark be made respecting the performance of any of the members, neither shall they report abroad any of the transactions of the society to the prejudice of any of its members." The society prospered. In 1816, when it joined with a Young Ladies' Society that had been formed in 1812 under another minister's guidance, and founded the Female Cent Society of Jericho, the new group had seventy members.[27]

Women's diaries reveal the efforts, and the high esteem, given to religious associations. As a young matron in Greenfield, Massachusetts, in 1815 Sarah Ripley Stearns joined a group of "youthful females" who hoped to improve themselves in piety. The same year she helped found a female charitable society, with the goal of aiding destitute children to attend school and church. She noted when the "band of associated females" met at her house, and remarked that their "Benevolent Institution" was one of her chief sources of enjoyment. In 1816 she endeavored to found a maternal association, a "Juvenile Institution," and a "heathen school society." She carried on these activities during the years in which she bore three children, despite her laments that household cares left her little time for diary writing, pious reading, or church attendance.[28]

Sarah Connell Ayer of Maine involved herself even more thoroughly. Although her youth had been frivolous, the deaths of four infants during her first five years of mar-

27. Documents of the Jericho Center, Vermont, Female Religious Society, Cent Society, and Maternal Associations. By 1824 the Cent Society had 120 subscribers.

28. Sarah Ripley Stearns diary, 1814–17, esp. Dec. 24, 1815, March 2, March 31, July 14, Oct. 13, 1816, June 1817.

riage turned her increasingly to religion and its community of consolation. (The deaths of children, in these years, may have given women more powerful motivation toward religiosity then ever did fears of their own mortality in childbirth.) By the time Sarah Ayer was twenty-four she saw nothing more pleasant "than to spend an evening in conversation with a few pious friends." In early 1816 she belonged to a female missionary society, prayer meeting, and donation society in Portland, and was devoted to her orthodox Congregationalist minister. After giving birth to two children who survived, she joined the Maternal Association and found its meetings "profitable." In 1822 her husband's appointment as surveyor of the port induced the family to move to Eastport. There Mrs. Ayer found the Congregationalist minister too Unitarian for her taste, and missed her Portland friends greatly. "We loved to meet together, to talk of Heaven as our final home, Christ as our Saviour; we shared each others joys and sorrows, and found the one heightened and the other alleviated by sympathy. Ah! how prone am I to murmur when things go contrary to my own inclinations," she wrote in her diary. Soon, however, she reestablished comparable activities in Eastport. At first she discovered a compatible community among the Baptists, and then worked with a small group of orthodox Congregationalists—seventeen women and three men—to set up a church to her preference. By the late 1820s she participated in a maternal association, a female prayer society, a benevolent society, and Sabbath School class.[29]

The ease with which women moved among evangelical societies, and participated in several at once, suggests that

29. *Diary of Sarah Connell Ayer 1805-1835*, pp. 209, 211, 213, 214, 215, 225, 226, 228, 231-33, 236-37, 239-40, 254, 278, 282-305. There is a gap in the diary between 1811 and 1815, the years in which Ayer bore and buried her first four children.

associating under the ideological aegis of evangelical Christianity mattered more to them than the specific goals of any one group. The founding members of the Female Religious Biographical and Reading Society (or "Berean Circle") associated in 1826 because they were "convinced of the importance and utility of the benevolent associations of the present day, and wish[ed] to unite our efforts in the same worthy objects, and also desir[ed] to improve and impress our own minds by obtaining religous instruction."[30] The occurrence of such associations in virtually every Protestant church implied that professing faith had come to include participating in group activity. Whether local ministers, state organizations, or pious individuals launched them, such associations created peer groups which became part of their members' definition of Christian piety.

The chosen Christian community also entered into a woman's self-definition. Rachel Willard Stearns, who set herself off from her Congregational family by converting to Methodism, exemplified that effect in a pronounced way. She appreciated the Methodist small-group meetings, she said, because "if we have been gay or trifling, or anger or revenge have had a place in our hearts, we do not wish to go, if we stay away, then the others will think there is something wrong. . . . I am thankful that I have placed myself under the watch-care and discipline of a church, where when I do wrong they will tell me of it. . . ."[31] Stearns's Methodism brought her to an especially intense religious self-concept; but religion performed an analogous social function for women in traditional denominations.

Within their Christian peer groups women examined their own behavior, weighed the balance between self and

30. Record book of the Female Religious, Biographical, Reading Society (the Berean Circle), 1826-32, EI. The society was probably located near Newburyport, though its exact location is not clear.
31. Diary of Rachel Willard Stearns, July 19, 1835, Stearns Collection, SL.

sacrifice in their lives, and sought appropriate models. In October 1828 the Berean Circle discussed the question, "Can an individual who is more strongly activated by selfish motives than by a view to the glory of God be a Christian?" They recorded their conclusions: "If their *habitual prevailing* motives are selfish they cannot; for the most important point in conversion is the change from selfishness to benevolence. We are not required to be so disinterested as to leave our own *chief* happiness out of view. This subject led to much interesting conversation." Several years later the group was engaged in similar topics, pursuing such questions as "Is an ungoverned temper, proof of an unsanctified heart?" Women's remarks in diaries suggest unanimously the deep satisfaction derived from occasions for discussion. One recorded that her meeting provided "much pleasure," another that it was "instructive and entertaining," a third that "I returned much refreshed in spirit."[32]

A shift in ministers' views also encouraged women's religious activities. The seventeenth-century clergy had tended to stress Eve's legacy, and hence to focus on woman being the "first in transgression." During the eighteenth century, ministers turned their attention from Eve to other promising models of female character in the Bible, in order to justify the idea that women could bear the standard of the religious community.[33] From the 1790s to the 1820s ministers of several denominations endorsed the view that women were of conscientious and prudent character, especially suited to religion. Drawing often on the text of Proverbs 31, they showed the model Christian woman to be a mod-

32. Record book of the Berean Circle, Oct. 15, 1828, Jan. 17, 1832; Mary Orne Tucker diary, April 12, 1802; *The Writings of Nancy Maria Hyde,* pp. 189–90; diary of Nancy Meriam, May 12, 1819, WHS.
33. See Malmsheimer, "New England Funeral Sermons."

est and faithful wife, an industrious and benevolent community member, and an efficient housekeeper who did not neglect the refinements of life. Fervently they described how pious women could influence others in the community and in their own families. From Baptists to Unitarians, clergymen agreed that family religion communicated from parents to children was the natural, divinely approved, most effective means of reproducing true Christian character.[34] By the pastors' own admission, mothers had more impact on children in this regard than fathers did. The reasoning of a Wolfborough, New Hampshire, Sabbath School convention reiterated the pervasive idea that mothers (and by extension, all women) propagated religion best. They resolved in 1834: "Whereas the influence of females on little children ordinarily determines their future character and eternal destiny, and as it has been most effectually exerted in bringing them to Christ, therefore, *Resolved,* that it is the sacred duty of all females to use every effort to promote the cause of Sabbath Schools."[35]

No other public institution spoke to women and cultivated their loyalty so assiduously as the churches did. Quickened by religious anxiety and self-interest, the clergy gave their formulations of women's roles unusual force. They pinned on women's domestic occupation and influence their own best hopes. Their portrayal of women's roles grew in persuasive power because it overlapped with republican commonplaces about the need for virtuous citi-

34. See, for example, Amos Chase, *On Female Excellence* (Litchfield, Conn., 1792); John C. Ogden, *The Female Guide* (Concord, N.H., 1793); George Strebeck, *A Sermon on the Character of the Virtuous Woman* (New York, 1800); William Lyman, *A Virtuous Woman the Bond of Domestic Union and the Source of Domestic Happiness* (New London, Conn., 1802); Nathan Strong, *The Character of a Virtuous and Good Woman* (Hartford, 1809); Ethan Smith, *Daughters of Zion Excelling* (Concord, N.H., 1814); Daniel Clark, *The Wise Builder* (Boston, 1820); and Cott, "In the Bonds of Womanhood," pp. 105–15.

35. Quoted by Henry C. Wright in his journal, 6:135, June 18, 1834, HCL.

zens for a successful republic. It gained intensity because it intersected with new interest in early childhood learning. Ministers declared repeatedly that women's pious influence was not only appropriate to them but crucial for society. "We look to you, ladies," said Joseph Buckminster, "to raise the standard of character in our own sex; we look to you, to guard and fortify those barriers, which still exist in society, against the encroachments of impudence and licentiousness. We look to you for the continuance of domestick purity, for the revival of domestick religion, for the increase of our charities, and the support of what remains of religion in our private habits and publick institutions."[36]

Ministers addressed women as a sex and, at the same time, as an interest group in the polity that had special civil and social responsibilities and special powers to defend its interests. "I address you as a class," said a Boston pastor to the mothers of the Mount Vernon Maternal Association, "because your duties and responsibilities are peculiar."[37] Ministers viewed women's sex-role as a social role, in other words. It meant no lessening of women's consciousness of the responsibilities borne to them by gender that the interests and obligations proposed to them were the ministers' own interests, and that the latter looked ahead to a rising generation of sons (the *men* who would lead society). Under ministers' guidance women could conclude that their sex shared not simply a biological but a social purpose. They were entrusted with the morals and faith of the next generation. According to prevailing conceptions of republican virtue, this was a task having political impact.[38]

36. Buckminster, "A Sermon Preached . . . 1810," pp. 24-25.

37. Pastor's address appended to *Constitution of the Maternal Association of the New Congregational Church* (Boston, 1843), p. 5.

38. E.g., Ward Cotton told the women of Boylston, Massachusetts, that bringing domestic missionaries to unchurched Western residents would be "the means not only of the salvation of their souls, but also of the political salva-

Maternal and moral reform societies—the two wings (as it were) of the women's religious-voluntary movement—illustrated vividly how women took to heart the social role proposed by ministers. Both kinds of societies institutionalized the idea that women's pious influence, especially as exerted over their own children, could reform the world. Maternal associations have left few traces because they were organized locally only (with no state or national superstructure) and had no official organ of communication.[39] They were grass-roots responses to the contemporary cultural and religious elevation of the mother's role. Their members felt obliged to prepare themselves to guide their children properly, in order to raise a generation of Christians and thus accomplish a moral reformation. The appearance of such associations suggests how the perception of motherhood as a social role as well as a personal role led women to seek supportive peer groups. The women who formed the Dorchester Maternal Association in Massachusetts in 1816 did so because they were "aware of our highly responsible situation as Mothers & as professing Christians" and wished to "commend our dear offspring" to God. They considered it each member's duty to pray and to read appropriate works, to pray with her children, and "to suggest to her sister members such hints as her

tion of our country." *Causes and Effects of Female Regard to Christ* (Worcester, 1816), p. 13.

39. The monthly *Mother's Magazine*, begun by Mrs. A.G. Whittelsey in 1833 in Utica, N.Y., served informally as an organ of communication, advising on programs and topics for maternal associations.

Mary P. Ryan's data from Utica indicates that the members of maternal societies there (c. 1825-35) were predominantly middle-class (wives of mechanics, shopkeepers, etc.) in contrast to the higher status of members of missionary societies formed there slightly earlier (c. 1805-15), who were predominantly wives of large proprietors, merchants, etc. See "A Woman's Awakening: Revivalist Religion in Utica, New York, 1800-1835."

own experience may furnish or circumstances seem to render necessary."[40] In Portland, Maine, mothers created in 1815 a widely copied format for a maternal association, providing for election of officers, monthly meetings for reading and discussion, and attendance at every third meeting of the members' daughters between age three and sixteen, and sons between three and fourteen.[41]

The spate of evangelically-oriented child-rearing books during the 1830s seems to have encouraged mothers to give institutional form to their developing consciousness, and maternal associations multiplied, John S.C. Abbott's *The Mother at Home* became a much-used part of the library of the Maternal Association of Jericho Center, Vermont, a group formed in 1833 by mothers "deeply impressed with the importance of bringing up children in the nurture and admonition of the Lord," who "associate[d] for the purpose of devising and adopting such measures, as may seem best calculated to assist us in the performance of this duty." Women who created maternal associations seemed burdened with the weight of responsibility in motherhood as well as impressed by its power. Mary Hurlbut, at twenty-eight the mother of four children, described the formation of her association in New London, Connecticut, in 1833: "11 mothers who feeling the greatness of their responsibilities & the need of Almighty aid, meet together unitedly to plead for their Children & for grace & strength to help—O that the Lord would bless this little band of sisters." Mothers in Hamilton, Massachusetts, began a maternal association in 1833 because "the immense influence we were exerting upon our beloved children, & that that influence would be felt

40. Constitution and rules of the Maternal Association in Dorchester, Massachusetts, Dec. 25, 1816, CL.

41. The constitutions of the maternal associations of Newburyport, Dedham, 2d Parish of West-Newbury, and New Congregational Church of Boston copied that format; see note 16.

through eternity, pressed upon our consciences." Every two weeks they met to discuss such topics as how "to train up our children for the service of the church" and "the best methods of instilling into our children habits of *Self-Denial*." The aim and the ambiance of the meetings are evoked in a member's intentions "that in order to make their meetings profitable to ourselves, there should be perfect and unreserved freedom & that the ladies should feel so much confidence in each other as to express their feelings and opinions without reserve—that our object in associating ourselves was mutual benefit & instruction & this could not be effected unless the sentiments of each other were elicited."[42]

Women who joined maternal associations thus asserted their formative power over their children's lives, took up evangelical goals, and complemented the private job of child rearing by approaching their common occupation cooperatively with their peers. Women joined moral reform societies to accomplish different immediate aims, but with similar reasoning. Moral reform societies intended to eliminate the sin of "licentiousness," which appeared in the permitted lust of men and the prostitution of women. The Boston Female Society for Missionary Purposes was

42. Constitution of the Jericho Center Maternal Association, CL; diary of Mary Hurlbut, Feb. 10, 1833 CHS (a penciled note added later on this page of the diary states that the maternal association continued to meet for 42 years); "Record Book of the Maternal Association, Hamilton, Massachusetts, 1834–1835, copied by A.W. Dodge for her friend Mrs. Judith N. Hill, 1835," EI. A member of the Hamilton association said that every one of her nine children had experienced religious conversion early; she explained that "she began when they were very young to discipline them. She thought children were subject to it at a much earlier age than we had generally any idea—she believed that it could be done at the expiration of one month after their birth—She also subjected them to habits of *self-denial* and *self-control* at an early age. And she made it a constant practice to pray with her children." I have no further evidence to corroborate *so* early an imposition of self-denial. But the document strongly suggests a link between mothers' new, evangelically-oriented concentration on child-rearing and the self-repressive "Victorian personality."

probably the earliest to adopt such goals, in 1817. The Boston Female Moral Reform Society and others similarly titled were formed for that purpose in the 1830s. These groups had four main tactics. Two were direct: to reform and resurrect "fallen" women, and to publicize and ostracize men who visited prostitutes. Two were long-term, preventive, moral education measures: to kindle self-respect in women and to bring up both sexes in the next generation to uphold chastity and marital fidelity. Twenty-nine local societies enlisted as auxiliaries when the Boston society became the "New England" Female Moral Reform Society in 1838, and scores more in New England towns affiliated with the New York organization.[43]

Like maternal associations, moral reform societies focused women's energies on the family arena in order to solve social problems. The Boston society's rhetoric breathed fire: "Our mothers, our sisters, our daughters are sacrificed by the thousands every year on the altar of sin, and who are the agents in this work of destruction? Why, our fathers, our brothers, and our sons." But the moral reformers' aim took them outside the family. It also gave them a unique sexual perspective on sin. Since they believed that men practiced licentiousness, and women suffered it, they were sensitive to prevailing sexual injustice. They opposed the double standard of sexual morality as much as they opposed licentiousness, resolving "to make the impure man lose his character as effectually as the impure woman," urging the virtuous to "esteem the licentious man as little as they do the licentious woman," and further insisting

43. The Boston Society for Missionary Purposes, originally a foreign mission group, became interested in a "city mission" to prostitutes in 1817–18 (see *A Brief Account,* and 1825 *Report,* cited in note 16); *Second Annual Report, Third Annual Report of the Boston Female Moral Reform Society;* on the New York Female Moral Reform Society, see Carroll Smith-Rosenberg, "Beauty, The Beast, and the Militant Woman," *AQ* 23 (1971), esp. 575–76, regarding the New England affiliates.

that "this work must begin with the ladies. They are the injured and they must rise and assert their rights."[44]

Although it portrayed women as sacrificial victims to male lust, the language of moral reform evoked women's power; power to avenge, power to control and reform. The visiting committee of the Boston Female Moral Reform Society described the city's prostitutes as "abandoned girls, who having been ruined themselves by the treachery and depravity of man, have sworn to glut their vengeance by dragging to their own depths in guilt and infamy such young men as might otherwise have been the flower and stamina of our country."[45] In moral reform activities women took up (literally with a vengeance) the power that ministers had for decades told them they possessed. Ministers taught that women had beneficial influence on men's habits; hence the moral reformers thought it possible to eliminate male lust, and devised a program to end licentiousness by ostracizing "impure" men. Ministers emphasized that women's power centered in their influence over their children; hence the moral reformers vowed to stop prostitution by rearing self-controlled children. Ministers told women that they had a special obligation to uphold Christianity and oppose sin, and also that women were especially suited to help one another; hence moral reformers believed that their collective opposition to sexual exploitation was valiant Christian service.

In taking up these sexually designated powers and duties moral reformers moved toward asserting women's "rights." They disavowed false delicacy, and urged women to acquaint themselves with human anatomy and physiology in order to understand their sexual nature and instruct their

44. *Second Annual Report; Advocate of Moral Reform,* New York (Sept. 1835), 1:72.
45. *Third Annual Report,* p. 16; cf. the report of the missionary of the Boston Female Society for Missionary Purposes, *A Brief Account,* p. 8.

children scientifically.[46] Their ideology encouraged women's self-esteem, denied female inferiority outright, and disapproved women's subservience to men's whims and wishes. In an address to the society in Worcester, Massachusetts, Mary Ann Brown counseled every young woman to "consider [her]self *inferior by nature to no man,"* and to marry no one but a principled man who would "receive her as *an equal and be willing that she shall stand upon the broad platform of human rights, free and untrammeled, and accountable only to her God."*[47] As far as was possible moral reform societies put into action and ideology the predisposition of evangelical associations to organize women and provoke their gender-group consciousness.

From the simplest prayer group, through "cent" and "mite" societies, education and missionary support groups to maternal and moral reform societies, women's religious voluntary associations had a dual potential: to encourage women's independence and self-definition within a supportive community, or to accommodate them to a limited, clerically defined role. Like women's religious involvement generally, therefore, they had an ambiguous effect on women's autonomy and status. Religious voluntary associations provided women with a community of peers outside the family, without contravening the importance of the family. For those who had to move around the country—more often for their fathers' or husbands' reasons than their own—the personal and national implications of these cooperative endeavors transferred easily. Women softened the shock of displacement and maintained a continuing

46. See *Third Annual Report,* p. 18, which notes approvingly Mary Gove's classes on physiology for women, held in Boston; and *Advocate of Moral Reform* for frequent rejections of false delicacy.

47. Mary Ann B. Brown, *An Address on Moral Reform, Delivered before the Worcester Female Moral Reform Society, Oct. 22, 1839* (n.p., n.d.), p. 14.

sense of belonging to a female Christian community by
finding or re-creating associations like the ones they had
left, as Sarah Connell Ayer did. Such evangelical activity
grouped women with one another, obviously, and put wom-
en's interests and capabilities in a category different
from men's. It reaffirmed members' shared womanhood
while giving each one perspective on her own life. She
could compare her experience with her peers, with the
poor widows or female orphans or the "heathen" whom
they hoped to benefit, or even with the ministers and
young men whom the women's "mites" would educate.
Since it illustrated different kinds and degrees of female
subordination—and disclosed the *social* as well as the "natural" construction of women's roles—that comparison
might lead some women to consider changes in their own
position. Furthermore, in their associations women wrote
and debated and amended constitutions, elected officers,
raised and allotted funds, voted on issues, solicited and
organized new members; in other words, they familiarized
themselves with the processes of representative government in an all-female environment, while they were prevented from it in the male political system.

Did women who contributed their "mites" to missionary
funds mark out new social boundaries for themselves, or
become pawns of manipulative ministers and conservative
laymen? Were women who united for religious self-improvement conforming more than graciously to their prescribed roles? Did anxious mothers in maternal associations forge new social power or resign themselves to the
domestic fireside? Lucy Stone, who became an early and
ardent supporter of the women's rights movement, and refused to have the word *obey* in her marriage contract or
give up her own name for her husband's, quickly rebelled
against the self-sacrifice implicit in women's evangelical
societies. While she was sewing for an education society it

occurred to her "how absurd it was for her to be working to help educate a student who could earn more money toward his own education in a week, by teaching, than she could earn in a month; and she left the shirt unfinished and hoped that no one would ever complete it."[48] Most women, however, did not move on from evangelical societies to advocate equal education, equal pay, and political rights for women.[49] Church-related voluntary associations commanded a much larger membership through the nineteenth century than did the women's rights movement proper. Powerful restraints inhered in the very concerns that brought women into evangelical association: religious conviction and family role. Because they brought women together on the basis of religious and familial definitions, voluntary societies could hinder the prospect of further change, especially if they diverted women from and compensated them for their isolation and subordination, and offered assurances of usefulness and sisterly companionship.

Women's religious associationism cannot be neatly classified either as a protofeminist or, on the contrary, as a crypto-conservative or merely compensatory phenomenon. It preserved conventional appearances but gave them a new direction. Evangelical activity fostered women's emergence as social actors whose roles were based on female responsibilities rather than on human rights. While evoking women's group-consciousness and sense of sex-identified social

48. Quoted from Alice Stone Blackwell, *Lucy Stone* (Boston: Little Brown, 1930), p. 20, in Eleanor Flexner, *Century of Struggle* (New York: Atheneum, 1970), p. 34. Lucy Stone's marriage protest, signed by herself and her husband, is reprinted in Aileen S. Kraditor, ed., *Up from the Pedestal* (Chicago: Quadrangle Books, 1970), pp. 149-50.

49. Keith Melder's article "'Ladies Bountiful'," while generally helpful, portrays the women's benevolent associations as predecessors of the women's rights movement without discerning their more complex and ambiguous overall impact.

purpose—both of which were requisite before any woman would perceive her sex-oppression—evangelical association-ism directly served to elucidate the doctrine of woman's sphere, a "different but equal" doctrine.

Ministers' addresses to women turned in the same direction. Positive appeals to women to contribute to society with benevolent works, pious influence, and child nurture dominated ministers' attitudes from 1790 to 1820, but in the next decades their sermons more often sprang from negative tenets, such as Gardiner Spring's of 1825 that "there are spheres for which a female is not fitted, and from which the God of nature has proscribed her."[50] Of course even their calls for women's social participation had implied this kind of constraint, for ministers defined women primarily as members of families and then, secondarily, as individuals in society. Women's contribution through domesticity was not a possible or preferred option but the only permissible role. Even ministers' promises of women's social power contained implicit threats about their limitations.

Between 1790 and 1820, however, ministers had seemed more interested in the promise. Their only explicit prohibitions pertained to clerical prerogatives. The Reverend Walter Harris, a Congregationalist of New Hampshire, explained in 1814 that women could considerably assist and advance the preaching of the Gospel, but "God has made known, that it is his will that females should not be public teachers of religion, nor take an active part in the government of his church on earth." As Methodist evangelists adopted the unorthodox tactic of encouraging women to pray aloud in public, ministers of opposing denominations strengthened their prohibition against women's preaching. George

50. Gardiner Spring, *The Excellence and Influence of the Female Character; Preached at the Request of the N.Y. Female Missionary Society* (2d ed., New York, 1825), p. 3. Spring was a conservative Presbyterian.

Keely, a Baptist, protested in 1819, "that woman appears to me lost to modesty and prudence, who has boldness enough to teach or exhort where men are present. If she were a relative of mine, I should request her to change her name and remove to a distance where her connections were not known."[51]

These strictures forboded a hardening of boundaries in ministers' appraisal of the social role of women. Without abandoning their earlier estimate of woman's influence, ministers clarified its limitations. Rather than the book of Proverbs, they chose texts from Titus and Paul, requiring women to be "keepers at home," and "silent in the churches." The Reverend Joseph Richardson of Hingham, Massachusetts, interpreted the text of Titus for the women there in 1832, advising them, "the world concedes to you the honor of exerting an influence, all but divine; but an influence you lose the power to exert, the moment you depart from the sphere and delicacy of your proper character."[52]

Ministers used the concept of "woman's sphere" to esteem female importance while containing it. In their sermons of the 1830s the theme of order in family and society took precedence, vividly emphasizing the necessity for women to be subordinate to and dependent on their husbands.[53] Clergymen focused on woman's place their own

51. Walter Harris, *A Discourse to the Members of the Female Cent Society in Bedford, New Hampshire, July 18, 1814* (Concord, 1814), p. 10; George Keely, *The Nature and Order of a Gospel Church . . .* (Haverhill, Mass., 1819), p. 24. On Methodist practices, see note 12, above.

52. Joseph Richardson, *A Sermon on the Duty and Dignity of Woman Delivered April 22, 1832* (Hingham, Mass., 1833), p. 15. Cf. Samuel P. Williams (a Presbyterian), in *Plea for the Orphan* (Newburyport, 1822), p. 3: "Christianity, alone, has marked with precision, the official boundaries between the two great divisions of mankind; clearly defined the duties of their several relations, and wisely assigned the stations which they may occupy with appropriate dignity."

53. For an extended view of women as dependent, see "Claims of Christianity on Females," *Universalist and Ladies' Repository* 2 (1834):309, 325, 340, 356, 388, 396. The magazine was conducted by Universalist ministers.

alarm at changing social patterns. The widespread tendency toward erosion of accustomed authority and deference made the fulfillment of women's promised social importance problematic. Ministers warned that women who betrayed their subordinate place in the family would destroy themselves. Inverting their reasoning about Christianity's special benefit to women, they threatened that women would suffer more than men if the Christian social order dissolved. Should "the wife who possesses a mind of superior cultivation and power to her husbands . . . be in subjection to his authority?" asked Richardson, and answered, "yes, because this is conformable to the general order God has established. Many private citizens may possess minds of powers and gifts superior to those of rulers and magistrates, to whose authority it is their duty to submit. Subordination to principles and laws of order is absolutely essential to the existence of the social state. Break up the order of the social state and woman must become the most abject and helpless of all slaves."[54]

Evangelical religion thus imparted a twofold message and possibility to women in these years, especially since its clerical guides needed both to elevate women as religion's supporters and yet (in order to sustain social stability, as they saw it) to reaffirm women's subordination to men. In most ministers' interpretation evangelical Christianity confined women to pious self-expression, sex-specific duties, and subjection to men. But by promoting women in activities deemed appropriate for their sex and "sphere" evangelical religion nourished the formation of a female community that served them as both a resource and a resort outside the family. And it endowed women with vital identity and purpose that could be confirmed among their peers.

54. Richardson, *A Sermon*, p. 13.

5

SISTERHOOD

Friendships between women have existed in all ages and cultures. But the diaries and correspondence of New England women suggest that from the late eighteenth through the mid-nineteenth century they invented a newly self-conscious and idealized concept of female friendship. This ideal became a subject of their conversation, reading, reflection, and writing. And in individual relationships women put their new perceptions into effect, making palpable the bonds of womanhood.

More compassion dwelled "within the soul of Woman" than in the soul of man, assumed the clergymen who urged women into Christian benevolence. In fact, a unified set of assumptions about women's qualities of "heart" structured all their exhortations regarding women's religious duties. Unitarian Joseph Buckminster used the most succinct phrasing when he said the female sex was "accustomed to feel, oftener than to reason." Others used more elaborate language. The rector of Boston's Episcopalian Trinity Church praised women for possessing "all the milder virtues of humanity," "those endearing sympathies," "a more exquisite sensibility than men." "The God of heaven has more exquisitively [*sic*] attuned their souls to love, to sympathy and compassion," said the Reverend Daniel Dana of Newburyport.[1]

1. Joseph Buckminster, "A Sermon Preached before the Members of the

In identifying women with "the heart" New England ministers followed the emphasis that had been devised during the eighteenth century, when traditional beliefs in many categories of thought were under attack. The placement of new authority in Nature and Reason engendered a kind of pseudo-scientific cataloguing of differences between the sexes. Rather than alter their belief in the subordination of women, "enlightened" thinkers altered, refined (even amplified) their reasons for it, discovering "natural" and "rational" explanations in place of solely God-given ones. "Deference and submission" was woman's part, declared a mid-eighteenth century American commentary on marriage, because of the "superior Degree of Knowledge and Understanding in the Man." The anonymous author claimed, without need to refer to divine command, that "REALLY *Nature* and the circumstances of human life, seem to design for Man that Superiority, and to invest him with a directing Power in the more difficult and important Affairs of Life."[2] American writers followed the British in converting cultural artifacts into nature's determinants, composing a litany, much-chanted, of the two sexes' qualifications: men were superior in strength and in all of the rational capacities (discernment, judgment, etc.) but women surpassed them in sensibility, grace, tenderness, imagination, compliance—the qualities of "the heart." In a Boston magazine of 1784 an essayist typically described "matrimonial felicity" as the union of complementary souls:

Boston Female Asylum, Sept. 1810," hand-copied and bound with other printed sermons to the BFA, p. 8, BPL; Samuel Parker, *Charity to Children, Enforced in a Discourse delivered . . . before the Subscribers to the Boston Female Asylum* (Boston, 1803), p. 10; Daniel Dana, *A Discourse Delivered . . . before the members of the Female Charitable Society of Newburyport* (Newburyport, 1804), p. 16.

2. [Mistakenly attributed to Benjamin Franklin], *Reflections on Courtship and Marriage* (Philadelphia, 1746), p. 31.

"the man all truth, the woman all tenderness; he possessed of cheerful solidity, she of rational gaiety; acknowledging his superior judgment she complies with all his reasonable desires, whilst he, charmed with such repeated instances of superior love, endeavors to suit his requests to her inclinations." These sex-role distinctions were universally employed in the literate Anglo-American world by the late eighteenth century.[3]

In pleas to improve women's lot as well as in rationalization of their subordinate status, the conventional distinctions held. Concluding her now-famous exchange with her husband about women's rights in the "new code of laws" of 1776, Abigail Adams disarmingly warned him, "we [women] have it in our power not only to free ourselves but to subdue our Masters. . . . 'Charm by accepting, by

3. *Gentleman's and Lady's Town and Country Magazine* 1 (Sept. 1784): 194. Dr. John Gregory's *A Father's Legacy to His Daughters,* originally published in London in 1774 but quickly, and repeatedly, republished in America, was significant in establishing the contrast between the "hard and masculine spirit" and feminine "softness and sensibility of heart" (p. 20 in edition of London, 1822). The Reverend James Fordyce's *Sermons to Young Women,* first published in England in 1765, and also widely reprinted on this side of the Atlantic, forcefully advised "those masculine women" who wished to participate in politics, commerce, abstract intellectual pursuits, or exercises of strength, to learn that woman's true "empire" had "the heart for its object," and was "secured by meekness and modesty, by soft attraction and virtuous love" (p. 61 in edition of Philadelphia, 1787). Cf. also the suggestion in a woman's letter to the editor of the Boston magazine above, that the two sexes could use their differing strengths to serve one another, "the men elevating our thoughts, and striving to improve our natural geniuses, which are generally too much curbed in education: while we, by a softness natural to us, should smooth the harshness of their tempers, and alleviate all their misfortunes." "Lucia," *Gentleman's and Lady's Town and Country Magazine* 1 (May 1784); 13. On the consistent employment of sex-role distinctions in eighteenth-century British and America writings, see Mary S. Benson, *Women in Eighteenth-Century America* (New York: Columbia University Press, 1935), pp. 37–39. Frank Luther Mott, in *A History of America Magazines,1741–1785* (Cambridge: Harvard University Press, 1957), pp. 64–65, remarks that essays and poems entitled "Counsel upon Female Virtues" and "Advice to the Fair" became "sickeningly frequent" during the last quarter of the eighteenth century.

submitting sway. . . . ' " Eliza Southgate, even while arguing
for more serious female education, assumed that sprightli-
ness, imagination, and pliability were the characteristics
of women's minds, profundity and astuteness the characteristics of men's. An "aged matron" who authored a feminist tract in New Haven, Connecticut, in 1801 did not
hesitate to declare that women transcended men in the
capacities of tenderness, morality, consideration for
others, and willingness to forgive.[4]

Literature of the period gave unprecedented attention to
sensibility and "improvement of the heart." Frank L.
Mott quotes from the *Christian's, Scholar's and Farmer's
Magazine* of 1789 a view representative of American magazine literature: "Everyone boasts of having a heart tender
and delicate, and even those who know themselves deficient
therein, endeavor to persuade others that they possess
these qualities." This valuation of the heart at once seemed
to raise esteem of women and to justify no change in their
assigned role. Excellence in "heart" was their essential
and their sufficient endowment. Another magazine con-
tributor acclaimed women for possessing "all the virtues
that are founded in the sensibility of the heart. . . . Pity,
the attribute of angels, and friendship, the balm of life,
delight to dwell in the female breast. What a forlorn, what
a savage creature would man be without the meliorating
offices of the gentle sex!"[5]

Prescriptions of women's duties and promises of praise
for them, both religious and secular, identified women

4. Abigail Adams to John Adams, May 7, 1776, in Charles Francis Adams,
ed., *Familiar Letters of John Adams and his Wife Abigail Adams, During the
Revolution* (New York, 1876), p. 169; Eliza Southgate to Moses Porter, June
1801, quoted in Nancy F. Cott, ed., *Root of Bitterness: Documents of the
Social History of American Women* (New York: Dutton, 1972), p. 106; *The
Female Advocate,* Written by a Lady (New Haven, 1801), pp. 14-17.

5. Mott, *History of American Magazines,* pp. 42-43; and p. 141, quoting
from "The Female Sex," *Literary Magazine* 15 (Jan. 1805).

with qualities of heart. There are occasional explicit references to the reign of this attitude in parents' upbringing of daughters, as well. Mary Lee, in a letter to her sister about the latter's children, distinguished the sons' need for book-learning from a daughter's different requirements: "you wish her heart to be more richly cultivated than the head, and this cannot be under any one's tuition so well as yours. A mother alone can do this, I believe." A wealthy Maine lawyer had clear preferences for his teenaged daughter's education in 1801: "She has enough [intellect], and too much to make her exactly what I wish her to be. I mean only that her thurst [sic] for reading, will probably obstruct the attainment of those amiable, condescending, and endearing manners, without which a woman is, in my estimation, but a poor piece of furniture." Eulogies of women unfailingly focused on their hearts, regardless of their other substantial achievements. An obituary notice for historian and religious controversialist Hannah Adams declared, "Indeed, literary claims are perhaps among the last that . . . present themselves to the minds of her friends. The virtues and excellences of her character, her blameless life, her sensibility, the warmth of her affections, her sincerity and candor, call forth a flow of feeling that cannot be restrained."[6]

The heart's ruling purpose was to express affections, sympathies, consideration and tenderness toward others —in short, to love. Sarah Connell, at eighteen, believed she understood her own character when she confided to her diary, "To love, is necessary to my very existence." The

6. Mary Jackson Lee to Hannah Jackson Lowell, Feb. 27, 1811, in Frances Rollins Morse, ed., *Henry and Mary Lee: Letters and Journals* (Boston: T. Todd, 1926), p. 100; Daniel Davis to James Freeman, Portland, April 18, 1801, in Katherine Minot Channing, ed., *Minot Family Letters 1773–1871* (Shelborn, Mass., privately printed, 1957), p. 97–98; *Memoir of Miss Hannah Adams, written by Herself, with additional notices, by a friend* (Boston: Gray and Bowen, 1832), p. 106. See also chapter 2, note 15.

identification of woman with the heart meant that she was defined *in relation to* other persons. "A true woman's heart never grows cold," wrote the female author of *Girlhood and Womanhood,* "even the most isolated of my sex will ever find some object, upon which her affections will expend themselves." Women's appropriate motivation was "affiliation" rather than "achievement" (to borrow psychologist David McClelland's terms); their cardinal goal was to establish positive affective relationships.[7] Didactic works on sex-roles and marriage from the late eighteenth through the nineteenth century named a woman's "stations" in life according to her personal relationships as daughter, sister, loved one, wife, and mother, not in terms of her discrete individual status or aims. An 1837 discussion of woman's character and influence on man furnished baroque detail, evidence of the intensification of rhetoric on the subject at the time:

> As a sister, she soothes the troubled heart, chastens and tempers the wild daring of the hurt mind restless with disappointed pride or fired with ambition. As a mistress, she inspires the nobler sentiment of purer love, and the sober purpose of conquering himself for virtue's sake. As a wife, she consoles him in grief, animates him with hope in despair, restrains him in prosperity, cheers him in poverty and trouble, swells the pulsations of his throbbing breast that beats for honorable distinction, and rewards his toils with the undivided homage of a grateful heart. In the important and endearing character of mother, she watches

7. *Diary of Sarah Connell Ayer,* pp. 92-93 (1809); Mrs. A.J. Graves (pseud.), *Girlhood and Womanhood: or, Sketches of my Schoolmates* (Boston, 1844), p. 210. On achievement and affiliation motivation see David McClelland, ed., *Studies in Motivation* (New York: Appleton-Century-Crofts, 1955), and Richard de Charms and Gerald H. Moeller, "Values Expressed in Children's Readers, 1800-1950," *Journal of Abnormal and Social Psychology* 64 (1962): 136-42.

and directs the various impulses of unfledged genius, instills into the tender and susceptible mind the quickening seeds of virtue, fits us to brave dangers in time of peril, and consecrates to truth and virtue the best affections of our nature.[8]

When they privately assessed their own characters, women used the same standard. "My happiness consists in feeling that I deserve the love of my friends," Sarah Connell went on in her diary, "in studying to make their life pass pleasantly, and in cherishing their esteem. I could not exist in a state of indifference. Nature never formed me for it." Nancy Hyde hoped that the students whom she taught in a female academy in Connecticut would be admired for "the excellent qualities of their hearts, and . . . for diffusing around them that happiness, which is the inseparable concomitant of virtue," as well as for their literary accomplishments. Catherine Sedgwick affirmed, even after she achieved fame as a novelist, that her true happiness derived "from the dearest relations of life," and that her "author existence" was "accidental, extraneous & independent of my inner self." Another woman whose literary aims were not so well rewarded as Sedgwick's consoled herself with the thought that "the heart, that is formed for friendship and affection, is in itself an inexhaustible storehouse of happiness, and the true secret of being happy is to love as many of human kind as possible."[9]

In truth, the identification of women with "the heart" was a gloss on the inequality of the sexes. The need for

8. *The Discussion: or the Character, Education, Prerogatives, and Moral Influence of Woman* (Boston, 1837), p. 90.

9. *Diary of Sarah Connell Ayer*, June 17, 1809, p. 103; *The Writings of Nancy Maria Hyde of Norwich, Conn.* (Norwich, 1816), pp. 150-51; diary of Catherine Maria Sedgwick, Dec. 17, 1835, Sedgwick Collection, MHS; Luella Case to Sarah Edgarton, Oct. 18, 1839, Hooker Collection, SL.

and inspiration of affiliative motives in women derived from their dependent status. "A woman of fine feelings cannot be insensible that *her constitutional condition is secondary and dependent among men,*" said the Reverend Amos Chase of Litchfield, Connecticut, in 1791, "nor can she long want conviction that the sure way to avoid any evil consequence . . . is to yield the front of battle to a hardier sex." If women were considered dependent on others (men) for protection and support, self-preservation itself demanded skill in personal relationships. Rousseau's portrayal in *Emile* (1762) was the most unequivocal and influential formulation of this reasoning in the eighteenth century: "Woman, weak as she is . . . perceives and judges the forces at her disposal to supplement her weakness, and those forces are the passions of man. Her own mechanism is more powerful than ours; she has many levers which may set the human heart in motion. She must find a way to make us desire what she cannot achieve unaided . . . without seeming to have any such purpose." Although a feminist such as Mary Wollstonecraft rejected Rousseau's formulation, and other Anglo-Americans—especially Evangelicals, who wished to efface the erotic content of women's influence over men—diluted it, his central meaning resonated through the decades as a description of women's social options and a prescription for their behavior.[10] To identify women with the heart was to imply that they conducted themselves through

10. Amos Chase, *On Female Excellence, or a Discourse in which Good Character in Women is Described* (Litchfield, Conn., 1792), p. 12; Jean-Jacques Rousseau, *Emile,* trans. Barbara Foxley (London: J. M. Dent, 1974; orig. 1762), p. 350. For Mary Wollstonecraft's opinions see *A Vindication of the Rights of Women,* ed. Charles W. Hagelman, Jr. (New York: Norton, 1967; orig. 1792), pp. 76-77, 88, 128-129; and on the Evangelicals' de-eroticizing of women's influence over men, Nancy F. Cott, "In the Bonds of Womanhood: Perspectives on Female Experience and Consciousness in New England, 1780-1830," (Ph.D. diss., Brandeis University, 1974), pp. 230-42.

life by engaging the affections of others. The cultural metonymy by which the nurturant maternal role stood for the whole of woman's experience further confirmed that "heartfelt" caring was woman's characteristic virtue.

Although it was intended to stress the complementary nature of the two sexes while keeping women subordinate, the identification of women with the heart also implied that they would find truly reciprocal interpersonal relationships only with other women. They would find answering sensibilities only among their own sex. The sex-role division of the eighteenth century impelled women toward friendship and sisterhood with one another for two corollary reasons. Women characterized by "heart" presumably would seek equivalent sympathies in their friends. And just as women were viewed as inferior to men in rationality, men could not be expected to respond in kind to women's feelings. "Who but a woman can know the heart of a woman?" Daniel Dana put the question in 1804.[11] In their actual friendships women answered him: no one.

One of the few times Esther Edwards Burr, daughter and wife of clergymen, lost her temper so far as to argue with a young minister, was in response to his scorn of women's capacity for friendship. She had a "smart combat" with Mr. Ewing, a tutor at the College of New Jersey, of which Aaron Burr was president, in April 1757. Ewing had criticized a woman friend of hers for being "full of talk about Friendship & Society & Such Stuff" and declared that women should talk about "things that they understood, he did not think women knew what Friendship was, they were hardly capable of anything so cool and rational as friendship." This outraged Esther Burr.

11. Dana, *A Discourse Delivered,* p. 18.

Although she had previously admired Ewing, she "retorted Several Severe things upon him before he had time to Speak again" and in an hour of dispute "talked him quite Silent."[12]

Esther Burr had good reason to defend the concept and reality of female friendship. The document that records her argument with Ewing was a letter in journal format to the "Fidelia" she loved, Sarah Prince, who lived in Boston. The two friends had begun to write journals for one another when Esther moved with her husband Aaron Burr from New England to New Jersey. Both women had grown up in large, patriarchal, ministers' families with numerous siblings and relatives. Both married, apparently happily. Yet as Burr's letter-journal reveals, the two considered their ties of friendship as important as, if not more important than, their other ties. "I esteem you one of the best, and in Some respects nerer [*sic*] than any Sister I have," wrote Burr. "I have not one sister I can write so freely to as to you the sister of my heart."[13]

Burr's relationship with Sarah Prince and her views of the friendship possible between women were symbiotic and mutually intensifying, and compelled her to differ with

12. Journal of Esther Edwards Burr, April 12, 1757, Beinecke Rare Book Library, Yale University. Esther Burr was a daughter of the Reverend Jonathan Edwards of Northampton. I am grateful to Laurie Crumpacker for allowing me to use the typescript of the journal that she and Carol Karlsen, a graduate student of Yale University, had prepared. See also Laurie Crumpacker, "The Journal of Esther Burr addressed to Miss Prince of Boston" (Ph.D. diss., Boston University, 1976).

13. Esther Edwards Burr journal, Oct. 11, 1754; see also April 22, 1756, and passim. In "Two 'Kindred Spirits': Sorority and Family in New England, 1839-1845," *New England Quarterly* 36 (1963): 23-41, a pioneer recognition of the importance of female friendships in nineteenth-century society, Christopher Lasch and William R. Taylor argued, with emphasis that now seems mistaken, that a "sisterhood of sensibility" arose because of the decline of the large patriarchal family, an increase in geographical mobility, and the desire of women to affirm that they were purer than men.

Ewing. She often dwelled on the theme of friendship in her letter-journal, alluding to the ideal while savoring her real (though long-distance) feeling for her "Fidelia." The sending and receipt of journals, together with her faith in the friendship, steadied her in difficult and lonely circumstances. The ties of friendship were sacred, Esther Burr believed, and "the spirit of, & relish for, true friendship" were "God-like." "When I speak of the *world,* & the things that are in the World, I don't mean friends," she wrote, "for *friendship* does not belong to the *world, true friendship* is first inkindled by a Spark from Heaven."[14]

The Edwardsean canon of the religious affections supplied Esther Burr with language in which to express her feelings for Sarah Prince. "Heart," "soul," and "spirit" were involved in what she saw as true friendship. When Jonathan Edwards had revivified Puritanism as a "religion of the heart," he made the religious experience of woman (his wife, Sarah Pierrepont Edwards) the prototype for all conversion.[15] The New Light of the 1740s fostered female religious friendships, by illuminating the "heart," at the same time that it induced men to approve and share similar religious affections.

Another enduring eighteenth-century friendship, between Susanna Anthony and Sarah Osborn of Newport, Rhode Island, also illustrates that trend. Both of these women were deeply affected by the revival preaching of the 1740s Awakening, and both subsequently became celebrated for

14. Esther Edwards Burr journal, Jan. 23, 1756, Feb. 15, 1755.

15. See Jonathan Edwards, "Some Thoughts Concerning the Present Revival of Religion in New England," in *The Works of Jonathan Edwards,* Vol. 4, *The Great Awakening,* ed. Clarence C. Goen (New Haven: Yale University Press, 1972), esp. part 1, section 5. I am sincerely indebted to Laurie Crumpacker (see note 12) for a dialogue that has enriched my knowledge of the Edwards family, Jonathan Edwards's conception of the religious affections, and the connection of the latter with sisterhood in the eighteenth century.

piety. They joined in a friendship and correspondence that lasted for four decades. Susanna Anthony's words suggest the quality of their attachment: "Into your breast, I have often poured out the joys and sorrows of my soul; and as often found compassion, tenderness, and sympathy there. . . . O, my dear, my bosom-friend, I feel my love to you to be without dissimulation, therefore wish you the same strength and consolation, with my own soul."[16] Such feelings doubly contradicted the line of argument that tutor Ewing took against Esther Burr, that women were not capable of anything so "cool and rational" as friendship. Friendship in the cause of Christ was not restricted to the cool and rational but encompassed the religious affections, and for women to exercise these affections was wholly "in character." (Ewing held a minority view in the dispute, in fact; the other gentleman present sided with Esther Burr.)

The eighteenth-century emphasis on the religious affections even created new possibilities for women's religious leadership. Sarah Osborn, who began in the 1740s to guide a group of young women in prayer, by the 1760s led scores of "hopeful converts" of many ages, two races, and both sexes in devotions at her home in Newport. The effect of the religion of the heart on personal relations was not limited to women, of course. If Sarah Osborn's friendship with Susanna Anthony stemmed from their religious feelings—Anthony hoped that their "highest ambition" would be "to join hand in hand, to promote the cause and interest of our infinitely worthy Redeemer"—so too did Osborn's friendship with the Reverend Joseph

16. *Familiar Letters written by Mrs. Sarah Osborn and Miss Susanna Anthony* (Newport, R.I.: Mercury Office, 1807), pp. 27, 60. See Samuel Hopkins, ed., *Memoirs of the Life of Mrs. Sarah Osborn* (Worcester, Mass., 1799), and Hopkins, ed., *The Life and Character of Miss Susanna Anthony . . . consisting chiefly in extracts from her writings* (2d ed., Portland, Me., 1810).

Fish, a mentor of hers, or *Aaron* Burr's friendship with
Sarah Prince.[17] Both men and women with religious aims
wished to be "tender-hearted." Both men and women used
the same language in recounting their religious experiences
in the first Great Awakening; the sex of the writer is not
apparent in printed narratives of conversions.[18]

The religion of the heart contributed a language appropriate to, and an ideal of, female friendship, but alone it
did not create "sisters of the heart." The sisterhood between Esther Burr and Sarah Prince, certainly, also drew
on their concerns for sexual and individual defense and
integrity. Burr once had to resist her temptation to confide
in a mutual friend about the journal-letter correspondence
because, she wrote, "I was affraid[*sic*] she would tell her
Man of it, & *he* knows so much better about matters than
She that he would Sertainly make some Ill-natured remarks
or other, & So these *Hes* [*sic*] shall know nothing about
our affairs *untill they are grown as wise as you & I are.*"[19]
Her account disclosed certain of her assumptions (confirmed elsewhere in the journal) respecting the marital relationship, friendship between women, and the relative virtues of
the two. Esther Burr trusted, dearly loved, and revered her
husband. She expected a husband and wife to sustain the
"nearest and dearest Relation." Yet she also recognized
that a husband was the "head & Governor" of his wife.
This closest of relations between a man and a woman made
the woman subordinate. Without Ewing's contribution,
Esther Burr knew that men generally slighted women's

17. *Familiar Letters,* p. 60. See also Mary Beth Norton, "'My Resting Reap-
ing Times': Sarah Osborn's Defense of Her "Unfeminine" Activities, 1767,"
Signs: A Journal of Women in Culture and Society, forthcoming, 1977.

18. This is one of the conclusions of Barbara Leslie Eaton's comparative
study of the First and the Second Great Awakenings, "Women, Religion and
the Family: Revivalism as an Indicator of Social Change in Early New England,"
(Ph.D. diss., University of California, Berkeley, 1974).

19. Esther Edwards Burr journal, Jan. 15, 1756.

intellects and denied knowledge to them, and that husbands could enforce intolerable demands on their wives— although she exempted Aaron Burr from accusation on these counts.[20] Friendships between women, on the contrary, required no such subordination or disparagement of women's capacities.

Esther Burr's exceptional friendship with her Fidelia struck a keynote for subsequent developments. The culture of sensibility of the late eighteenth century proved fertile for female friendships, allowing, in effect, a secular replacement for the religion of the heart which was most in evidence among young women, especially those who read sentimental literature. When Hannah Adams's father lost his fortune during the Revolutionary war, the daughter consoled herself in a circle of "a few dear friends (for novels had taught me to be very romantic,) who were chiefly in indigent circumstances, and like myself had imbibed a taste for reading. . . . Our mutual love of literature, want of fortune, and indifference to the society of those whose minds were wholly uncultivated, served to cement a union between us." Persons who held and acted upon "the highest ideas of friendship," as Adams saw it, "considered their earthly happiness as dependent upon the life of one beloved object, on whose judgment they relied, and in whom they found comfort and support in every difficulty and affliction. . . ."[21]

The diaries and letters of young women of the late eighteenth century (particularly those of the well-to-do, which are the most accessible documents for that period) record extensive social life in which both sexes shared, but also suggest a pattern of reliance on female friendship for emotional expression and security. While Patty Rogers of

20. Esther Edwards Burr journal, Oct. 21, 1756 (quotation); see also April 15, 1755, Dec. 20, 1755, April 12, 1757.
21. *Memoir of Miss Hannah Adams*, pp. 7, 18.

Exeter, New Hampshire, fluttered with concern over male
suitors, she derived her deepest pleasure from her relation
to a married woman friend. Friendships between Hannah
Emery of Exeter and Mary Carter of Newburyport, and between Susan Kittredge of Andover and Eliza Waite of
Salem, around 1790, showed similar division of feelings.
The friends engaged in gossip about suitors and assemblies,
but made their reciprocal affections, their longings to see
one another, and their feelings of loss at parting their
major themes. Sarah Connell yearned and sighed "for the
presence of *mes chere amies,* Lydia and Emily," when her
family moved from Newburyport to Concord, New Hampshire, in 1809, and she immediately pursued similar attachments. After a social call from two female neighbors, she
fell into a reverie about the younger of them (who seemed
"interesting, sensible, and cheerful"), and imagined how
they would love one another and "ramble" together. Not
long after, she fell "quite in love with" a young married
woman upon their first meeting. Her greatest satisfaction
at this time came from "receiving letters from [her] female friends."[22]

To the point here, in her *Strictures on the Modern System of Female Education* (1799) Hannah More warned
against "imprudent and violent friendships" and elaborate
correspondences between young women, because she felt
that they produced affectation and mutual flattery. In one
aspect, epistolary friendships between young women in
this period simply defined a mode of discourse. Susan Kittredge began one of her letters to Eliza Waite with the

22. Diary of Patty [or Polly] Rogers, 1785, AAS; correspondence between
Hannah Emery (Abbott) and Mary Carter, 1787-91, Cutts Family Manuscripts,
EI; correspondence of Eliza Waite and Susan Kittredge, 1786-91, EI; *Diary of
Sarah Connell Ayer,* pp. 92-93, 114, 122. For other evidence of the social life
of young women in the late eighteenth century, see diary of Jerusha Leonard,
1791-92, HD; and "Diary of Elizabeth Porter Phelps, 1763-1805," ed.
Thomas Eliot Andrews, *NEHGR* 18-22 (1964-68).

hope that her friend would be "prepared with indulgent candour to listen," explaining that "these lines so expressive of my feelings I have borrow'd from a Magazine. I delight to see flow from another pen the sensations I feel but am unable to express." In another aspect, they showed young women's motive to seek true companions among their own sex. "If I might find one real female friend I would be satisfied," was the thought of newly-wed Peggy Dow when she embarked on an ocean voyage with her husband in 1806.[23]

Eunice Callender of Boston carried on a model epistolary friendship with her country cousin, Sally Ripley of Greenfield, at the beginning of the eighteenth century. In youth the two lived at each other's houses on extended visits, during which they spent all their time together, shared confidences, and even carved their names on "two united trees." Callender called her cousin "the dearest Friend of my heart." She prized their correspondence because it allowed her to "breathe forth the sentiments of my soul," she wrote Ripley. "Oh could you see with what rapture . . . all your epistles are open'd by me . . . then would you acknowledge that *my* Friendship at least equals your own, and yours I believe is as true as pure a flame as ever warmed the breast of any human Creature." Callender weighed their own against the abstract possibility of true friendship and found it not wanting; she had "heard of certain people continuing their most fervent affections for each other until the latest hour of their existence, & such I trust will be ours firm & united to the last." In fact, their friendship and correspondence lasted for at least three decades, through Ripley's marriage and widowhood. But, during

23. Hannah More, *Strictures on the Modern System of Female Education* (9th ed., London, 1801), 1:256-57; Susan Kittredge to Betsy Waite, March 24, 1792, EI; Peggy Dow, "Vicissitudes, or the Journey of Life," in Lorenzo Dow, *History of Cosmopolite* (Cincinnati, 1859), p. 613.

young womanhood at least, Ripley found an even more intimate friend in Rachel Willard of Greenfield. These two were childhood playmates, and at school "pursued the same studies & the same recreations." They wrote to each other when they were apart, and "each in the friendly bosom of the other, could repose their secret thoughts, in perfect confidence." Upon Willard's sudden death very shortly after her marriage, in 1808, Ripley appeared inconsolable; she could hardly believe that she would "no more behold her lovd [sic] countenance, meeting with the smile of welcome, no more hear her soft voice . . . speaking from the feelings of her heart; . . . to me her loss seems irreparable, I have not a friend on earth, to who [sic] I could so freely communicate my feelings, at any time."[24] Attesting to the strength of their attachment, Ripley gave the name Rachel Willard to her first child, born in 1813.

Sally Ripley's and Rachel Willard's shared education at Dorchester Female Academy added a dimension to their friendship. Willard had attended first, in the summer of 1803, and in the following summer (when Ripley was nineteen) both of them enrolled. Their experience as well as numerous others' suggests that academies for girls propagated friendships better than almost any other institution. A few days after Ripley arrived at the academy she noted, "A number of the Young Ladies formed themselves into a society to be called 'the Band of Sisters.' . . . We . . . are all to live in perfect harmony & friendship & no young Lady belonging to the Society is to speak unkindly to a Sister." Apparently, both the students' parents and their teachers encouraged the sisterly impulse. The aunt and guardian of orphan Mehitable May Dawes wrote to her at school in

24. Eunice Callender to Sarah Ripley, May 21, 1803, May 26, 1810, Sept. 8, [1808], Oct. 19, 1808, Stearns Collection, SL; diary of Sarah Ripley Stearns, Nov. 12, 1808, Stearns Collection, SL.

1810, when she was fourteen, "be a good girl, and make
the utmost use of this very important period of your life.
. . . Endeavour to make your Self beloved by your young
associates, and be above the little tattle of a boarding
school." Lydia Huntley advised the pupils at her academy
in Hartford in the 1810s to "consider yourselves as a little
band of sisters united for a time in one family with frequent opportunities of retarding or advancing each others
enjoyment." Another headmistress early in the century
tried, as a former student recalled, "to make us feel that
we were a band of sisters, and that in the eye of God we
were all equals."[25]

The philosophy of female education that triumphed by
1820 in New England inclined women to see their destiny
as a shared one and to look to one another for similar sensibilities and moral support. By providing both convenient
circumstances and a justifying ideology, academies pro-
moted sisterhood among women. Even though most individuals spent only a few months at an academy at a time
(perhaps only a few months altogether) the experience attuned them to female friendship with a force out of proportion to its duration. Sally Ripley regretted departing
from Dorchester since she felt "to many of the young
Ladies . . . a degree of attachment which I flatter myself is
reciprocal." Similarly, Mary Endicott of Danvers, Massachusetts, hated to be "parted from my dear associates that
I have daily conversed with" when she ended a term of
school in 1818. "The union which subsisted among us
[school companions] bound our hearts with no feeble

25. Sarah Ripley (Stearns) diary, June 14, 1803, Sept. 19, 1803, May 19,
1804. A. Prescott, Boston, to Mehitable May Dawes, Oct. 7, 1810, May-Goddard Collection, SL; Lydia Huntley, "Letters to the young ladies under her
care, Copied by Frances Ann Brace, August 25, 1814," CHS; Graves, *Girlhood
and Womanhood*, p. 15.

ties," Sophronia Grout also reflected, after a short period of education in 1822. "Never was a separation so painful I think to any of us as at the close of this school."[26]

When academy education was combined with religious revival the impulse toward female friendship was doubly forceful. The letters surviving from a circle of young women who went to an academy in Hartford, Connecticut, together and shared revival experience there around 1812 are revealing. They corresponded for years after they parted— past the time when several of them married—and continued to reiterate their friendship, their nostalgia for the past, their desires to see one another, and their fears of being forgotten. Not long after their separation Rebeccah Root wrote to Weltha Brown about her depression of spirits and her longing to see their common friend Harriet Whiting, adding, "since our first acquaintance I have felt more at liberty in her company could converse with her more freely than with anyone else, here is Mama but I cannot say any thing to her although the best of Mothers, My sisters feel differently from me therefore cannot participate in my feelings. I often think if I could see you or Harriet a few moments I should feel much more contented." If Brown's correspondence slackened, Root became anxious and fearful that she no longer cared. "My heart often sunk [sic] within me," she confessed, "when I reflected on former joys . . . and past scenes in which we had alike engaged, and professions of friendship which each from each received, and the thought unpleasant as it was often intruded, that Weltha had forgotten her friend; . . . but I would drive it from me as injurious to the character of that friend whom I so dearly love." Another one of this circle acknowledged how female revival meetings had cemented

26. Sarah Ripley diary, Sept. 8, 1804; diary of Mary Endicott, March 3, 1818, EI; diary of Sophronia Grout, May 1822, Pocumtuck Valley Memorial Association Library Collections, HD.

their friendships when she wrote to Weltha Brown, after she moved from Hartford, "I regret very much that we do not have conferences oftener here, they serve to keep the affections warm and make us friendly to each other as well as animated in the glorious cause of Christ."[27]

Intense attachments between women were often rooted in shared or similar experiences of conversion to Christianity. More inclusive than the female academy in its social range, the church was even more instrumental, overall, in shaping female friendships. Two young women who had made public professions of faith along with her at the First Church in Boston in 1796 became Abigail Brackett's best friends. "How much more valuable the friendship founded on Religion," the latter mused in 1802, "—hearts seem as it were to incorporate and become one and indivisible—the deciples [sic] of Jesus are engaged in one common cause— have the same enemies to encounter & the same gracious portions to obtain—they feel bound by sacred obligations to seek others good." Similar feelings lay behind Nancy Meriam's confidence to a friend, "you, Irene, well know my heart, to you I have never been afraid to express my sentiments without reserve, and with you have enjoyed many a pleasing hour of reciprocal friendship. I say reciprocal, I believe it so, and that our friendship is built on a sure foundation Jesus Christ himself being the chief cornerstone." Because they had both professed faith, she did not fear that death would part them. Friends could hope that they would one day be united forever in Heaven. Sophronia Grout, a minister's daughter, was saddened to discover that a friend who had "professed to be on the

27. Rebeccah Root to Weltha Brown, Aug. 7, 1815, and 1817 (date uncertain); Almira Eaton, Monson, to Weltha Brown, Hartford, May 7, 1815, Hooker Collection, SL. The Weltha Brown Correspondence in the Hooker Collection includes letters of Almira Eaton, Rebeccah Root (Buell), Eliza Perkins (Gunnell), C. Lloyd, Mary Cogswell, Marcia Hall, and Lucia Hall.

Lords side on the same day" had to move away. "Her heart is united to mine with the strongest ties," she testified, "Many sweet hours have I spent walking the field and viewing the works of the Almighty and conversing upon the best of subjects with my Julia. . . ." She sustained hope that God would allow them to meet "where we never shall again be parted."[28]

During the Second Great Awakening, religious sisterhood was invested with a self-consciousness about gender that had been absent from a friendship of the earlier revival such as Susanna Anthony's with Sarah Osborn. Women and men narrated their conversion experiences in the Second Great Awakening in two different "dialects," in contrast to the case a century earlier, when converts' language was indistinguishable by sex.[29] Because of the sex-segregated forms it took, the religious activism of the revivals accentuated women's consciousness of sexual differentiation and of their own sisterhood. Another case in point occurred in the Female Temperance Society of West Bradford, Massachusetts. It was founded by fifteen women who had organized in 1825 for religious self-improvement but then transformed their group into a teetotalers society, with a pledge to abstain from alcohol and not to serve it to guests. They gained adherents during the next five years as they pursued the twofold aim of abstinence and religious conversion among their number. Rather than attempting to reduce intemperance in general, they focused on eliminating *women's* drinking. They took the direct step of

28. Journal of Abigail Brackett Lyman, Oct. 13, 1802, in Helen Roelker Kessler, "The Worlds of Abigail Brackett Lyman," (M. A. thesis, Tufts University, 1976), appendix A; see also chap. 1, p. 16, and journal entries of Feb. 3, and 22, March 12 and 30, 1800; Nancy Meriam, Charlton, Mass., to Irene Hartwell, Oxford, Mass., April 16, 1813, Meriam Collection, WHS; diary of Sophronia Grout, June 15, 1816.

29. See Easton, "Women, Religion and the Family," esp. pp. 12-22, 101-02, 164-74.

sending to women who made "too free use" of liquor a
written "remonstrance," which warned of consequences
such as illness, loss of reputation, suicidal passion, or an
eternity in hell, and then appealed on grounds of female
solidarity: "Do regard your reputation, your influence, the
happiness and respectability of your friends—regard the
honor and dignity of the female sex."[30]

If Christian sisterhood promised to confute death, in
eternity, it also intended to cross earthly barriers of wealth
and station. After her conversion Nancy Thompson found
her spirits buoyed up by conversations with the hired girl
in her family, whom she described as her inferior in
"talents, education and circumstances"—"and yet a Christian." Rachel Willard Stearns's religious convictions came
to her aid when she had to earn her living, after her father's death. "I thank the Lord for many things," she
wrote in her diary in 1835, "first that he has humbled my
proud heart, and made me willing to go to Mr Humes, and
sew for a girl who once lived as a maid in my grandfather's
family, she is now a devoted Christian, and I try to be so,
also, and I love her dearly."[31] Ministers stressed, in spon-
soring women's charitable and evangelical organizations,
that since women were united by their "preeminent sus-
ceptibility of heart" and their "correspondent obligations,"
only they could understand adequately and relieve the
needs of members of their sex. "To whom shall the friend-
less orphan girl repair," asked Daniel Dana, "but to one
who knows the feelings, the exigencies, the distresses, the
dangers of the sex, and in whom she may hope to find the
care and sensibilities of a mother indeed?" Middle-class

30. Record Book of the Female Temperance Society, West Bradford, Mass.,
1829-34, EI.
31. "A Short Sketch of the Life of Nancy Thomson [*sic*]," autobiographical
fragment in the diary of Nancy Thompson (Hunt), CHS; diary of Rachel Willard
Stearns, Oct. 19, 1835, Stearns Collection, SL.

and upper-class women's founding of institutions to aid
indigent widows and female orphans involved the idea that
women's shared characteristics—epitomized in "heart"—
belittled the economic differences among them.[32]

Aware of their alliance on the basis of sex, women
friends elicited a new intensity of feeling which, in turn,
shaped their concept of friendship. Eliza Chaplin of Salem
and Laura Lovell of Bridgewater, Massachusetts, shared a
remarkable attachment stretching from 1819, when they
were both single, living with parents and siblings and trying
to earn support by teaching and handiwork, to 1869,
thirty–seven years after Eliza Chaplin's marriage. They
were able to visit each other only infrequently. Chaplin
indicated the significance of their correspondence as she
wrote, in 1820, "when a letter from you was announced,
my dear friend, the letter which I had so long, but vainly
expected, a tremour pervaded my whole frame. Surely,
famishing indigence could scarcely hail food with more
delight. I loosed the seal & read its contents with the same
eagerness that we may suppose such an individual to par-

---

32. Dana, *A Discourse Delivered*, p. 18 (quotations). Ministers supported
these charitable institutions, which were the first to be founded by women,
because they feared that the female sex posed a unique threat, as it promised a
unique benefit, to society. The Reverend Samuel Stillman, in *A Discourse Delivered before the Members of the Boston Female Asylum* (Boston, 1801),
p. 11, approved that institution's aim to house female orphans because "Such
is the delicacy and importance of the female character—such is its influence on
society, that it ought to be removed, especially in early life, as far as possible
from the very appearance of evil." Thaddeus Harris, in *A Discourse, Preached
before the Members of the Boston Female Asylum* (Boston, 1813), p. 9, was
more direct about the threat embodied in female orphans: "there is the utmost reason to apprehend that, instead of being, as their sex should be, the
ornament and charm, they will become the scorn and pest of society." The
female charitable societies' object, to aid widows and female orphans, itself
singled out women from the rest of the population, admitting that women
were less competent in self-help than men (and implying, conversely, that able-
bodied men who did not succeed at self-help did not deserve any particular
sympathy). See Cott, "In the Bonds," pp. 273–80, on these charitable societies.

take of a meal." She claimed that she would "have pined like the lover, doomed to a separation from his mistress" without the letters that filled in between their visits, apologizing half-seriously, "if this is romance, romance imparts the most exquisite delight. And never can I desire to be divested of that which savors so much of heaven."[33]

The subject of friendship occupied much of their letters. "Your observation respecting disinterested friendship is certainly very just—" Eliza Chaplin wrote, "my heart fully subscribes to it—for I have met but with a few instances to which I could apply so sacred a name. It cannot be given to those vague unions which are formed only [to] pass away a tedious hour—for in such connexions the sentiments of the heart have no share." Their own friendship was founded on "reciprocal views and feelings." Every one of Laura Lovell's sentiments "[met] with a respond in my heart," Chaplin said. For the mutuality of their views their

33. Eliza Chaplin (Nelson), Salem, to Laura Lovell, Bridgewater, Mass., July 27, 1820, June 24, 1821, EI.

In her path-breaking article, "The Female World of Love and Ritual: Relations between Women in Nineteenth-Century America," *Signs: A Journal of Women in Culture and Society* 1 (1975):1-29, Carroll Smith-Rosenberg has dealt explicitly with what appears, to twentieth-century minds, to be the paradox of these nineteenth-century friendships, that they were "both sensual and platonic" (p. 4). She argues persuasively that "the twentieth-century tendency to view human love and sexuality within a dichotomized universe of deviance and normality, genitality and platonic love, is alien to the emotions and attitudes of the nineteenth century and fundamentally distorts the nature of these women's emotional interaction" (p. 8), and proposes that in order to fathom nineteenth-century society we must "view sexual and emotional impulses as part of a continuum or spectrum of affect gradations strongly effected [*sic*] by cultural norms and arrangements, a continuum influenced in part by observed and thus learned behavior" (pp. 28-29). Her perspective is crucial to the understanding of nineteenth-century women's history. I regard the nature and meaning of female friendships as changing rather than stable from the mid-eighteenth through the nineteenth century, however, as I question the "middle-class" basis of her eighteenth-century sources and differ from her assessment of how "generic and unself-conscious" (p. 9), and how far rooted in mother-daughter rather than in peer relationships, such friendships continued to be.

sex was an implicitly necessary basis, though not a sufficient one. Chaplin often compared Lovell to other women
in order to praise her. But their friendship was strongly
shaped by preconceptions such as Chaplin revealed in writing that she had "seldom met with individuals of the
opposite sex, who have appeared feelingly alive to the
beauties of nature." When Lovell wrote about her rejection
of a suitor, Chaplin replied that she, too, had never given
her heart to an "individual of the other sex"; and added,
"*you* my friend possess it—or possess it in common with
my father's family." After a period of neglecting her correspondence, Chaplin assured Lovell that she was "not forgotten by that friend who so long has loved you. . . . I
always love you, Laura. . . . To you I unfold my whole
heart, without apology."[34]

A similar relationship between Luella Case and Sarah
Edgarton in the 1830s and 40s originated in their common Universalist religion and literary ambitions. The religious grounding of their friendship was evident in Sarah
Edgarton's assurance to her friend that "I love you far too
well ever to breathe a word to you that comes not from
the soul," and in her comforting hope that their "earthly
love" would attain permanence when they ascended to the
"heavenly coterie." Luella Case, who was ten years older
and of a "darker" cast of mind, hesitated to affirm the
reality of true friendship. "I have looked upon friendship,
as one of those lovely dreams never meant to be realized
on earth, one of the beautiful impossibilities of life, but to
be known in the world beyond the grave. . . ," she wrote.
"Friendship is something more to be worshipped as an
ideal good, than a real, and possible thing, something that
may be, rather than something *that is.*" Yet she verged on
admitting that the relationship with Sarah Edgarton ful-

34. Eliza Chaplin to Laura Lovell, April 18, 1819, June 24, 1821, March 13,
1828, June 24, 1821, April 17, 1827.

filled her criteria; after discovering a poem that the younger woman had written to her, she replied, "words seem inadequate to express the sense I feel of your—what shall I say, *friendship?* no, I will rather call it affection, for you know I confessed as one of my weaknesses, an inordinate desire *to be loved.*" Although Luella Case was married and worked off and on with her husband (a journalist and publisher), her model for friendship was female. As a visit from Sarah Edgarton ended, she felt "most lonely," having "no gentle voice to talk with, or read to me, no sweet, beaming, countenance to echo the feelings expressed, none of that gentlest of all sympathies, that of a pure, and truehearted female. . . ."[35]

What had appeared in the latter part of the eighteenth century in the romantic effusions of adolescent (and mostly upper-class) girls became, by the early part of the nineteenth century, the common experience of middle-class women, youthful or not. In the vast growth of voluntary associations this emotional phenomenon had an institutional expression. "Heart"-felt friendship between women became a way of life.[36]

The character of women's friendships resulted partially from general cultural valuation of "the heart" and emphasis on women's superiority in sensibility. At the same time, the "introspective revolution" broadened ideas about the

35. Sarah Edgarton to Luella Case, 1838 or 1839, quoted in A. D. Mayo, ed., *Selections from the Writings of Mrs. Sarah C. Edgarton Mayo, with a Memoir* (Boston, 1850), pp. 32–33; Sarah Edgarton to Luella Case, Jan. 8, 1840; Luella Case, Lowell, Mass., to Sarah Edgarton, Shirley, Mass., Oct. 18, 1839; Luella Case to Sarah Edgarton, "Thursday Morning"; Luella Case, Lowell, to Sarah Edgarton, Nov. 30 [before 1842]; all in Hooker Collection, SL. The article by Lasch and Taylor cited in note 13 is based on the Case-Edgarton correspondence.

36. In "The Female World of Love and Ritual" Carroll Smith-Rosenberg describes in detail the way of life founded on female friendships.

purpose and content of friendship.[37] Only when individuals recognized and dwelled on private feelings, and deemed them worthy of communication to others, would one seek an intimate to whom she could "unfold her whole heart." In the religious sphere, revivalism had similar kinds of impact, both actual and rhetorical, because it solicited the religious affections and required the individual to search her heart. Revivalism provided unimpeachable justification and circumstances for mutual outpourings of feeling and also identified the flow of affections with the soul, with Heaven, with nonworldly and "disinterested" temperament: exactly the prerogatives of woman's sphere. Nonevangelical Christians, too, adopted the concept that friendship was sacred and separate from "the world." "If you were not my Sister my dear Frances—your friendship —the friendship of a heart so ardent & warm as yours would amount to more than all the *world* has ever offered to me," Unitarian Catherine Sedgwick wrote in a solacing letter.[38] The very use of the word *friend* altered. In the eighteenth century women often used "my friends" to refer to their kin. As time went on, the verbal distinction between family members and unrelated friends became clearer. Of the members of the family only the husband continued to be called a "friend," the "nearest" or "best" friend, or "friend and companion."[39] Thus language released "friendship" from blood ties so that it existed purely in elective relationships and became subject to idealization.

37. Fred Weinstein and Gerald M. Platt, in *The Wish To Be Free: Society, Psyche, and Value Change* (Berkeley: University of California Press, 1969), use the quoted phrase to characterize what is more typically called Romanticism in the late eighteenth and early nineteenth centuries.

38. Catherine Sedgwick to [her sister] Frances Watson, March 9, 1831, Sedgwick Collection, MHS.

39. The latest usage of "friend" to mean "kin" cited in the *Oxford English Dictionary* is in 1721.

Even more important, female friendships assumed a new value in women's lives in this era because relations between *equals*—"peer relationships"—were superseding *hierarchical* relationships as the desired norms of human interaction. In the seventeenth century an ideal of orderly, reciprocal relations between acknowledged superiors and inferiors had guided politics, vocations, and family roles (though perhaps imperfectly). During the eighteenth century it was increasingly eroded. By the post-Revolutionary years the moral justification behind apprentices' service to masters, the people's deference to governors—even children's obedience to parents—was undermined by newer ideals of individual achievement, equal representation, and popular rights. Both the libertarian rhetoric of the American Revolution and the renewed emphasis on the equality of persons before Christ in the religious revivals hastened this process. Myriad voluntary associations in the young republic reaffirmed the decline of deference and its replacement by an activist conception of a polity of peers.[40]

Women's frequent interest in the ideal of friendship and especially in the mutuality of friends' views was a key indication that the peer relationship had arrived (so to speak)

40. On seventeenth-century norms, see Edmund S. Morgan, *The Puritan Family* (rev. ed., New York: Harper Torchbooks, 1966); for changes during the eighteenth-century, especially the later part, see Daniel Scott Smith, "Parental Power and Marriage Patterns—An Analysis of Historical Trends in Hingham, Massachusetts," *Journal of Marriage and the Family* 35 (1973): 419–28; Daniel Scott Smith and Michael Hindus, "Premarital Pregnancy in America, 1640–1966," *JIH* 6 (1975):537–71; Philip J. Greven, Jr., *Four Generations* (Ithaca: Cornell University Press, 1970); Edward Burrows and Michael Wallace, "The American Revolution: The Ideology and Psychology of National Liberation," *Perspectives in American History* (1972), pp. 167–302; David Hackett Fischer, "America: A Social History, Vol. 1, The Main Lines of the Subject 1650–1975," unpublished MS draft, 1974, chap. 6, pp. 19–28; Richard D. Brown, "Modernization and the Modern Personality in Early America, 1600–1865," *JIH* 2 (1972):201–28, and "The Emergence of Voluntary Associations in Massachusetts, 1760–1830," *Journal of Voluntary Action Research* 2 (1973):64–73.

as a cultural *desideratum*. Women would value peer relationships among their own sex all the more because they
were not regarded as peers of men, despite the gains in
women's education, religious leadership, and family influence. In innumerable small as well as great ways—from
John Adams's compliment to Mrs. Hancock in 1775 that
"in large and mixed company she is totally silent as a lady
ought to be" to the clearly warmer welcome of a boy's
than a girl's birth in the Robert Sedgwick family in the
1820s—it was obvious throughout this period that men and
women were not peers.[41] Amidst the weakening of traditional dependency relationships the only hierarchy vocif-
erously maintained (outside of racism) was women's
subordination to men, or more specifically, wives' subordination to husbands. In traditional society the subordination and dependency of wives had been one instance
of a kind of relationship typical in religious, economic, and
political life; but in the early nineteenth century women's
ascribed "place" was unique. Women therefore sought and
valued peer relationships where they could find them: with
other women.

The conventional sex-role distinctions represented more
powerful, multiple, and overlapping structures in society at
large that encouraged women to view one another as peers
par excellence because of their shared sexual destiny.
While production, exchange, and training for livelihoods
moved out of the household, the persistence of married
women's occupation there, demanded by their obligation
of housekeeping and child care, provided the material basis
for separating the qualities of women *as a sex* from those
of men. If eighteenth-century "rational" analysis and observation of "nature" had exaggerated the contrast and

41. John Adams to Abigail Adams, Nov. 4, 1775, in C. F. Adams, *Familiar
Letters*, p. 121; Elizabeth Ellery Sedgwick, journal of the first years of her
child's life, Jan. 1824 and March 1825, HCL.

complementarity between the sexes, early nineteenth century ideology effectively rooted these differences in the characteristic locations of adult women and men, "home" and "world." Religious and secular rhetoric elevated women's household occupations into a sexual vocation, making their typical work-role into their sex-role. Women practicing the domestic vocation perceived it as an experience that united them with other women. The canon of domesticity made motherhood a social and political role that also defined women as a class, and became the prism through which all expectations of and prescriptions for women were refracted. The mainstream of women's education carried these ideas along. Both ideology and practice in reawakened Protestantism confirmed that women had a discrete social, civil, and religious role owing to susceptibilities and responsibilities dictated by gender. Furthermore, evangelical Christianity's championing of the spirit over the flesh, together with its reliance on a female constituency, insinuated the idea that women's moral nature overcame the physical, freeing them from carnal passion. Though that notion (so central to nineteenth-century sexual ideology) has frequently been interpreted as oppressive to women, it not only implied women's moral superiority but also created proud solidarity among women, and encouraged them to view their own friendships as more honorable than heterosexual relationships because they excluded carnality. "I do not believe that men can ever feel so pure an enthusiasm for women as we can feel for one another," wrote Catherine Sedgwick, transported with delight after meeting Fanny Kemble, "—ours is nearest to the love of angels."[42]

42. Catherine Maria Sedgwick diary, May 16, 1834. Cf. Mary Grew's end-of-the-century vindication of her enduring friendship with Mary Burleigh: "Love is spiritual, only passion is sexual." Mary Grew to Isabel Howland, April 27, 1892, quoted in Carroll Smith-Rosenberg, "The Female World of

A woman discovered among her own sex a world of true peers, in valuing whom she confirmed her own value. In one sense, the female friendships of this period expressed a new individuality on women's part, a willingness and ability to extract themselves from familial definition and to enter into peer relationships as distinct human beings. In another sense, these attachments documented women's construction of a sex-group identity. Women had learned that gender prescribed their talents, needs, outlooks, inclinations; their best chance to escape their stated inferiority in the world of men was on a raft of gender "difference." Female friendships, by upholding such attributes as "heart" as positive qualities, asserted that women were different from but not lesser than—perhaps better than—men.

Women's appreciation of friends of their own sex to whom they could "freely communicate . . . their feelings at any time," or "express . . . their sentiments without reserve," as Sarah Ripley and Nancy Meriam phrased it (and find in return "a sweet, beaming countenance to echo the feelings expressed," in Luella Case's words) reflected the psychological distance placed between the sexes by sex-role typing. Exaggerated sex-role distinctions may have succeeded in making women uncomfortable with men (and vice versa) as often as rendering the two sexes complementary. "I should have been really gratified if a pleasant companion had been with me," wrote a twenty-five-year-old woman patient at a spa, recounting her feelings about dining at a table with forty men, "but as it was I found such beauties in my cup and saucer I look'd at nothing else—how like a fool one acts, and feels, in such a situation, while those high and mighty Lords of the Creation, as they

Love and Ritual," p. 27. I have discussed the development of these ideas in "In the Bonds of Womanhood," pp. 217–64, and "Passionlessness: An Interpretation," unpublished MS.

call themselves, will pick their teeth and stare confidently in your face, fast heeding the confusion it occasions." A stagecoach journey with six men as co-passengers prompted similar feelings from another young woman, who wrote to her mother: "the gentlemen were civil, but I was in no enviable situation. I sat in a corner, seldom unclosing my lips excepting when spoken to and that was an unfrequent occurrence. When silence was interrupted by conversation it was upon subjects that ladies are not often consulted about, such as the presidential election, tariff, canals, slave trade, smuggling, &c &c. Some part of the time I felt somewhat more alone, than if alone."[43]

If women were not consulted about wordly events, neither did many men share the feelings closest to women's hearts. Before Catharine Beecher's career in advancing woman's sphere had yet begun, she appraised men's and women's heartfelt needs differently, in the process of deciding whether or not to marry the scholar seeking her hand. To a good friend she wrote, "The truth is Louisa I feel more & more every day that talents learning & good principals [sic] never could make me happy alone—I shall need a warm & affectionate heart—& whether I can find it in this case I know not . . . I could not dispense with the little attentions & kindnesses that in domestic life constitute a great share of a womans happiness & which a cold hearted man never could bestow—The more I think of it the more I am sure that I ought to guard my heart from the fascination of genius & the flattery of attentions till I am sure that my happiness is not risqued."[44]

43. Diary of Abigail May, 1800, May-Goddard Collection, SL (she undoubtedly meant "a pleasant *female* companion"!); Sarah Bradley to Abigail Bradley, Nov. 7, 1828, Bradley-Hyde Collection, SL. Sarah Bradley was about 29 at the time.

44. Catharine Beecher, New London, Conn., to Louisa [Wait], Litchfield, Beecher-Stowe Collection, SL., n.d. but approximately June 1821, when Beecher was 21.

The feminization of religion presents a case in point. How often did women, sincere believers and evangelical activists, have to lament their husbands' failure to join the church or to conform to religious behavior? In how many marriages did this difference in commitment provoke friction—diminution of respect—or despair? In light of the predominance of women among communicants, many must have prayed as did Mrs. Smith of Woodmont, Connecticut, "that the time is not far distant when I shall see my companion my bosom-friend engaged in the same glorious cause. May he be as a guide and example to me and to his children and as an ornament to the church of Christ." If they professed faith during adolescence women might plan to accept none but a man with the same qualification, but not all could succeed. The many besides who joined the church after marriage often regretted their spouses' skepticism or inattention. Sarah Connell Ayer expressed distress at her husband's continuing neglect of his "immortal peace" after fourteen years of marriage.[45]

The irony of the situation was that without marriage supplying women with home and children, the central prerequisite of their sex-role disappeared. Nineteenth-century women—even birth control reformers deemed extremists—considered the fate and advancement of women conjoined with those of the home and family (and, necessarily, marriage), not opposed to them.[46] Catherine Sedgwick revealed how deep this belief ran in a diary entry written when she was forty-five (in 1830) and already acclaimed as a novelist. Having never married, she relied on her siblings and their children for emotional support, but wished for something more, as she admitted in a somewhat

45. Diary of Mrs. S. Smith, Oct. 28, 1821 or 1823, CSL; *Diary of Sarah Connell Ayer*, Oct. 9, 1825, p. 254.

46. Cf. Linda Gordon, "Voluntary Motherhood: The Beginnings of Feminist Birth Control Ideas in the United States," in Mary Hartman and Lois Banner, eds., *Clio's Consciousness Raised* (New York: Harper Torchbooks, 1973).

depressed mood, "Never perhaps was a condition of inferiority & dependence made by the affection of friends more tolerable than mine—Still I hanker after the independence & interests & power of communication of a home of my own."[47] She associated "inferiority and dependence" with her *single* life, despite her public prestige and commercial success, and assumed that "a home of her own"—that is, implicitly, where she was mistress, wife, and mother—would allow "independence and interests and power of communication," when her novels had given her a vaster, and willing, audience.

Catherine Sedgwick may have been taken in by her own sentimentalization of domesticity. (A stronger personal priority prevented her from actually undergoing the "thralldom" of marriage.) But even aside from the rhetorical inflation of woman's power in the home, there was for most women no appealing alternative to marriage in its economic, sexual, and social aspects. The best chance to have both worlds was to balance marriage with conscious sisterly relations. Wives who had female friends or relatives living with them seemed the most contented of women. When Rebeccah Root wrote to Weltha Brown after her marriage and move to upstate New York, she called her husband a "Christian companion & the most tender affectionate friend," yet added, "but I could not bear to live so far from sisters, and by pleading have succeeded in getting Sister Ann with me, & this adds very much to my happiness." Elizabeth Ellery Sedgwick, whose wife-and-motherhood apparently incarnated the ideal of domesticity, described the winter of 1827-28, "in addition to our other pleasures, sister Catherine passed the winter with us. She is the most delightful companion in the world—and her society the greatest treat, that can be enjoyed—Of course she

47. Catherine Sedgwick diary, Aug. 5, 1830. Her use of "friends" to include kin here shows that the usage disappeared only gradually.

helped to make our domestic circle perfect." Although Luella Case generally balked at her lot during the years of her correspondence with Sarah Edgarton, for the period when she and her husband lived in her sister's household her spirits were "so good," she wrote to Edgarton, "that I cannot by any contrivance of mental incapacity work myself into even a decent fit of the 'blues.'"[48] Women who did not have sisters or peers at home found analogous companionship and support in voluntary associations.[49]

Sisterhood expressed in an affective way the gender identification—the consciousness of "womanhood"—so thickly sown and vigorously cultivated in contemporary social structure and orthodoxy. Women's reliance on each other to confirm their values embodied a new kind of group consciousness, one which could develop into a political consciousness. The "woman question" and the women's rights movement of the nineteenth century were predicated on the appearance of women as a discrete class and on the concomitant group-consciousness of sisterhood. Both the feminists who began to expose and to protest women's oppression in the 1830s and the educators, writers, and social reformers who intended more conservatively to improve women's status took for granted this double-headed assumption. All of them recognized gender as the most important determinant of the shape of their lives. Feminists moved from acknowledging that to sensing the disabilities imposed by gender roles. In the year of the Seneca Falls Convention, for example, Elizabeth Cady Stanton looked toward the achievement of women's rights

48. Rebeccah Root Buell, Geneseo, N.Y., to Weltha Brown, Hartford, June 24, 1822; Elizabeth Ellery Sedgwick, journal of the first years of her child's life ("sister Catherine" was her husband's sister, Catherine Sedgwick); Luella Case, "Westbrook," to Sarah Edgarton, May 17, 1842.

49. Cf. Carroll Smith-Rosenberg's conclusion in "Beauty, the Beast, and the Militant Woman," *AQ* 23 (1971):576–77, that New York moral reform activists of the 1830s sought sisterhood, through their association, in order to combat their experience of isolation and status inferiority in their families.

and declared, "Woman herself must do this work—for woman alone can understand the height, and the depth, the length and the breadth of her own degradation and woe. Man cannot speak for us—because he has been educated to believe that we differ from him so materially, that he cannot judge of our thoughts, feelings and opinions by his own."[50]

If political feminists viewed women's allotment as inequitable and debasing and—perhaps more offensive—imposed on them without their consent, most women were willing to accept a sphere they saw as different but equal. To strengthen women's position within that sphere by reaffirming their powers of moral suasion vis-à-vis men, by improving their educational opportunities, and by enhancing the social role implicit in their child-rearing duties, seemed sufficient reform. The growth of women's schools, publications, and associations during the 1830s showed progress toward these aims. But in the same decade, confrontation with voices of incipient feminism (such as those of antislavery speakers Angelina and Sarah Grimké) clarified the fact that the ideology of woman's sphere had inherently limited utility to reform woman's lot.[51] The doctrine restrained women's initiative because of its central distinction between womanly self-abnegation and manly self-assertion. More potently, since it derived from woman's difference from man, and defined women in specifically sexual rather than human terms, it deprived the sexes of their common ground and opened the door to anti-femi-

50. Speech at Waterloo Convention, Aug. 2, 1848, Stanton Papers, Library of Congress, quoted in Andrew Sinclair, *The Emancipation of the American Woman* (New York: Harper and Row, 1965), p. 257.

51. See, e.g., the negative responses of moral reformers to Sarah Grimké's *Letters on the Equality of the Sexes and the Condition of Women*, discussed in Carroll Smith-Rosenberg, "Beauty, the Beast, and the Militant Woman," pp. 581–83; and the conflict of opinion between Catharine Beecher and Angelina Grimké evident in the former's *Essay on Slavery and Abolition* and the latter's *Letters to Catharine E. Beecher*.

nist and misogynist philosophies. For the duration of the nineteenth century, nonetheless, most women honored their separate sphere, especially when they had sisterhood to secure it. They had little objective reason and still less subjective cause to envision advancement (or even comfort) outside it.

CONCLUSION
On "Woman's Sphere" and Feminism

By 1830 "different" had overwhelmed "inferior" in usage to depict woman's place, budged by the leverage of belief in "woman's sphere." Feminist historians in recent years have sought the meaning of domesticity and "woman's sphere" in successive interpretations, which—running the risk of oversimplifying—I can divide into three. The first to appear in historical writing tended to see women as victims, or prisoners, of an ideology of domesticity that was imposed on them between 1820 and 1850 in order to serve men's view of social utility and order. The second, a refinement and revision, observed that women made use of the ideology of domesticity for their own purposes, to advance their educational opportunities, to gain influence and satisfaction, even to express hostility to men. The third, more literally a re-vision, viewed woman's sphere as the basis for a subculture among women that formed a source of strength and identity and afforded supportive sisterly relations; this view implied that the ideology's tenacity owed as much to women's motives as to the imposition of men's or "society's" wishes. The three interpretations primarily derived from three different kinds of sources: the first from published didactic literature about woman's place and the home, the second from the published writings of women authors, and the third from the private documents of non-famous women. It is worth pointing out that the more historians have relied on women's personal documents the more positively they have evaluated woman's sphere.

The relation between the ideology of woman's sphere

and feminism—or, to put it more broadly, the relation between the former and women's social, educational, political, and legal advancement—has always been of underlying interest. The first interpretation, adopting nineteenth century feminists' emphasis on the "disabilities" of their sex, voiced the constraints of woman's sphere, and drew domesticity and feminism as virtual opposites. The second interpretation turned around to find the roots of feminism, in a shrewdly adapted form, in domesticity itself. The third view bypassed familiar appraisals of women's progress to examine women's discovery and creation of psychic and social resources in their given situations.[1] Having gained

1. I regret that my categorization here underestimates (as must any such division into categories) the subtleties and the distinct contributions of individual historians. The "first" perspective was offered by Barbara Welter, "The Cult of True Womanhood, 1820-1860," *AQ* 18 (1966):151-74; and refined and ramified by Gerda Lerner, "The Lady and the Mill-Girl: Changes in the Status of Women in the Age of Jackson," *Mid-Continent American Studies Journal* 10 (1969):5-15, and Mary P. Ryan, "American Society and the Cult of Domesticity, 1830-1860," (Ph.D. diss., University of California, Santa Barbara, 1971). The "second" was implied in Keith Melder, "Ladies Bountiful: Organized Women's Benevolence in 19th-Century America," *New York History* 48 (1967):231-54 and more explicit in Glenda Riley, "The Subtle Subversion: Change in the Traditionalist Image of the American Woman," *The Historian* 32 (1970):210-27, and Ann Douglas Wood, "Mrs. Sigourney and the Sensibility of Inner Space," *New England Quarterly* 45 (1972): 163-81; it was foreshadowed by an idiosyncratic work of popular literary history, Helen Papashvily's *All the Happy Endings* (New York: Harper Bros., 1956). The "third" has been best presented in Kathryn Kish Sklar, *Catharine Beecher: A Study in American Domesticity* (New Haven: Yale University Press, 1973), the work of Carroll Smith Rosenberg, especially "The Female World of Love and Ritual," *Signs: A Journal of Women in Culture and Society* 1 (1975):1-29, and Johnny Faragher and Christine Stansell, "Women and Their Families on the Overland Trail," *FS* 2 (1975):150-66; Daniel Scott Smith's article "Family Limitation, Sexual Control, and Domestic Feminism in Victorian America," in Mary Hartman and Lois W. Banner, eds., *Clio's Consciousness Raised* (New York: Harper Torchbooks, 1974), is also consonant with this interpretation. Aileen S. Kraditor, in her introduction to *Up from the Pedestal* (Chicago: Quadrangle Books, 1968), which preceded all of these, succinctly identified a link between proponents of woman's sphere and feminism by focusing on the issue of "autonomy."

from these interpretations, I intended this essay to cast another light on the intents and contents and portents of woman's sphere. My first prerequisite was to judge domesticity on its own terms, as of its own time. The intrusion of mid-twentieth-century assumptions entails a particular distortion of this subject because women of the past centuries rarely perceived, as many modern feminists do, an antithesis between women's obligations in the domestic realm and their general progress.

Long before publicists began to harp on woman's "separate sphere," women traditionally conducted their daily business in the household. For several mutually reinforcing reasons, as I have tried to show, that domestic sphere became more conspicuous and more clearly articulated as woman's prerogative at the end of the eighteenth and beginning of the nineteenth centuries. The shift of production and exchange away from the household, and a general tightening of functional "spheres" (specialization) in the economy and society at large, made it seem "separate." But a cultural halo ringing the significance of home and family—doubly brilliant because both religious and secular energies gave rise to it—reconnected woman's "separate" sphere with the well-being of society. Statesmen of the Revolution had said that the republic of the United States would be great or weak as its citizens' characters were so; they believed as John Adams said in 1778, linking the Puritans to the Jacksonians in a chain of sentiment, that "the foundations of national Morality must be laid in private families."[2] This ideology—colored by customary belief in women's domestic influence on men, strengthened by

2. Quoted from John Adams' diary in David Flaherty, "Law and the Enforcement of Morals in Early America," *Perspectives in American History* 5 (1971):247. Gordon Wood effectively presents this aspect of Revolutionary ideology in *The Creation of the American Republic, 1776–1787* (New York: Norton, 1972).

awareness of women's child-rearing obligations and by
faith in the malleability of infant character—hinged the
success of the national experiment on women's success in
their sphere. The clergy, in addition, tended to focus the
general concern for character formation specifically on
women's performance as mothers. To accomplish their
own social aims they solicited women, who comprised the
majority of their congregations, to rear the next generation
in piety. Religious and secular ideology thus made explicit
what had been beneath the surface, for the most part: that
women's domestic influence and maternal duties composed
a positive social role. This was a social role that inherently
justified certain greater opportunities for women—notably
in education—without contradicting their family obligations. Its configuration took shape as early as 1780 and
was well established by 1820.

The doctrine of woman's sphere opened to women (re-
served for them) the avenues of domestic influence, religious morality, and child nurture. It articulated a social
power based on their special female qualities rather than
on general human rights. For women who previously held
no particular avenue of power of their own—no unique
defense of their integrity and dignity—this represented an
advance. Earlier secular and religious norms had assumed
male dominance in home, family, and religion as well as in
the public world. (Husbands' legal authority over their
wives and children, indeed, remained unchallenged until
the 1830s.[3]) The ideology of woman's sphere formed a
necessary stage in the process of shattering the hierarchy
of sex and, more directly, in softening the hierarchical relationship of marriage.

3. In "Family Limitation, Sexual Control, and Domestic Feminism," Daniel
Scott Smith similarly argues that, viewed from the perspective of the earlier
centuries, women's attainment of the domestic sphere as their own constituted
a distinct improvement in their position.

But woman's sphere had the defects of its virtues. In opening certain avenues to women because of their sex, it barricaded all others. It also contained within itself the preconditions for organized feminism, by allotting a "separate" sphere for women and engendering sisterhood within that sphere. It assigned women a "vocation" comparable to men's vocations, but also implying, in women's case, a unique sexual solidarity. When they took up their common vocation women asserted their common identity in "womanhood," which became their defining social role: gender ruled, in effect, their sentiments, capacities, purpose, and potential achievements. Without such consciousness of their definition according to sex, no minority of women would have created the issue of "women's rights."

At this point it may be useful to offer a sketch—regrettably abstract—of the evolution of "group-consciousness" among women in New England, beginning with the seventeenth centuries. In those early years a woman customarily perceived her gender and the tasks it dictated as her biological (and in her eyes, God-given) fate. The sisterhood women knew was the sharing of "woman's lot." If civil and religious institutions defined them as "weaker vessels," in day-to-day interaction with men women were less conscious of inferiority than of *subjection,* an order that they accepted along with other hierarchical and deferential relationships prescribed by God and demanded by social order. In the later eighteenth century this perception began to change. (To explain why would require another book.) The erosion of patriarchal order in the civil, economic, and religious spheres stripped away the adjuncts, supports of, and similes to women's subjection to men, revealing its immanent logic to be women's *inferiority.* Feminists at the end of the century such as Judith Sargent Murray ("Constantia") brought into focus and then aimed their sharpest arrows at the belief that women were inferior to men (in the all-important Enlightenment capacity of reason, especially), and protested the neglect and restriction of women's minds. Women's "group-consciousness" in this period (c. 1770–1800) consisted in a common sense of their shared weakness relative to men; but they had laid open the question whether this weakness was natural or artificial, biological or cultural. Such "consciousness of (ascribed) inferiority" was the first group-consciousness likely to produce a feminist movement, because it acknowledged cultural and social determinants of women's capabilities as well as divine and natural ones, and thus allowed for the possibility of change.

In the last decade of the eighteenth century two reforming interpretations of woman's role appeared. One—best known via Mary Wollstonecraft's *Vindication of the Rights of Women,* in England, and probably best represented in New England by "Constantia"—may be called the equalitarian feminist view.[4] In broadest outline, it stressed women's common humanity with men and their equal endowment with mental and moral powers; it denied no venture to women categorically because of their sex. The other was the program of woman's sphere. Its formulators detoured the question of sexual equality by stressing sexual propriety. These two schools of thought nevertheless shared considerable common ground: both deplored the treatment of women as sexual objects or domestic drudges, advocated improvement in women's education, upheld models of women as responsible mothers of citizens.[5] This

4. Male feminists, such as Charles Brockden Brown, also voiced their sentiments publicly in this decade.

5. It is instructive to compare the writings of contemporaries Hannah More and Mary Wollstonecraft, in this regard; while their styles of life, their politics, and their ostensible views of womanhood stood in conflict, their actual critiques and proposals respecting the role of women overlapped considerably.

is not to deny the crucial, deep-lying difference between them.

In New England, reawakened Protestantism overcame the equalitarian feminist view almost as soon as it arose. (Mary Wollstonecraft's opinions were deemed akin to the doctrines of "godless" revolutionary France—even aside from the moral finger pointed at her convention-defying life and early death.) Around the turn of the century some New England women consciously used Wollstonecraft's ideas as a foil to clarify their own understanding of woman's role.[6] Ministers' wives or female kin were particularly adept at handling the distinctions.[7] The success of the Second Great Awakening insured that belief in woman's sphere, not equalitarian feminism, would dominate the first several decades of the nineteenth century. Following the logic of woman's sphere, women developed an instrumental conception of their gender role (c. 1800–1830) and a new group-consciousness based upon it. I say "instrumental," because they justified this role on the grounds of its usefulness in society as well as its ordination by God and nature. Encouraged by their religious mentors, women adopted that instrumental view, rather than a feminist ideal, to resolve their previously ascribed "inferiority"; by accentuating the difference between men and women they got around the question of inferiority and superiority.

Because it was instrumental the program of woman's sphere was flexible, accommodating a range of specific choices for venturesome women so long as they subsumed

6. E.g., diary of Mary Orne Tucker, April 13, 1802, EI; Eliza Southgate to Moses Porter, June 1801, reprinted in Nancy F. Cott, ed., *Root of Bitterness: Documents of the Social History of American Women* (New York: Dutton, 1972), pp. 107–08.

7. E.g., diary of Susan Mansfield Huntington, Jan. 22, 1813, John Trumbull Collection, SML; Hannah Mather Crocker, *Observations on the Real Rights of Women, with Their Appropriate Duties, Agreeable to Scripture, Reason and Common Sense* (Boston, 1818).

these under the rubric of *female* duties (that is, preserving the home, caring for the young or helpless, upholding morality and religion). Nonetheless it had severe limits. For many women it utterly failed to "resolve" the problem of inferiority, becoming instead a wellspring of strain.[8] And as the ideology of woman's sphere improved women's education, it built tension in its own boundaries. The internal dynamics of woman's sphere, by encouraging women to claim a social role according to their sex and to share both social and sexual solidarity, provoked a minority of women to see and protest those boundaries. Organized feminism in the following decades was a revolution of rising expectations.[9] The dual bonds of womanhood in woman's sphere prompted the reappearance of the equalitarian feminist view, on a substantial social base, after 1835. What precipitated some women and not others to cross the boundaries from "woman's sphere" to "woman's rights" is not certain; but it seems that variation on or escape from the containment of conventional evangelical Protestantism —whether through Quakerism, Unitarianism, radical sectarianism, or "de-conversion"—often led the way.[10]

8. Carroll Smith-Rosenberg has most fruitfully explored women's experience of role-stress, especially in "Beauty, the Beast and the Militant Woman: A Case Study in Sex Roles and Social Stress in Jacksonian America," *AQ* 23 (1971):562–84, and "The Hysterical Woman: Sex Roles and Role Conflict in 19th-Century America," *Social Research* 39 (1972):652–78.

9. Cf. Gerda Lerner's judgment in "The Lady and the Mill-Girl" that the Seneca Falls feminists, "like most revolutionaries, . . . were not the most downtrodden but rather the most status-deprived group"; Lerner maintains that middle-class women's rising expectations, confronted with a relative deterioration in their political status and an actual deterioration in their economic status, between 1800 and 1840, produced the frustration that fueled the feminist movement. Alice Rossi develops a "status-deprivation" argument in her outstanding essay "Social Roots of the Woman's Movement in America," *The Feminist Papers* (New York: Columbia University Press, 1973).

10. My thoughts here have been clarified by conversations with Ellen Dubois, over a long period of time, about "de-conversion"—i.e., ideological disengagement from the convincing power of evangelical Protestantism (or inability to accept the whole of it)—and reignited by Mary Ryan's suggestion, during the

Yet how much of what they learned in woman's sphere feminists carried with them! Throughout the nineteenth century feminists saw women's progress not in opposition to but at one with esteem for home and family; their radical demand was to include a role in the civil and public sphere among women's rights and prerogatives.[11] It is a lapse of historical vision to fault nineteenth-century feminists for "trailing clouds of glory," as it were, from the veneration of domesticity, as much as to call the ideology of woman's sphere reactionary and constraining from its inception. The latter had those aspects, of course, ever more visible as feminist eyes sharpened. But the majority of women upheld woman's sphere in order to enhance their status; they staked their major claim to social power on their "vocation." Proponents of woman's sphere largely agreed with feminists' desires to develop women's self-esteem and to free them from obeisance to men's whims, and the two views concurred on the need to advance educational opportunities and encourage women to be useful members of society. On the other hand, it oversimplifies to call woman's sphere ideology "protofeminist" or to give both principles the same lineage. The link between the one and the other was women's perception of "womanhood" as an all-sufficient definition and of sisterhood implicit in it. That consciousness had mighty portents. "We are a band of sisters—we must have sympathy for each other's woes," wrote a woman operative in the *Voice of Industry*

session "Women in God's Growing Kingdom" at the Third Berkshire Conference on the History of Women, Bryn Mawr College, June 10, 1976, that feminists in Utica, N.Y., likely came from among the Unitarians rather than the evangelicals.

11. See Ellen Dubois, "The Radicalism of the Woman Suffrage Movement: Notes Toward the Reconstruction of Nineteenth-Century Feminism," *FS* 3 (1975):63–71.

in 1847, alluding to *women* workers when she mentioned "that class to which it is my lot to belong." "Womanhood is the primal fact, wifehood and motherhood its incidents," Elizabeth Cady Stanton proclaimed.[12] Not until they saw themselves thus classed by sex would women join to protest their sexual fate.

12. Letter from "An Operative," Manchester, Dec. 21, 1846, *Voice of Industry* (Lowell, Mass.), Jan. 8, 1847. I am indebted to Lise Vogel for bringing this reference to my attention. Elizabeth Cady Stanton MSS No. 11, Library of Congress, undated, quoted in Linda Gordon, "Voluntary Motherhood: The Beginnings of Feminist Birth Control Ideas in the United States," in Hartman and Banner, *Clio's Consciousness Raised*, p. 60.

LIST OF
WOMEN'S DOCUMENTS CONSULTED

A. *Unpublished manuscripts in the possession of, and used by permission of, the libraries cited in abbreviated form:*

Alcott, Abigail (b. 1800, d. 1877), Philadelphia, Boston, et al., Journals and correspondence, 1825-35, Alcott Family Papers, I, folders, 24, 25, 26, II, folder 28, VII, folders 3, 4, 5, HCL.

Almy, Lydia Hill, Rhode Island, Diary, August 1797-June 1799, EI.

Bancroft, Elizabeth (b. 1773, d. 1867), Pepperell, Mass., Diary, June 1793-October 1795, AAS.

Barrett, Samantha (b. 1780s, d. 1830), New Hartford, Conn., Account Book, 1812-16, and Diaries, 1828-30, CHS.

Barrett, Zeloda (b. 1786), New Hartford, Conn., Diaries, 1804, 1820-21, 1830-31, CHS.

Beckley, Lucy, Berlin, Conn., Journal-book, May-June 1819, CHS.

Beecher, Catharine E. (b. 1800, d. 1878), New London and Hartford, Conn., Letters to Louisa Wait, 1819-25, and letter to Lyman Beecher, 1821, Beecher-Stowe Collection, SL.

Bemis, Martha Wheatland (b. 1807), Lowell and Cabotville, Mass., Letters, 1833-46, EI.

Bliss, Hannah, Longmeadow, Mass., Diaries, 1814-18, MHS.

Bowen, Elizabeth (b. 1735), Marblehead?, Mass., Diary 1778-1808, EI.

Bradford, Sarah (b. 1793, d. 1867), Boston, Mass., Letters, 1807-12, Sarah Bradford Ripley Collection, SL.

Bradley, Abigail and Sarah, Stockbridge, Mass. and Bolton, Conn., Letters, 1814-29, Bradley-Hyde Collection, SL.

Brainard Family Manuscripts, including letters of Huldah Foote Brainard, 1780s, and Jerusha Brainard, 1818-28, CHS.

Bryant, Sarah Snell (b. 1766, d. 1847), Cummington, Mass., Diaries, 1795-1847, HCL.

Burr, Esther Edwards (b. 1732, d. 1757), Newark and Princeton, N.J., and Stockbridge, Mass., Journal, written in the form of letters to Sarah Prince, 1754-57, Beinecke Rare Book and Manuscript Library, Yale University, New Haven.

Cabot, Eliza Perkins (b. 1791, d. 1885), "Reminiscences" (typescript), Cabot Family Papers, SL.

Callender, Eunice (b. 1786), Boston, Mass., Diaries, 1808–24, and letters to Sarah Ripley (Stearns), 1801–30, Stearns Collection, SL.

Carter, Mary, Newburyport, Mass., Correspondence with Hannah Emery, Exeter, N.H., 1787–91, Cutts Family Manuscripts, EI.

Challoner, Martha Church (b. 1723), Newport, R.I., Diary, 1765–70, CHS.

Chandler, Mary Ann Tucker (b. 1801), Boston, Charlestown, Concord, Mass., Diary, 1829–35, NHHS.

Chaplin (Nelson), Eliza, Salem, Mass., and New Canaan, N.H., Correspondence with Laura Lovell, Bridgewater, Mass., 1819–69, EI.

Cilly, Lavinia Bailey Kelly (b. 1818), Northwood, N.H., Diaries, 1828–30, 1834–37, NHHS.

Cleaveland, Mary (b. 1722), Ipswich, Mass., Diary, 1742–62, EI.

Cleveland, Elizabeth, Salem, Mass., Diary, 1824–49, EI.

Cobb, Eunice Hale Wait (b. 1803, d. 1877?), Hallowell and Waterville, Me., Diary, 1821–26, BPL.

Drew, Abigail Gardner (b. 1777, d. 1868), Nantucket, Mass., Diary, 1799–1818, AAS.

Elliott, Amanda (b. 1787, d. 1839), Guilford, Conn., Diary, 1813–21, CSL.

Endicott, Mary (b. 1800, d. 1877), Danvers, Mass., Diary, 1816–35, EI.

Farnum, Mary Barker (b. 1784, d. 1861), Nantucket, Mass., Diary, 1811–20, AAS.

Foote, Abigail, Colchester, Conn., Diary, June 1775–July 1776, CHS.

Foote, Elizabeth (b. 1750), Colchester, Conn., Diary, January–October 1775, CHS.

Gray, Frances Elizabeth (b. 1812), Roxbury, Mass., Journals and letters, 1831–60, MHS.

Gray, Lucy, Letters to husband Joshua Gray, 1814–29, SL.

Grout, Esther (b. 1806), Hawley, Mass. and Hamilton, N.Y., Diary, May 1830–June 1835, Pocumtuck Valley Memorial Association Library Collections, HD.

Grout, Sophronia (b. 1800), Hawley, Mass., Diary, 1816–37, Pocumtuck Valley Memorial Association Library Collections, HD.

Hall, Mary (b. 1806), Concord and Exeter, N.H. and Lowell, Mass., Diary, 1826–36, NHHS.

Henshaw (Miles) (Bascom), Ruth (b. 1772, d. 1846), Leicester, Deerfield, Fitzwilliam, and Ashby, Mass., Diary, 1789–1814, AAS.

Hook, Elizabeth, Salisbury and Newbury, Mass., Diary and account book, 1786-1844, EI.

Hooker, Mary Treadwell (b. 1755), Farmington, Conn., Diary, 1795-1812, CSL.

Hooker Collection, miscellaneous letters of numerous women, 1800-65, including Weltha Brown Correspondence, 1812-22, and correspondence between Luella Case and Sarah Edgarton, 1839-46, SL.

Huntington, Susan Mansfield (b. 1791, d. 1823), Boston, Mass., Diary, 1812-23, John Trumbull Collection, Box 11, SML.

Huntley, Lydia, Hartford, Conn., "Letters to the young ladies under her care, copied by Frances Ann Brace, 1814-1815," SL.

Hurlbut, Mary (b. 1804), New London, Conn., Diary, June 1830-April 1836, CHS.

Johnson, Betsy Graves, Reading and Nahant, Mass., Diary 1812-30, MHS.

Leonard, Jerusha, Sunderland, Mass., Diary, 1791-92, Pocumtuck Valley Memorial Association Library Collections, HD.

Lyman, Abigail Brackett (b. 1779, d. 1803), Northampton, Mass., Journal, 1800-03, and Letters, 1796-1803, appendices A and B in Helen Roelker Kessler, "The Worlds of Abigail Brackett Lyman," M.A. thesis, Tufts University, 1976.

Lyman (Mills), Elizabeth, Middlefield, Conn., Correspondence, 1832-46, CSL.

May, Abigail (b. 1775, d. 1800), Journal of residence in Portland, Maine, 1796, MeHS. (See also May-Goddard Collection.)

May-Goddard Collection, SL, including:

May, Mary Goddard, Account books, 1809-12;

White, Nancy, Diary, 1781-86;

Dawes (Goddard), Mehitable May (b. 1796, d. 1882), Brookline, Mass., School prizes, 1802-08, correspondence, 1805-32, and Diary addressed to her cousin Lucretia Dana Goddard, 1815-18;

May, Abigail (b. 1775, d. 1800), Diary, May 24-August 30, 1800.

Meriam, Nancy (b. 1792, d. 1822), Oxford, Mass., Religious notes and Diary, 1811-21, Meriam Collection, WHS.

Mills, daughter of the Reverend, near Hadlyme, Conn., Diary 1809-10, VHS.

Morris, Mercy Flynt (b. 1788, d. 1831), Belchertown and Wilbraham, Mass., Diary 1808-31, and letters to, 1808-30, CHS.

Munroe, Sophia Sewall, Boston, Mass., Diary, December 1815-May 1816, CHS.

Nichols, Sarah Pierce (b. 1804), Salem, Mass., Diary, 1833, EI.

Norton, Elizabeth Cranch (b. 1763, d. 1811), Braintree and Weymouth, Mass., Diaries, 1781–89, 1794–1808, MHS.

Noyes, Rebecca (b. 1759), Stonington, Conn., Diaries, 1801–29, CHS.

Otis, Harriet, Journal and letters of a trip from Boston to Niagara, 1825, HCL.

Parker (Quincy), Lucilla P., Boston, Mass., Diary, 1832–33, HCL.

Parrott, Sarah (b. 1800), Portsmouth, N.H., Correspondence, 1820s, John Fabyan Parrott Family Collection, NHHS.

Pickman, Mary Tappan (b. 1816), Salem, Mass., Diary, I, 1831–34, EI.

Pierce, Elizabeth (b. 1804), Northampton, Mass., Diary, November 1815–December 1816, and Letters, 1813–19, Poor Family Collection, SL.

Pierce, Lucy Tappan, Brookline, Mass., Letters, 1803–42, Poor Family Collection, SL.

Prescott, Caroline, Page on Female Education, 1817, Frances Merritt Quick Collection, SL.

Read, Lucinda (b. 1797), Greensboro, Vt., Farmington and Canton, Conn., et al., Diaries, 1815–21, two books of extracts, 1815, and book of song lines, MHS.

Ripley (Stearns), Sarah [or Sally] (b. 1785), Greenfield, Mass., Diaries, 1799–June 1801, October 1805–September 1808, AAS. (See also under Stearns).

Robbins, Meroa, Colchester, Conn., Letters to her family while at Miss Pierce's school in Litchfield, 1811, CSL.

Rogers, Patty [Polly], Exeter, N.H., Diary, 1785, AAS.

Russell, Mary (b. 1768, d. 1839), Middletown, Conn., Diary, 1796–1801, CHS.

Searle (Curson), Margaret (b. 1787, d. 1877), Newburyport, Mass., Diaries, January–November 1809, January 1812–July 1813, Curson Family Papers, HCL.

Sedgwick, Catherine Maria (b. 1789, d. 1867), Stockbridge and Lenox, Mass., and N.Y.C., Diaries, 1811–12, 1829–39, and Letters, 1798–1838, MHS.

Sedgwick, Elizabeth Ellery, N.Y.C., Journal-book of the first years of her child's life, 1824–29, HCL.

Smith, Anna Bryant (b. 1763), Portland, Maine, Diary 1805–07, MeHS.

Smith, Hannah Hickok (b. 1767, d. 1850), Glastonbury, Conn., Account books, 1819–31, Diary, 1832–40, and Letters to Abigail Mitchell, 1796–1816, CSL.

Smith, Margaret Everston, Sharon, Conn., Diary, 1807-10, CHS.

Smith, Mrs. S., Woodmont, Conn., Diary, 1822-25, CSL.

Staples, Eliza Ann Hull (b. 1804, d. 1832), Diary, 1818-32, CSL.

Stearns, Rachel Willard (b. 1813), Greenfield, Leominster, Mass., Diaries, October 1834-December 1837, Stearns Collection, SL.

Stearns, Sarah Ripley (b. 1785), Greenfield, Mass., Diaries, 1801-05, 1808-18, Stearns Collection, SL. (See also under Ripley.)

Storrs, Lucinda Howe (b. 1757, d. 1839), Mansfield, Conn., and Lebanon, N.H., Diaries, 1776-80, 1812-38, CHS.

Talbot (Capen), Betsy Estey (b. 1807, d. 1884), Stoughton, Mass., Journal, March 1838-December 1844, SL.

Thompson (Hunt), Nancy (b. 1789, d. 1865?), Connecticut, Diary, 1809-65, including "A Short Sketch of the Life of Nancy Thomson [sic]," CHS.

Tucker, Mary Orne (b. 1775, d. 1806), Haverhill, Mass., Diary, 1802, EI.

Waite, Eliza [Betsy], Salem, Mass., Correspondence with Susan Kittredge, Andover, Mass., and others, 1786-91, EI.

Watson (Dana), Sarah (b. 1814), Hartford, Conn., Diary, 1833-35, SL.

Wildes, Elizabeth (b. 1765, d. 1844), Arundel, Maine, Diary, 1789-93, MeHS.

Williams, Paulina Bascomb, Diary, 1830-33, VHS.

Wood, Mrs. Hartley, Diary, 1809-11, SML.

B. *Published Works:*

Adams, Charles Francis, ed. *Familiar Letters of John Adams and his Wife Abigail Adams, during the Revolution.* New York: Hurd and Houghton, 1876.

Adams, Hannah (b. 1755, d. 1831). *A Memoir of Miss Hannah Adams, written by Herself, with additional notices, by a friend.* Boston: Gray and Bowen, 1832.

Adams, Horace. "A Puritan Wife on the Frontier." *MVHR* 27 (1940): 67-84.

Almy, Mary Gould, "Journal, 1778." In *Newport Historical Magazine* 1 (July 1880):17-36.

Ballard, Martha Moore (b. 1735, d. 1812). "Diary, 1785-1812." In Charles Elventon Nash, ed., *The History of Augusta [Maine].* Augusta: Charles Nash and Sons, 1904, pp. 229-464.

Barns, Lucy. *The Female Christian: Containing a Selection from the Writings of Miss Lucy Barns.* Portland, Me.: Argus Office, 1809.

Bessie: or, Reminiscences of a Daughter of a New England Clergyman of the Eighteenth Century. By a Grandmother. New Haven: J. H. Benham, 1861.

Channing, Katherine Minot, ed. *Minot Family Letters 1773-1871.* Shelborn, Mass., privately printed, 1957.

Clark, Laura Downs (b. 1798). "Diary, June 21–October 26, 1818." *Firelands Pioneer*, n.s. 21 (1920):2308-26.

Codman, Martha, ed. *The Journal of Mrs. John Amory, 1775-1777* (b. 1731). Boston, privately printed, 1923.

Coit, Mehetabel Chandler (b. 1673, d. 1758). *Her Book, 1714.* Norwich, Conn.: Bulletin Print, 1895.

Cook, Clarence, ed. *A Girl's Life Eighty Years Ago: Letters of Eliza Southgate Bowne* (b. 1783, d. 1803). New York, 1883.

Davis, Almond H. *The Female Preacher, or Memoir of Salome Lincoln* (b. 1807). Providence, R.I.: Elder J. S. Mowry, 1843.

Diary of Sarah Connell Ayer 1805-1835 (b. 1791, d. 1835). Portland, Me., 1910.

The Diaries of Sally [b. 1807] and Pamela Brown [b. 1816], 1832-1838, Hyde Leslie, 1887, Plymouth Notch, Vermont. Blanche B. Bryant and Gertrude E. Baker, eds. Springfield, Vt.: Wm. L. Bryant Foundation, 1970.

Dow, Peggy. "Vicissitudes, or the Journey of Life; and Supplementary Reflections to the Journey of Life." In Lorenzo Dow, *History of Cosmopolite.* Cincinnati: Anderson Gates and Wright, 1859.

Earle, Alice Morse, ed. *The Diary of Anna Green Winslow.* Boston: Houghton Mifflin, 1894.

Familiar Letters written by Mrs. Sarah Osborn and Miss Susanna Anthony. Newport, R.I.: Mercury Office, 1807.

Fuller, Elizabeth (b. 1775?). "Diary, 1790-1792." In Francis E. Blake, *History of the Town of Princeton [Massachusetts].* Princeton, 1915. 1:302-23.

Higginson, Thomas Wentworth, ed. "Cambridge Eighty Years Since—Letters in the form of a diary by Louise Higginson, 1827-1828." *Cambridge Historical Society Publications* 2 (Cambridge, Mass., 1907):20-32.

Hopkins, Samuel, ed. *The Life and Character of Miss Susanna Anthony [b. 1726, d. 1791] . . . consisting chiefly in extracts from her writings . . .* 2d ed. Portland, Maine, 1810.

———. *Memoirs of the Life of Mrs. Sarah Osborn* (b. 1714, d. 1796). Worcester, Mass., 1799.

Kendrick, A. C., ed. *The Life and Letters of Mrs. Emily C. Judson*

(b. 1817). New York: Sheldon and Co.; Boston: Gould and Lincoln, 1861.

Larcom, Lucy (b. 1824, d. 1893). *A New England Girlhood*. New York: Corinth Books, 1961; orig. 1883.

Mayo, A. D., ed. *Selections from the Writings of Mrs. Sarah Edgarton Mayo [b. 1819], with a memoir*. Boston: A. Tompkins, 1850.

Memoir of Mrs. Ann H. Judson [b. 1784, d. 1826], Late Missionary to Burmah. 10th ed. Boston: Gould Kendall and Lincoln, 1838.

Memoirs of Catharine Seely and Deborah S. Roberts, late of Darien, Connecticut. New York: Daniel Godwin, 1844.

Morse, Frances Rollins, ed. *Henry and Mary Lee [b. 1783]: Letters and Journals*. Boston, 1926.

Moseley, Laura Hadley, ed. *The Diaries of Julia Cowles*. New Haven: Yale University Press, 1931.

Phelps, Elizabeth Porter (b. 1747, d. 1817). "Diary, 1763–1805." Edited by Thomas Eliot Andrews. *NEHGR* 18–22 (1964–68).

Smith, Ethan, ed. *Memoirs of Mrs. Abigail Bailey*. Boston: Samuel T. Armstrong, 1815.

Smith, Lydia, "Journal, 1805–1806." *Massachusetts Historical Society Proceedings* 48 (1914–15):508–34.

White, Tryphena Ely (b. 1784). *Journal, 1805*. New York: Grafton Press, 1905.

The Writings of Nancy Maria Hyde [b. 1792] of Norwich, Connecticut, Connected with a Sketch of her Life. Norwich: Russell Hubbard, 1816.

LIST OF
MINISTERS' SERMONS CONSULTED

Abbot, Abiel. *A Discourse, Delivered before the Members of the Portsmouth Female Asylum . . . August 9, 1807.* Portsmouth: Stephen Sewall, 1807.

——. *The Duty of Youth, in a Sermon Occasioned by the Death of Miss Sarah Ayer, April 7, 1802.* Haverhill: Galen H. Fay, 1802.

Alden, Timothy, Jr. *A Discourse, Delivered before the Members of the Portsmouth Female Asylum . . . 16 September 1804.* Portsmouth: J. Melcher, 1804.

Allen, William. *Sermon Preached before the Auxiliary Society for Promoting Good Morals, and the Female Charitable Society of Williamstown, June 7, 1815.* Pittsfield: Phinehas Allen, 1815.

Appleton, J. *A Discourse, Delivered before the Members of the Portsmouth Female Asylum . . . August 10, 1806.* Portsmouth: S. Whidden, 1806.

Baldwin, Thomas. *A Discourse, Delivered before the Members of the Boston Female Asylum, September 26, 1806 . . .* Boston: Russell, and Cutler, 1806.

Barnard, Thomas. *A Sermon Preached before the Salem Female Charitable Society . . . July 6, 1803.* Salem: William Carlton, 1803.

Beasley, Frederic. *A Sermon Delivered at the Request of the Ladies Society . . . Albany, January 10, 1808.* Albany: Websters and Skinner, 1808.

Bentley, William. *A Discourse, Delivered . . . September 2, 1807, at the Annual Meeting of the Salem Female Charitable Society.* Salem: Pool and Palfray, 1807.

Bodwell, Abraham. *Sermon, Delivered at the Request of the Female Cent Society in Sandbornton, N.H., December 23, 1813.* Concord: George Hough, 1813.

Bolles, Lucius. *A Discourse, Delivered before the Members of the Salem Female Charitable Society, September 27, 1810 . . .* Salem: Thomas C. Cushing, 1810.

Buckminster, Joseph. *A Discourse Delivered before the Members of* the *Portsmouth Female Charity School, October 14, 1803.* Portsmouth: N.S. and W. Pierce, 1803.

———. *A Sermon Delivered before the Members of the Female Charitable Society in Newburyport, May 22, 1809* . . . Newburyport: Edward Little, 1809.

———. "A Sermon Preached before the Members of the Boston Female Asylum. September 1810." Hand-copied and bound with other sermons to the Boston Female Asylum, Boston Public Library rare book room.

Bullard, John. *A Discourse, Delivered at Pepperell, September 19, 1815, before the Charitable Female Society* . . . Amherst, N.H.: R. Boylston, 1815.

Chaplin, Daniel. *A Discourse Delivered before the Charitable Female Society in Groton, October 19, 1814.* Andover: Flagg and Gould, 1814.

Chase, Amos. *On Female Excellence, or a Discourse in which Good Character in Women is Described.* Litchfield: Collier and Buel, 1792.

Church, John Hubbard. *Female Liberality Acceptable to Jesus Christ, A Sermon Preached before the Female Heathen School Society of Dracutt, Massachusetts, August 27, 1818.* Concord, N.H.: George Hough, 1818.

Clark, Daniel A. *The Wise Builder, A Sermon Delivered to the Females of the First Parish in Amherst, Massachusetts.* Boston: Ezra Lincoln, 1820.

Clarke, Pitt. *A Discourse Delivered before the Norton Female Christian Association, . . . June 13, 1818.* Taunton: A. Danforth, 1818.

Cotton, Ward. *Causes and Effects of Female Regard to Christ, Illustrated in a Sermon Delivered before the Female Society in Boylston . . . October 1, 1816.* Worcester: William Manning, 1817.

Dana, Daniel. *A Discourse Delivered May 22, 1804, before the Members of the Female Charitable Society of Newburyport* . . . Newburyport: Edmund M. Blunt, 1804.

Dehon, Theodore. *A Discourse Delivered in Providence, September 6, 1804, before the Female Charitable Society* . . . Providence: Heaton and Williams, 1804.

Eaton, Asa. "A Sermon Preached Before the Members of the Boston Female Asylum, September 1812." Hand-copied and bound with other sermons to the Boston Female Asylum, Boston Public Library rare book room.

Eckley, Joseph. *A Discourse, Delivered before the Members of the*

Boston Female Asylum, September 24, 1802 ... Boston: Ornamental Printing Office, [1802].

Emerson, Brown. *A Discourse Delivered October 1, 1811 ... before the Salem Female Charitable Society.* Salem: Warwick Palfray, 1811.

Emerson, William. *A Discourse Delivered before the Members of the Boston Female Asylum, September 20, 1805* ... Boston: Russell and Cutler, 1805.

Gardiner, John S. C. *A Sermon, Delivered at Trinity Church, September, 22, 1809, before the Members of the Boston Female Asylum.* Boston: Munroe, Francis and Parker, 1809.

Harris, Thaddeus. *A Discourse, Preached before the Members of the Boston Female Asylum, September 24, 1813.* Boston: Russell, Cutler and Co., 1813.

Harris, Walter. *A Discourse to the Members of the Female Cent Society in Bedford, New Hampshire, July 18, 1814.* Concord: George Hough, 1814.

Hyde, Alvan. *The Conjugal Relation Made Happy and Useful, A Sermon Delivered at Lee, Massachusetts, December 24, 1815.* Stockbridge: Berkshire Star Office, 1816.

———. *Essay on the State of Infants.* New York: Cornelius Davis, 1830.

Keely, George. *The Nature and Order of a Gospel Church ... stated in a Sermon Preached at the Baptist Meetinghouse, Haverhill, Massachusetts ... 1818, with an appendix containing an enquiry into the Standing of Females in a Christian Church ...* Haverhill: P. N. Green, 1819.

Kimball, David T. *The Obligation and Disposition of Females to Promote Christianity, An Address Delivered June 15, 1819, before the Female Education and Charitable Societies ... Ipswich.* Newburyport: Ephraim W. Allen, 1819.

Lathrop, John. *A Discourse Delivered before the Members of the Boston Female Asylum, September 21, 1804* ... Boston: Russell and Cutler, 1804.

———. "A Sermon Preached before the Members of the Boston Female Asylum, September 1815." Hand-copied and bound with other sermons to the Boston Female Asylum, Boston Public Library rare book room.

Lyman, William. *A Virtuous Woman the Bond of Domestic Union, and the Source of Domestic Happiness.* New London: S. Green, 1802.

Miltimore, James. *A Discourse, Delivered before the Members of the Female Charitable Society of Newburyport . . . May 20, 1807.* Newburyport: Thomas Whipple, 1807.

Morse, Jedidiah. *A Sermon, Preached . . . September 25, 1807, before the Managers of the Boston Female Asylum . . .* Boston: Russell and Cutler, 1807.

Nott, Samuel, Jr. *A Sermon, on the Idolatry of the Hindoos, Delivered November 29, 1816, at the Annual Meeting of the Female Foreign Mission Society of Franklin, Connecticut.* Norwich: Hubbard and Martin, 1817.

Parish, Elijah. *A Sermon Preached before the Members of the Female Charitable Society of Newburyport . . . May 17, 1808.* Newburyport: Thomas and Whipple, 1808.

Parker, Samuel. *Charity to Children, Enforced, in a Discourse delivered . . . before the Subscribers to the Boston Female Asylum, September 23, 1803.* Boston: Russell and Cutler, 1803.

Perrine, Matthew La Rue. *Women Have a Work to Do in the House of God: A Discourse Delivered at the First Annual Meeting of the Female Missionary Society for the Poor of the City of New York* . . . New York: Edward W. Thomson, 1817.

Prince, John. *Charity Recommended from the Social State of Man, A Discourse Delivered before the Salem Female Charitable Society, September 17, 1806.* Salem: Joshua Cushing, 1806.

Proudfit, Alexander. *The Female Laborer in the Gospel, A Sermon to the Members of the Female Society for the Promotion of Religious Knowledge in Salem [N.Y.], August 6, 1805.* Title page missing—Andover-Harvard Library copy.

——. *A Word to Mothers, on the Religious Instruction of their Children.* Bound in *The One Thing Needful.* Salem [N.Y.]: Dodd and Rumsey, 1812.

Richardson, J. *A Sermon on the Duty and Dignity of Woman, Delivered April 22, 1832.* Hingham: Jedidiah Farmer, 1833.

Smith, Ethan. *Daughters of Zion Excelling, A Sermon Preached to the Ladies of the Cent Institution, in Hopkinton, New Hampshire, August 18, 1814.* Concord: George Hough, 1814.

Snell, Thomas. *Women Ministering to Christ, A Discourse Delivered in the West Parish of Brookfield before the Female Bible Cent Society.* Brookfield: E. Merriam and Co., 1815.

Society for Promoting Christian Knowledge, Piety and Charity, Religious Tracts No. V. Boston: Isaiah Thomas, jun., 1814. Sermon IV, 66-95, "The Effect of Christian Principles in Rendering the

Female Heart Benevolent." Preached before the Boston Female Asylum (no author, no date).

Spalding, Joshua. *A Sermon Preached . . . at the Annual Meeting of the Salem Female Charitable Society, September 8, 1808.* Salem: Pool and Palfray, 1808.

Spring, Gardiner. *The Excellence and Influence of the Female Character.* 2d ed. New York: F. and R. Lockwood, 1825.

Stearns, J. F. *Female Influence, and the True Christian Mode of Its Exercise, A Discourse Delivered in the First Presbyterian Church in Newburyport, July 30, 1837.* Newburyport: John G. Tilton, 1837.

Stillman, Samuel. *A Discourse Delivered before the Members of the Boston Female Asylum . . . 1801.* Boston: Russell and Cutler, 1801.

Strebeck, George. *A Sermon on the Character of the Virtuous Woman.* New York: the author, 1800.

Strong, Nathan. *The Character of a Virtuous and Good Woman, A Discourse . . . [to] the Female Beneficent Society, Hartford, October 4, 1809.* Hartford: Hudson and Goodwin, 1809.

Stuart, Moses. *A Sermon, Delivered by Request of the Female Charitable Society in Salem . . . August A.D. 1815.* Andover: Flagg and Gould, 1815.

Thompson, James W. *A Sermon Delivered by Request of the Female Charitable Society in Salem . . . June 24, 1832.* Salem: Foote and Brown, 1832.

Tullar, Martin. *A Concise System of Family Duty . . . in six sermons.* Windsor, Vt.: Nahum Mower, 1802.

———. *The Virtues of a Prudent Wife Illustrated in a Sermon . . . December 5, 1799.* Hanover, N.H.: Moses Davies, n.d.

Turner, Edward. *A Discourse, Delivered before the Female Benevolent Society in Charlestown . . . November 5, 1822.* Boston: J. Howe, 1822.

Wadsworth, Benjamin. *Female Charity an Acceptable Offering, A Sermon Delivered . . . at the Request of the Charitable Female Cent Society in Danvers and Middleton . . .* Andover: Flagg and Gould, 1817.

Weston, John E. *Claims of the Poor, A Discourse, Delivered at Charlestown, . . . November 8, 1829, before the Female Benevolent Society, and at East Cambridge, . . . December 18, 1829, before the Female Charitable Society.* Boston: True and Green, 1830.

Whittemore, Thomas. *A Discourse Delivered in the Central Univer-*

salist Church, Boston, before the Female Samaritan Society, October 26, 1828. Boston: Trumpet Office, n.d.

Wilbur, Hervey. *Female Piety Demanding Assistance, Two Sermons, Delivered in Bradford, Second Parish, January 5, 1812.* Haverhill: William Brown Allen, 1812.

Williams, Samuel P. *Plea for the Orphan, Delivered on the Anniversary of the Female Charitable Society of Newburyport, May 21, 1822.* Newburyport: W. and J. Gilman, 1822.

Woodbridge, Timothy. *A Sermon, Preached April 20, 1813, in Compliance with a Request of the Gloucester Female Society For the Promotion of Christian Knowledge and Practical Piety.* Boston: Samuel T. Armstrong, 1813.

Worcester, Samuel. *Female Love to Christ . . . [A Sermon Preached] before the Salem Female Charitable Society, September 27, 1809.* Salem: Pool and Palfray, n.d.

Wright, Chester. *A Sermon, Preached before the Female Foreign Mission Society in Montpelier, 1816.* Montpelier, Vt.: E. P. Walton, 1817.

INDEX

221